To Jean,
Buon Appetito, I hope you enjoy many Friday Evening meals in your own cucina!

Michele Carbone

Venerdì Sera
Friday Evening

Creating La Dolce Vita, one bite at a time.

Venerdì Sera
Friday Evening

Creating La Dolce Vita, one bite at a time.

Michele Carbone

PUBLISHED BY

Pentola Press
Post Office Box 719
Summerland, CA 93067-0719
(805) 570-0896

www.pentolapress.com
orders@pentolapress.com

Friday Evening: Creating *La Dolce Vita*, one bite at a time.
by Michele Carbone

Copyright 2009 by Michele Carbone
Foreword Copyright 2009 by Doug Margerum

All rights reserved. NO part of this book may be reproduced
or transmitted in any form or by any means, electronic or mechanical,
including photocopying, recording or by any information storage and
retrieval system, without written permission from the author,
except for the inclusion of brief quotations in a review.

First Edition

ISBN 978-0-615-21919-6
Library of Congress Control Number: 2008930519

Design, Digital Production and Printing by Media 27, Inc., Santa Barbara, California

WWW.MEDIA27.COM

Printed and bound in China

For Kristin

Contents

8	Foreword	
9	Preface	
11	Chapter 1	The Kitchen Rules!
23	Chapter 2	Shopping
37	Chapter 3	The Menus
49	Chapter 4	*L'autunno*/Autumn
85	Chapter 5	*L'inverno*/Winter
127	Chapter 6	*La Primavera*/Spring
169	Chapter 7	*L'estate*/Summer
209	Chapter 8	The Proper Kitchen
225	Chapter 9	The Proper Pantry
235	Chapter 10	Your Refrigerator
241	Chapter 11	The Functional Freezer
247	Chapter 12	Closing
250	Acknowledgments	
252	Glossary	
256	The Thanksgiving Soup	

Foreword

BY DOUG MARGERUM

In the Italian culture, food is more than a means to sustain life. Meals are central to what Americans view as "the Italian lifestyle." Italians socialize around food and wine; at open air markets and especially around the abundent table surrounded by family and friends engaged in lively conversation. American's have a whirlwind lifestyle, even the internet seems too slow, and the pleasures of food and wine at the table are often lost as eating a meal becomes just another errand. Nearly everyone is guilty of picking up that preservative-laden, trans-fat-filled, greasy snack while rushing off to do whatever task was deemed more important than eating a healthy meal and enjoying the company of family and friends.

In *Friday Evening: Creating La Dolce Vita, one bite at a time,* Michele Carbone inspires us to truly enjoy the often overlooked special place that is the table. In her book she inspires us to bring the family back to the table for delicious dinners at home. During her transition from corporate engineer to full-time caregiver for her disabled daughter Kristin, she came to realize the value of a glass of wine with friends, an iced-cold piece of melon with the kids, and most importantly a good conversation over a platter of pasta. She inspires us to take the tips and tricks she learned here and in Italy to bring a bit of the Italian good life, *La Dolce Vita*, to our own tables and lives.

Michele reveals to us her techniques for shopping, taking advantage of fresh seasonal produce, equipping a kitchen and producing authentic meals the Italian way. Her seasonal menus and humorous stories will inspire you to begin your own culinary adventure and to take the time to enjoy what you can create. Michele observes that the Italian *moda di vita* (way of life) centers around the foundation of food, family and local food production from which centuries of art, religion and culture evolved. She reminds us that this important aspect of living begins with Friday Evening, *la cucina e la famiglia* (food and family). Pull up the chairs, set the table for many, pour the vino, eat slowly, savor every bite, and enjoy your time at the table!

A tavola non s'invecchia
AT THE TABLE ONE DOESN'T GET OLD

This was the path of my life prior to June 14, 1996. I lived in Montecito, California with my husband Jim and two lovely daughters, Kristin and Kate. I worked as a project engineer for a government contractor. I wore navy blue suits and high heels. My girls went to private school and had nannies. I didn't go to the farmers' markets, cooked dinners quickly, and drank my coffee while driving to work or sitting at my desk. I thought I was living "*La Dolce Vita*" (the good life). I had plenty of money, and although my friend Joe did get his Mercedes before me, I knew I could get one if I really wanted to; a used one, but a Mercedes after all. I had chosen a career and family and had little time for anything else.

On June 14th, 1996 my life changed forever. Kristin suffered a brain injury during what should have been routine, although complicated, heart surgery. My career ended. For an entire year I left the house less than ten times for recreation. My cooking style went from fry to simmer. My life became centered on therapy, doctor's visits, and puréed food. To keep from going insane, I turned to slow cooking, the Food TV Network, and "What could we put into Kristin's mouth that might help her get her mouth functioning again?"

Life eventually got a little bit better, and I began to accept the simple pleasures in life as the only rewards I was going to receive in life. I didn't realize it at first, but I began to live *La Dolce Vita*. It started with a few trips to the farmers' market for recently-harvested, local, seasonal produce.

We eventually got to Italy to meet the Italian cousins. It took five people and a rather large, handicapped-accessible van. It was not your standard Italian vacation. Again, my life was changed forever. Now I understood. "*La Dolce Vita e una moda di vita*" (the sweet life is a way of life), and it doesn't take much money to live. It happens in your head, by way of your taste buds and stomach, while your heart stands guard.

Now, when people ask me about myself, I tell them that I'm the kind of person you call when you need five prime ribs cooked medium rare and ready to carve at a teacher's luncheon the day after tomorrow. They usually think I'm kidding. Some time later, it will come up in conversation that I have a severely brain-injured daughter. They will feel sorry for me and wonder how I manage to do it. This part of my life has been the happiest part of my life. Do I wish Kristin never had her brain injury? Yes; and no. I am a better person for being her parent. I am definitely a better cook.

The Kitchen Rules!

CHAPTER I

I live in Montecito, California, one of the most beautiful places in the world. The climate is right for growing many foods—fresh seafood is always available, and the wine country and ranches are just over the hill. My living room looks out over what used to be an old orchard of a Jesuit Novitiate. Over the years I have seen the beehives, avocado trees, and citrus trees give way to some really exquisite mansions. While these houses were being built, we would wander through them with the dog. The kitchens were usually half the size of my entire house. I would dream of dinner parties in these amazing homes. Though I hoped to be a guest, over the years I've come to realize that hanging out in these kitchens would be even more fulfilling.

There's an old saying that there are two kinds of people in the world: those who eat to live and those who live to eat. I would of course be one of the second types. If you love to eat good food, love to shop at specialty markets and farmers' markets, and occasionally pull something out of the ground and bring it, covered in dirt, into your kitchen, this book is for you. If you want to begin living *La Dolce Vita* (The Good Life) or just love to eat delicious food, this book tells you my secrets about how I transformed my life, starting with the Friday evening meal. You can do it, too.

They say that the Mediterranean diet is the healthiest diet in the world, but it's more than diet, it's the lifestyle. As you read the chapters in this book, and begin consciously creating your own Friday evening *La Dolce Vita* menus and moments, you too will begin to reap the benefits of a healthy lifestyle.

My daughter Kristin is brain injured and in a wheelchair. Though I don't leave the house to work, my work is constant. If I can make these kinds of meals, you can do it, too. Yes, I do make everything from scratch, and I do spend a lot of time during the day prepping for these meals. But I prepare them every day, while also walking my dog for an hour each morning, shopping for food 2-4 times a week, driving kids to therapy and school, taking care of many of my husband's daily needs like dropping off dry-cleaning, and frequently dragging a hose all over the yard, paying bills, and keeping some of the household books.

> *Eat cream, butter, sugar, and salt, but don't be an idiot; eat it in moderate quantities, and put it into your foods yourself.*

Many of the meals and recipes in this book can be adjusted for faster preparation. You can, of course, buy many of the items pre-prepared. Strive to learn how to prepare your own basic ingredients and meals. The lifestyle is about spending time with your food and its preparation. If you must buy some items pre-prepared, try to use the very best ingredients

you can find (while remembering that taking the time to find them is part of the lifestyle). I won't be too upset with you if you occasionally must sacrifice preparation time for your other time demands. This book is about living the lifestyle, not building a facade and populating it with take-out food.

If you get up each day, get yourself moving, spend time thinking about what you have to do and what you want to do, managing your time and starting a "holistic kitchen," you may find you don't need to pay someone to make your food. You don't have to drive somewhere to get prepared food, and you may not need to join a gym because you'll be carrying heavier bags of groceries, bending over to pick herbs, greens, and veggies out of the ground, and spending more time moving around your kitchen getting exercise.

The lifestyle I'm promoting centers around keeping the family at the table at the end of the day for seven or so courses of simply prepared and delicious foods, with wine, and, of course, a *dolce* (dessert), with spirited and intelligent conversation. This lifestyle requires a lot of thought about food, some time, but most of all, time management. If you merely adjust your habits, you can achieve happiness through this simpler lifestyle while still having time to pursue many of your other interests.

I recently found an advertisement from a kitchen equipment manufacturer. I cut out the photo and keep it as an example of the dream kitchen I hope to have someday. Warm, yellow sunlight streams in through bright, airy windows. It has everything a cook could possibly want. There are four ovens, each filled with some item being prepared for the evening's meal. A pan of crusty rolls is slowly baking, as the aroma of bread fills the room. Another oven has a casserole, perhaps with a chicken, some vegetables glazing in the simmering pan juices, or perhaps a roast to be left standing on the table to rest while wine glasses are being filled. There are two separate cook tops, one has a pot of water just starting to steam as the water begins to boil, and it cries out for a pound or two of pasta. The second cook top contains a covered stock pot, slowly simmering with the vegetable pieces not used in the main dish of the evening, but quietly gathering flavors to build the foundation of another night's meal. In the large farmhouse sink, a colander of freshly washed herbs stands in the sunlight, drying slowly as beads of water drip into the porcelain basin. In the middle of the room stands a large table with chairs and stools for any number of friends. Bowls of flour, butter, and eggs stand on the table with boxes of berries brought in from the

> *"Chi ben comincia è alla metà dell'opera.*
> (Who starts well is half way to a masterpiece.)"

garden earlier in the day. Pie crust dough is spread out on the table with two large rounds cut and resting inside one of several tin forms.

The knives are right next to the stove, on a magnetic strip. Ladles are hanging above it, and wooden spoons are at the ready on the counter. Another oven has a plate rack above it. The platters are ready to grab at a moment's notice when something hot is coming out of the oven and is ready to serve. The pots are stacked in an open space under the second cook top, and a range hood with a wood-burning oven are tucked next to one of the big farmhouse sinks.

A large wrought iron chandelier covers the ceiling, though in my kitchen there would be pots and herbs hanging from it. A separate butcher block table stands next to the farmhouse table, and baskets of newly harvested fruits and vegetables are stacked on chairs, hand carts, and the floor. A colander of recently washed herbs is in the sink, and on the counter you can see a cutting board, bottles of oil and vinegar, pepper grinders, bowls of butter, and baskets of fresh bread. The doorway to the outside (presumably to the kitchen garden) is arched, with wide plaster ledges, and the walls are painted a mottled mustard yellow. The thick mud-colored bricks make for a very uneven floor. Kristin would be severely jostled in her wheelchair while navigating in this kitchen, but the tastes for her to savor would be exquisite.

This kitchen has the biggest refrigerator you could want. It has shelves for produce and plenty of room for one person to be grabbing a beer or a chilled bottle of Pinot Grigio while another is hunting for

heavy whipping cream. It will serve them both, with elbow room to spare. The dream kitchen is as big as my living room and is anchored by a used brick floor. It is the perfect marriage of the latest in high tech stainless steel components with an old world feel. This kitchen could be home to many a political argument, or discussions about religion, education, fashion, or gardening.

There was one thing missing from this kitchen, and it is the most important ingredient of all: people. There is no life to a kitchen without the sound of animated voices, shouting over the din of scraping chairs, chopping, bubbling, and the chink of stainless against wood, or steel or concrete. The smiles which come about when an elbow is bumped, or a sauce is offered to taste, or a freshly plated dish of pasta, or a vegetable casserole is brought to the table are the reward for hours of labor preparing food for the family meal. How do we put the joy of working silently side by side, one chopping and another stirring, into the photo of the perfect kitchen? We begin by living in our kitchens, they are the tools of our lives, lives which are made better by the meals created and shared in them.

When I first saw the dream kitchen photo, I didn't wish for a remodel to put it into my home. My first wish was to have the opportunity, just once, to be cooking in this kitchen with my favorite *foodie* friends. Kate, my younger daughter, would be there, in the pastry side of the room, pulling together some

tasty dessert, always watching what we were doing and always eager to push her way to the big pot on the stove to stir, to taste, to approve, or to surreptitiously add some missing ingredient to suit her taste when I wasn't looking.

In the next room, or lounging around the farmhouse table with several bottles of opened wine, would be Jim and Kristin, and any number of friends, both real and imaginary.

I direct the reader to place yourself in this kitchen, in your mind. In this kitchen we will let the smells of the food erase the cares of the world and begin living *La Dolce Vita*.

Let's start with *Venerdì sera* (Friday night).

Most of us don't have these dream kitchens, and many of us who do don't fully appreciate the lifestyle they can so easily support. After visiting Italy, after many hours of imaginary conversation between my favorite food television stars and myself, and years of striving to prepare culinary masterpieces in the kitchen, I decided to write down what I've learned. My hope for you is that no matter what your kitchen is like, and no matter how busy your lifestyle, you'll realize that living *La Dolce Vita* is an achievable reality, not just reserved for dreams and vacations.

> *One really good knife is far better than several stupid gadgets that will probably break anyway.*

Okay, the title of this chapter is *The Kitchen Rules!*, so let's discuss the rules:

1

Eat local organic foods, preferably recently harvested, produced, or butchered (to the maximum extent possible).

2

Eat whole foods, minimally processed.

3

Drink water—lots of it—wine, and coffee. Squeeze your juices. Take time out in the evening to have a sip of an after-dinner drink, and follow up with evening tea, and then more water.

4

If it comes in a box, is instant, or is new and improved, try not to buy it. The only way to improve on fresh fruits, vegetables, and grains is to serve them fresh, properly cooked, and/or anointed with the finest extra virgin olive oil you can find (also, with a little freshly cracked pepper and sea salt). If it's processed more than once, it's not going to be as healthy for you. It certainly isn't going to have the flavor, texture and nutritional value of the original ingredient, and you're wasting your money paying someone to process the food.

5

Buy wild, organic, or free ranging meats, fish, and poultry. God knows what they put into it otherwise, and I certainly don't want it in my body. (And we wonder why there is so much cardiac disease and cancer in our modern human bodies!) You've heard the phrase "Garbage in, garbage out." What people forget is that some of the garbage stays in!

6

Eat cream, butter, sugar, and salt, but don't be an idiot; eat it in moderate quantities, and put it into your foods yourself. That way you'll know how much you're actually consuming.

7

Buy large pieces of meat, with bones attached. Your foods will taste better, you'll spend less money, you'll start creating leftovers—which become the basis for secondary menu items—and you'll start producing the by-products you need to create excellent stocks, soups, and sauces (BONES!).

8

Buy fresh foods that look good to you and catch your eye at the markets, then figure out your menus based on what you've bought. Take a second stroll around the market and get whatever else you need. When you buy seasonal produce and combine fresh local ingredients, your food will automatically start to taste better.

9

Replenish all your old spices and start growing or buying fresh herbs. Put them into everything and definitely chop them up and put them on top of the plated dish, especially with some coarse salt and a drizzle of the fruitiest olive oil you can find. Yes, the expensive little bottle, or from your farmer, if you live in olive-producing regions.

10

Shop the perimeter of your market. They deliberately spread the healthy basics around the store so you have to walk past the entire selection of over-produced, high profit margin, impulse-buy foods in order to get your basic kitchen necessities like meats, dairy, produce, and baked goods.

11

Another good measure is to keep an eye on the trash produced by your eating habits. If you're throwing out a lot of non-recyclables and trash, you are probably buying foods that are over-processed, or non-foods, as I like to call them.

12

Buy the best and simplest of kitchen tools you can afford. One really good knife is far better than several stupid gadgets that will probably break anyway. If you're buying something for your kitchen, think about whether it will survive to be handed down to the next generation. If not, it probably isn't that well made. Buy copper pots, even if only one. Copper has excellent heat transfer characteristics, which allows you more control over the cooking process. The ascetic pleasure of cooking with the finest pots and pans will provide pleasure and inspiration. Rise to the challenge and strive to make each meal more delicious than the last. Don't be embarrassed to get a cast iron pan at the local second hand store.

13

Dishes are fun, but remember it's about the food. Yes, we do eat first with our eyes. A simple white plate or glass dish full of thoughtfully prepared delicious food is still far better that an expensive, elegant platter full of warmed up deli selections, or boring, tasteless food.

14

Participate in the production of your food. Get to know your suppliers. Talk to them about their processes. Understand how and where your food comes from. Perform your own preparations. Participating with your own foods in your own kitchen with your own family is a good thing. There's plenty of time to have a conversation while you're working together to prepare a meal. Using a *moka* (an Italian style coffee pot) to prepare your morning cup of coffee forces you to engage in the food preparation process. You do not set a timer the night before and awake to a freshly brewed cup of weak coffee made from stale grounds or, worse yet, grounds made (when?) by an unknown supplier. A *moka* forces you to be in your kitchen and anticipate the arrival of perfectly brewed coffee. A morning ritual of grinding your own coffee beans, filling the basket, and gently tamping them down, screwing on the top of the pot, setting the pot on a low flame and waiting for the coffee to completely express becomes one of the savored food moments of your life. It may take five to ten minutes, but that's a lot less time than to park your car, stand in line and grab a $3.00 espresso and then drink it while in traffic.

15

Make soup. It is a natural by-product of a well-stocked and organized kitchen. Stop to think about the pieces of meat and vegetables that you are currently cutting off of your daily foods. If they're not spoiled, they're probably the ingredients for soups that you're discarding instead of consuming. If you make one meal a week a soup-based meal—using foods that are already in your kitchen—you might even save money. If you estimate that you would have spent a minimum of $10.00 per person for a take-out or restaurant dinner for a family of four, it translates to over $2,000 a year. On top of that, consider the hidden costs of packaging, transportation, and waste removal. You can buy a very nice set of copper pots and pans for $2,000 and reward yourself for recycling your leftovers and doing something good for your environment, too.

16

Last, but not least, keep it simple. It must be visually appealing, it must be fresh, and it must be properly prepared. It doesn't need to be fussy, architecturally arranged, or complicated. That's what restaurants and professional chefs are for. If you decide to leave your simply prepared meals at home for dining out, remember to not pay for food in a restaurant that's worse than what you can make at home. It's never a good idea to reward someone for bad behavior.

> *"Fill your life with exciting food moments. You may find that along the way you have no more time for the usual stressors that fill up your day."*

Shopping

CHAPTER 2

Shopping is a perpetual necessity. You never actually get to a state where you can say, "I've finished all my shopping." It's something you just have to do. However, it can become an adventure where you look forward to finding new foods to play with in your kitchen. Shopping is a major part of living *La Dolce Vita*. The open-air *mercato* (market) in the *piazza* (square) in Italy is the center of a community. Yes, the church is, too. In my advanced Italian language tapes, they spend an entire section on learning the words, "*Dov'è la strada per andare alla piazza del Duomo?*" "Where is the street for going to the cathedral square?" Why do they emphasize this phrase? In Italy, the *piazza* is where it's all happening. The various markets one would need to visit in the course of a day's shopping are strategically located near the square. Do you know any American who would want to go to their cathedral square? Of course not, because we don't have many open air markets here! Our grocery stores have become large mega-stores with the life of the *piazza* removed.

I realize that not all of you look forward to doing your grocery shopping as I do. You do, however, need to procure food in some manner. Some of us have other people who can do our shopping for us. Some of us do less shopping and spend a lot of time eating out. You can definitely live a part of *La Dolce Vita* if you're able to spend most of your year living like you are on vacation. Wealth has its advantages, but sometimes it comes with hidden costs.

Every time you purchase an item, it contributes to your local community's pollution, because it comes with some level of individual packaging and some level of transportation cost. Count the number of trash containers that are removed from your household every week. Now think about the number of trash containers that are thrown away in your name from every vendor or supplier of your household services, or meals provided off site. Living *La Dolce Vita* requires some level of personal responsibility for your levels of consumption, and the mark you make upon our planet. Living your life with an open heart and mind, taking time to walk the extra mile to not support suppliers who overwhelm the planet's resources, and reducing the amount of your personal contribution to our trash dumps need to be included in your shopping experience. Remember the new adage

"Reuse, reduce, recycle." Tell your market's manager that you want less packaging, not more. Has anyone but me noticed that the spinach that was not in the plastic bags doesn't seem to have been tainted with E. coli bacteria?

Purchase fresh organic produce from your local farmers. Bring it home in your own organic cotton shopping bags. Say, "I don't need a bag, thank you, I have two hands." Make sure the packaging of your purchases can be recycled. Better yet, buy items that are unpackaged. Fruits and vegetables have their own protective skins after all. Treat them with respect on the trip home and they won't be all mangled up when you get them to your counter.

Now let's discuss the three Rs (reuse, reduce and recycle). It takes less planetary resources to reuse than to recycle. It takes more planetary resources to fill landfills with our trash (aka refuse) than to recycle.

> *Dal mattino si vede il buon giorno.*
> (A bad morning doesn't see a good day.)

> *" I don't need a bag, thank you. I have two hands. "*

It takes no planetary resources to refuse products that are unnecessarily packaged. Just say NO!

I maintain that there should be four Rs (reuse, reduce, recycle, and refuse). If an item you want to buy has too much packaging, try to find what you're looking for at another market, but don't waste your gas driving all over town. Support your small local organic markets. Yes, it may cost more money, in the short run, but in some cases you may even save money. Your money will directly support a farmer and a worthy cause. In the long run, the large markets are already beginning to feel the pinch from the organic movement. Be a part of the solution, not the problem. And do recognize that you and your planet ultimately pay the price for cheaper food at your big box grocery stores. You get what you pay for, and if you want to put quality food into your body, you'll have to pay the price. The good news is that even Wal-Mart is beginning to recognize the need for providing organic produce. Hopefully it will not take a jumbo jet to fly the organic produce to your market.

Talk to your food suppliers. Ask them what's fresh today. Ask them to grow what you like to eat. They just might do it. If there's no sign, ask them if their produce is organic. Sometimes it's almost organic, and they may tell you why or why not. Perhaps it's not organically fertilized and it's not sprayed with chemical pesticides (not fully organic but on the way towards getting there). If it's not organic, perhaps they'll notice that you walk away and purchase your produce at the next market or booth. I say, very politely, "Well, I may be able to find it down the street," (at their competitor's store) if they don't seem to have a particular item. Sometimes I'll ask for an organic item I know they don't have, just to remind them they have competition. Sometimes I'll buy it anyway because I'm tired or in a hurry, or just plain defeated. I usually feel guilty and tell myself I will *not* do that the next time. Strive. Start out with a small portion of your foods being organic. The more you purchase, prepare and eat fresh, organic foods, the more you'll find non-organic foods to be unsatisfying.

> *" L'unione fa la forza. (The union makes the force.) "*

When shopping, if you see something you don't recognize, buy it. Ask the vendor questions. "What is it? Do you eat it?" If someone next to you is exclaiming about how wonderful something looks, or is buying a bunch of them, ask them, "What do you do with it?" Pay attention, buy some, go home and try it in a small amount. If it works, great, do it again. If it doesn't, analyze it. What didn't you like about it? How could you change it? Did you do something wrong in the preparation or cooking, or is it a flavor that isn't preferred? Should it be discarded, or attempted again? Was more time necessary to prepare it properly?

Here's another shopping habit you can change. Can you imagine going to a grocery store and having them not bag your groceries for you? In Italy you bag your own groceries, and frequently it's in the bag that you brought with you. Is this absurd? No. It helps you develop some personal responsibility with your shopping habits and shopping by-products. Can you imagine having to pay a coin deposit to take a grocery cart from the corral? You are required to deposit a 2€ (almost $3) coin every time you take a cart, and you don't get your money back until you responsibly return the cart. Here's another great idea: if you are only buying a few items, why not skip the cart and the bag and say to our grocery checkers "I don't need a bag, thank you. I have two hands."

Another idea is to begin buying your food in reusable or recyclable containers. My local grocery store just started providing Sicilian olive oil in bottles that they will refill for you when you bring it back. This is a great idea. Now I'm trying to convince them that our local olive oil should also be available in this manner. It may seem like it's only one bottle, or it's only one piece of cardboard but it's not only one. It's many of them, all the time, accumulating infinitely. Think about how much trash *you*, personally, are putting into the planet. If the trash pile was in your back yard, would you want to bring all of this unnecessary and non-recyclable packaging home with you? Fresh foods frequently come in their own packaging. For instance, an apple has a skin. It doesn't need a plastic bag so it can cozy up with its friends.

Make shopping part of your lifestyle. Take a little more time and go to the specialty stores. Reward yourself with a special food you may not be able to afford very often. Reward yourself with a cup of freshly brewed or expressed coffee. It can be fun. Talk to the people you see along the way. If you have to do it anyway, why not make it an enjoyable experience? Yes, I sing to myself while I'm shopping, and I'm frequently smiling. It is, after all, a beautiful sunny day, or a beautiful rainy day, and I'm privileged

to live in a beautiful place where I can get excellent foods from some really interesting people.

Okay, here's how I shop: Randomly, with only a small list, which I usually forget because it's still on the refrigerator underneath the magnet. I rarely take a recipe with me. My style of cooking is to buy everything that looks really interesting and then take it home and figure out how to put it together into a delicious meal. Once I get a concept, sometimes I'll look into a cookbook.

I wonder how James Beard would prepare French onion soup, for instance. Oh, he adds a little _____, sure I can do that, too. Or, no, I don't have parsley today. Let's try it with cilantro....

After I do my shopping, I put most of the produce on the counter so I can look at it and get inspired.

I have many conversations with myself about various things to do with the five red bell peppers I brought home; Like, *Okay, stuffed with that bit of leftover rice in the fridge, no, how about roasted and added to steak with a little onion?* Or, *If I have any lemons on the tree I can make fajitas.... Well, if I make spaghetti sauce tonight, then I'll have some tomorrow and the stuffed peppers will be even better.* Sometimes the conversations are more like, *I'd better cook those zucchini soon or I'll have to throw them out. They don't really go with tonight's dinner; maybe I can get away with grating them onto the salad plate.*

❝ *Part of living* La Dolce Vita *is to have a good time doing what you want to do.* ❞

So here's an example. Today, it's one of those days that lets you know that summer is definitely over, and I'm not yet in the mood for the fall soups, stews, and squashes. I'm making steaks, because the men like them after a hard week at work. But I'm not particularly inspired just yet. I did go to the farmers' market. I purchased the ubiquitous anthuriums (my favorite), lettuces, zucchini, dandelion greens, raspberries and apples. It's not a particularly inspiring lot. I picked some of the remaining scraggly tomatoes. (It wasn't my best year for tomatoes.) My thoughts are to grill the steaks, which I seasoned with a spice rub that my husband purchased on a business trip to Texas. (Texans, like Florentines, know how to grill a great steak.) Then I'll pull together a pasta dish with the dandelion greens and the red and orange tomatoes.

Oh, yes, I bought artichokes, and they have been steamed and will be ready for an appetizer so the hungry ones don't push me too quickly in the kitchen. So, artichokes with a light mayonnaise dressing, green salad with the accompanying red plate of whatever I can pull together (it may just contain pickled artichoke stems. Guess where they came from?), a big bowl of spaghetti or linguine *con pomodori*, steaks, and things are starting to sound better already. For dessert, I'll try to talk Kate into spooning a small amount of ice cream over a 1-inch square of a defrosted chocolate cake and top it with a few raspberries. Now, how hard was that?

This is a great meal, it'll be well received, and it really isn't too hard to prepare. Soon I'll show you some of my more adventurous Friday evening meals. Although the title of the book is *Friday Evening*, for me the name of the book is *Venerdi Sera*. Oh yes, I bought a cauliflower for another night this weekend, and fresh bread, a chicken, and a very large piece of pork shoulder. After twenty years of smothering cauliflower under cheese sauce, my family has finally learned to love it and can now eat it just with a light dressing of olive oil or butter, Tomorrow, I'll probably roast the chicken, because I don't spend a lot of time working in the kitchen on weekends. On Sunday, if I'm energetic, I'll cube the pork, and sauté some onions, add a can of *tomatillo* (small edible yellow to purple tomato-like fruit enclosed in a bladder-like husk) or red enchilada sauce, and let it cook itself all day.

> *"In order to change your shopping and eating habits, you may need to break your old habits."*

This is an example of my thought processes when I shop. I try to think ahead about two to three days, while also looking back on what needs to be consumed from past meals. For instance, remember those steaks? I'll probably reheat the baked beans from last weekend and serve them with the steak. Either that, or there'll have to be a bean soup coming along shortly. I didn't make any broth this week because it's been too hot to think about soups, but if I cook that chicken, there'll be a carcass to start a stock with as early as Sunday morning.

Imagine yourself in the grocery store. If you find that it's not a pleasurable experience, could it be because you're not shopping properly, or at the correct market? When I'm at my favorite farmers' market, or my favorite organic market, I frequently find myself smiling and singing. This is a good thing. Part of living *La Dolce Vita* is to have a good time doing what you want to do. If you shop in the more upscale markets, yes, you'll probably pay a bit more. Have you noticed that when you sacrifice, or scrimp and save for a big purchase, or just go ahead and buy that thing you really can't afford, you only have a moment of guilt, and then you really begin to enjoy your new item? These splurge items can be translated into food purchases. I maintain that if you spend a little more on food, you'll take the preparation and eating parts more seriously and probably spend less time shopping for all of those other things you think you have to buy. Most of us have to purchase and/or consume food anyway, so why not make it a more important part of our budgets and lifestyles?

Yes, occasionally something gets thrown away because I didn't get to it in time. Sometimes, things that I bought for dinner that night get hastily put into the freezer because a neighbor shows up with a bag of tomatoes, or my father-in-law tells me he found a nice salmon, and will I cook it tonight? You have to remain flexible. Sometimes I do run back to the store because the original concept turns into something else at the last moment, and a key ingredient is missing. Luckily, I live within a mile of a small, well-stocked market. Those last-minute trips to the market are great times to pick up a loaf of fresh bread. Please, please, please buy fresh bread that came from an in-town bakery. (We'll talk about what to do with the leftover bread pieces later).

In order to change your shopping and eating habits, you may need to break your old habits. This means staying away from most of the items in the freezer section of the store, and especially staying away from most of the canned and packaged food items (except for items discussed in Chapters 9-10). Try shopping the perimeter of the store, buying only consumable items. Usually, a store is laid out so that you can do a sweep of the meats, fish, dairy, produce and fresh bakery. The majority of things you should be buying are in these major sections. Your shopping list for

> *“It doesn't take a rocket scientist to learn how to shop for wholesome fresh foods that minimize their impact on your local landfill.”*

these items should be in your head, because these items are the foods you use the most and run out of the fastest. Your shopping list can therefore be used for the items you don't use as often but still need to buy; toilet paper, batteries, mustard, cereals, flour, etc.

As you begin filling your freezer with large pieces of meat and ingredients for your *La Dolce Vita* meals, you won't have room for over-packaged, over-processed, pre-prepared junk food. You will stop going to the freezer first when you're hungry. Perhaps that apple, or a slice of the fresh French bread with some cheese, or some yogurt, will become a snack. Or you'll find leftover pasta in the refrigerator. These are the foods you should be eating when hunger appears in the middle of the day. If you begin to shop and cook in this manner, the variety of foods available to you will slowly begin to change. Sooner or later you'll realize that you've made the switch.

Now, back to shopping the perimeter: Look for a variety of meats, fish, and poultry. If you feel like chicken, buy one—a whole one. If you're single, this may be harder to do, but armed with a good knife and some plastic zipper bags, you can create smaller portions. The tradeoff is between spending some time to cut the meats yourself and paying the butcher to do it, plus now you've also paid for the additional packaging, and you've incurred a higher risk of food-borne pathogens getting into your food supply.

Here's another thing to think about while buying chicken. You know those large volume big-buy packages of boneless chicken breasts? How many chickens were killed so that your family of four can eat eight chicken breasts tonight for dinner? Yes, eight, or maybe four if they're double breasts. If you purchase a whole chicken, your family of four can still eat, and only one animal had to die for your consumption. My family doesn't like chicken legs, you say? Cut the meat off and make chicken salad, *ravioli*, or enchiladas out of them.

Buy eggs and cheese even if they're not a part of the recipe you have in your hand right now. In fact, throw away the recipe. The ingredient list is what you really want to shop with. Now, down to the dairy section. Milk is usually a part of everyone's household; why not try some plain yogurt? Once you get over the tanginess and get beyond the taste of no sugar in your yogurt, the flavor will grow on you. Plus, plain yogurt is much more versatile because you can use it in savory dishes as well as sweet. Tortillas are usually found near the dairy and are good to keep on hand for consuming leftovers at lunch.

Take a stroll through the produce section. Buy lettuce for a few days' meals, and whatever vegetables are in season and look good to you. Nothing looks good to you today? If it's fresh, buy it anyway. You can figure out what to do with it once you get it home. Broccoli is by far one of the healthiest and easiest to cook vegetables available to the American consumer. Consume some. Depending on how your market is set up, sometimes the vegetable section is the first you come to. Pick up several day's worth in portions that are enough for one and a half night's meals for the number of people you have at your table. If someone else shows up unexpectedly, you'll have enough. If not, you'll have leftovers for either a lunch or a *contorno* (vegetable side dish) another night.

Now, once you have picked out some meats and veggies, look at your basket and think about ways you can marry them.

Broccoli and steak? Maybe I should get some potatoes to go with that.

Chicken and mushrooms? If I add some fresh pasta or risotto rice, I could get a great braising thing going....

Make a second pass through the store and pick up any extras you may need or want to complete the meals with the items you've put into the cart. Not sure what all the ingredients are? Some markets have cookbook sections and/or recipe cards on hand. Look it up and get any other ingredients you may need. Forget about the recipe measurements; think about the number of people you're feeding and the

amount they may consume. For instance, when you're purchasing green beans, grab a handful for each adult and a couple of beans for smaller children. If you have too many, put them in someone's lunch the next day, even yours.

If the wealth of fresh produce has not yet inspired you to create the night's meal, you may look at the deli counter's pre-prepared foods. If something looks good to you, why not try making it yourself? Again, if your budget allows and you have no time to make your own meals, by all means go ahead and purchase some foods at the deli counter. Try not to make it a habit. Instead, make it a habit to buy some fresh fruit before leaving the market, and buy some fresh bread (unless your next stop is the bakery).

You don't read a manual to learn how to swim. You have to have some guidance, and you have to get into the water. The same is true for cooking your way to the good life. You have to get into your kitchen and start cooking. Use your head. It doesn't take a rocket scientist to learn how to shop for wholesome fresh foods that minimize their impact on your local landfill. It doesn't take a rocket scientist to learn how to cook. You just have to try. Learn from your mistakes, but above all *learn*. It's okay with me if you don't want to cook. You can always pay someone to cook and shop for you. Just please don't tell me you *can't* cook.

> *Al contadino non far sapere quant' è buono il formaggio con le pere.*
> (Don't let the farmer know how good the cheese is with the pear.)

The Menus

CHAPTER 3

In Italy, and in many restaurants in the U.S., menus are divided into appetizers, mains, and desserts. Sometimes you see a pasta or pizza section. Frequently, you'll see salads as a separate listing. In some of the finer restaurants, you'll even see the cheese and fruit courses listed at the back, after the dessert course, and if you're really lucky, you'll see a selection of after dinner drinks.

In the United States, many people are accustomed to eating one main plate, which is usually heaped with food. This is the standard American meat and potatoes meal. You are therefore dividing your attention between all the foods that are crowded onto your plate at one time. Just like a stolen television cable signal, each time you divide the signal, the signal strength is degraded.

I believe that with foods, you should keep the input signal strong by focusing on each individual food item, one at a time. In developing an *a la carte* approach, I recommend and try to follow the Italians. In general, start with an *aperitivo*, followed by an *antipasto*, *a primo*, maybe a *secondo*, *piatto principale*, with a *contorno*, and *a dolce*. More and more often we'll have a *digestivo* after we leave the table, sometimes with a piece of fruit shared by all.

No one in my family is fat. In fact, I have lost about ten pounds since I started eating in this manner. I highly recommend Mireille Guiliano's book, *French Women Don't Get Fat*. She talks about this at length. So why don't the French and Italian women get fat? They don't eat huge portions. Each item, as a small portion, is savored and appreciated. Rather than eating a huge amount of one thing, your body becomes more satisfied because you are presenting

it with delectable morsels of many interesting tastes and textures. Mireille is right. I've tried it, and it is certainly working for me.

And yes, try drinking water. It's a no-brainer. Don't tell me it tastes bad, put a slice of citrus in it. Save your money and cut out some of the sugar in your diet. In Europe you will see a bottle of mineral water in an ice bucket at almost every table. Again, if you get the finest, sip it slowly, and you'll enjoy it more. And maybe you'll have one less glass of wine with dinner, and that's probably healthier, too.

Before I give you some of my menus, I want to discuss the philosophy behind some of the courses. When you start preparing your own foods, you'll find that many of the small courses in one day's meal are really re-presentations of leftovers from previous meals. That's the beauty of this style of eating. Nothing gets thrown away.

> " *Non si puo avere la botte piena e la moglie ubriaca.*
> (You can't have a full cask and a drunk wife.) "

Aperitivo 1

For me, the consumption of the *aperitivo* begins during the production of the meal.

When I come running in the door before a meal, I usually have some idea about what I'm preparing for that night's dinner. I know what things are in my refrigerator. Some of them I have specifically purchased for tonight's dinner, some are leftovers from previous meals, and some are foods I purchased because they caught my eye at the farmers' market and need to be consumed or they will no longer be at the peak of their freshness.

I pour myself a glass of chilled white wine and either begin or peruse the current meal plan. A meal plan is a blank sheet of paper (for me, usually 8 ½" x 11" computer paper, for consistency, though sometimes it's the back of the shopping list or an envelope). I date it, I write down my menu ideas, and who will be at the table. Then I get going. This five minute period is like the quiet before the storm. If I'm not alone, we pour a glass of wine for each of the people present. Now, of course there are entire books written about *aperitivi*, so you can choose which one works for you.

I recently tried my first glass of Campari, and tonight's celebration is starting off with a Campari and soda. If I like it, I may start my weekends off with a little bit of the bitters.

Aperitivo 2

This is the refreshing of the first glass (remember they're not tumblers) and the pouring for the late arrivals, prior to the completion of cooking. At this time, I will set out the *assaggino*.

Assaggino

This course is an appetizer, or *uno spuntino* (a simple small snack), to distract the starving diners from breathing down your neck while you're trying to pull the rest of the meal together. It's frequently a bowl of nuts, or some grapes and cheese, some form of *bruschetta*, or even cheese and crackers. It is not an entire box of crackers with three whole wedges of cheese. It's a snack, and should do nothing more than stave off hunger until the meal is ready. The French call it *amuse bouche* (a mouth teaser). One or two pieces per person, small, very tasty if you have time to make it, or salty and crunchy if you're pulling it out of the pantry. This course is an excellent way to pair yesterday's bread with a puréed and re-seasoned *contorno* from the night before. Sometimes, last night's *piatto principale* is cut into bite-sized pieces and served with toothpicks. *Assaggini* are usually eaten in the kitchen, while standing. Sometimes they are taken into the office by someone who has been away for awhile and wants to check an email before dinner.

> *L'appetito vien mangiando.*
> (The appetite comes when we eat.)

Antipasto

This course may be necessary if your diners are starving and your meal is not going to be ready for quite a while. It should still be small, and can even be the *bruschetta*, if the nuts were served as the *assaggino*. The *antipasto* is often served at the table, though the hostess (me, aka cook) may not be seated at this time, depending on the formality of the evening.

Primo

By this time, the courses have all been prepped, the primo is ready to consume, and the cook takes a break to sit and eat for the first time. In our family, there may be a soup. If so, it comes out now. A small bowl of soup, about ½ to 1 cup is served. Remember, even though the soup may be fantastic, you don't want seconds because there are more courses coming. (Chances are there'll be soup for lunch tomorrow.)

If there isn't a soup planned for this meal, in our family, the primo is usually an *insalatina verde*. Our Italian cousins served their salads plain. I thought it was very strange, at the time. I remember thinking, *Well, we Californians have certainly improved on this part of the meal. Our salads are some of the best in the world. We put SO much into them. They're simply delicious.*

While we were serving ourselves from the bowl of simply-dressed lettuce, other plates came out: a plate of tomatoes, and maybe a small plate of *salumi* or prosciutto. I waited and saw my cousin pick from each plate those items that he wanted for his salad.

> " *I buy boxed pasta because it's inexpensive, and I am neurotic about natural disasters and not having enough food to sustain an army for at least one week.* "

Simple. Everyone chooses what he or she likes and puts it on their plate, as opposed to fishing out the things they don't like from the bowl. Now they're focusing on their food, participating, and beginning to make decisions that lead to dining, as opposed to gobbling up a gigantic meal loaded with calories before the next course comes to the table.

Since that meal, we never put anything but a simple dressing into our bowl with the lettuce. On the side, as a *contorno* to the *primo*, comes *Il Piatto Rosso* (The Red Plate). This plate is reserved for the featured items to go with the night's salad: a slice of feta, a sliced tomato, and some olives or zucchini. Pick from the freshest of produce that you bought recently, the things that looked really fresh at the farmers' market. We put some of these items on The Red Plate. If anyone wants to help in the kitchen, all I have to say is "Would you like to make The Red Plate?" If they've been here before, they know exactly what to do. These items get dressed with some coarse sea salt and the very freshest, fruitiest olive oil I can find. Then give it a "scritch" of pepper. (You are using a pepper grinder by now, aren't you?)

Secondo

The *secondo* can be the salad, as discussed above, or the *secondo* can be the pasta, or another small featured dish, depending on how your menu comes together. It can be a plate of freshly grated zucchini, with just a drizzle of olive oil, and, again, salt and pepper. Serving dishes like this, which can be prepared ahead of time, gives me a chance to check what's next, or to drop the pasta into the boiling water, while everyone is serving themselves. While the pasta is cooking, or while the *piatto principale* is resting before being carved or plated, I can come back to the table to eat. We eat, we talk, we pour some more wine, and the meal progresses.

> *"Now, in a culture whose meals developed over time during periods of poverty, all the previous courses would have been used to stretch the meal so everyone would get full and thereby not eat the main course, which would have been scarce and very expensive."*

Pasta e gli altri

I typically make dinner for five or six people, more if another couple is invited to dinner. So, when I make the pasta, I inevitable make the entire box of pasta. Now, you're wondering, a box of pasta? There is nothing like making fresh pasta and consuming it later that night. I know people who do this all the time. They're cooking for one or two. Kate will make pasta sometimes, when she's not in school. It's fun and it definitely is another whole taste away

> **" *I'll drink that evening cup of caffeine and have wild and crazy dreams all night long.* "**

from boxed pasta. This is one area of cuisine where I don't venture too often. I will buy fresh pasta at the market (make sure it's really fresh, and from a local company, or it really isn't fresh pasta) for special occasions. I buy boxed pasta because it's inexpensive, and I am neurotic about natural disasters and not having enough food to sustain an army for at least one week. At this exact moment, I have *cannelloni* (1), lasagne (5), *fettuccine* (3), *linguine* (1), *pappardelle* (1), *riso* (1), *capellini* (5), *spaghetti* (5), *orzo* (1), *fregola sarda* (1, for a future experiment), and *rusticane* (1, similar to two inch lasagne noodles). I rarely know which pasta I will choose until I determine how thick the sauce or condiment will be. This will usually happen sometime during the chopping phase. If I'm lazy and feel like cutting things into bigger pieces, I will choose a heartier pasta to go along with it.

Pasta will usually come to the table by itself as its own course unless the *piatto principale* contains gravy, or is meatballs or some similar item. This holds true for *risotto*, potatoes, and *couscous*. Bread and tortillas are usually not served as a course, and are served earlier in the meal, like with the soup, and stay on the table throughout the meal.

Piatto Principale

The *piatto principale* is, of course, the main dish, literally, the principle plate. By this time, if you're consuming American-sized portions, you will be quite full and could probably walk away from the table fully stuffed, ready to fall asleep in front of the television. Sometimes some of us do. But, if you didn't pace yourself and leave now, you'd be missing the best part. Now, in a culture whose meals developed over time during periods of poverty, all the previous courses would be used to stretch the meal so everyone would get full and thereby not eat the main course, which would have been scarce and very expensive. It's true even today. A household of hearty eaters could break the bank if they only ate meat, which is typically the most expensive item on the menu. All these cleverly-fashioned small courses were designed to curb the appetite while sustaining the hearty eaters in times of poverty. Cutlets are the embodiment of that very principle. Take a piece of meat, cut a thin slice for each person, pound it to make it more tender (and it also looks bigger) and put eggs and breadcrumbs on it to make it more flavorful and bigger yet, and *bruscamente*! You have a meal!

> **" *The secret is not to make more of what you already were planning to serve, but to add additional courses to the menu.* "**

My husband is a big meat eater. He is not big; he is a big eater of meats. So, you will see a lot of meat-related main dishes. If you are not a meat eater, you can move from the pasta course directly to the desserts. I would next offer a *contorno*, which in my house would be a vegetable dish, but in yours it may be instead a vegetarian main course.

Contorno

The *contorno*, or side dish, is usually a vegetable, unless the pasta is served with the meat, as in spaghetti and meatballs. It's very easy to prepare the locally grown seasonal vegetable that's dominating the farmers' market. Prepare it steamed, and anointed with a small amount of your very best olive oil. A drop or two of lemon juice is also very good. Cook it gently, keeping it still a bit firm. I always buy a larger amount of this vegetable so I will have leftovers for the next day's lunches or a second *contorno*. I believe it is better to have too much than not enough for my hungry dinner companions. The next night's *contorno* may have the same *al dente* vegetable, but with a dusting of toasted breadcrumbs or parmesan.

Dolci, Formaggi e Frutta

I don't like to bake, so I will hand off this menu item to whoever is willing to accept it, usually Kate. I do like to eat a sweet at the end of the meal. My mother is notorious for having her picture taken behind a very large piece of the gooiest chocolat-iest cake she can find. I tried that for awhile; now I am into the very small, elegantly served sweet. The rest of my family prefers the single serve size of Ben and Jerry's ice cream, elegantly served *"nel pacco con un cucchiaio"* which is a translation of "in the container with a spoon." It sounds much more elegant when put into Italian don't you think?

Caffé e Digestivo

Most nights don't end with a coffee after dinner because we are now at the age where a cup of coffee after two P.M. can ruin your whole night's sleep. I would be more than happy to make a pot of decaffeinated coffee, but it's very hard to talk someone into sharing it with me. I'm always happy when someone comes to dinner, plans to drive home afterwards, and is willing to go for that cup of Joe (or Giuseppe) for the road. I'll drink that evening cup of caffeine and have wild and crazy dreams all night long.

It's always worth it to have another excuse to bring out a treasured glass of a sweet Sicilian, or a local late harvest wine, some Tuaca or *Grappa*. Lingering at the table a little while longer with your best friends and family members before having to face the road, or the dishes, or homework is really what it's all about, anyway. Sometimes, if you're lucky, a card game may start up at this time. Chances are you'll have other reasons to sleep in late the next morning. If you're really lucky, someone has spent the night and you get to wake up and start thinking about the next evening's feast while at breakfast. Sometimes there's even a little leftover espresso to help you get that first morning pot onto the stove. Remember the famous scene from *The Big Chill* where Jeff Goldblum says "Are we the first ones up?" Ahh, houseguests....

> **"** *I may not make it to Oprah's show, but at least my grandchildren will know a little bit more about Grandma and why their mother has developed her own idiosyncratic food habits.* **"**

The Menus

The menus in the following chapters were developed over a series of years. Many of these are the actual meals we consumed over a variety of Friday evenings. Occasionally, I will add a menu which may have been consumed on other weeknights, or add typical courses to notes where I have only recorded a main dish or successful experiment. None of these meals are from large parties. (I'm reserving them for my next book.) The menus are arranged in seasonal order, which hopefully will allow you to prepare similar meals from the seasonal offerings at the local markets in your area.

These menus, or shall I say menu plans, evolved because there were times when I had to leave in the middle of the meal preparation to pick someone up from volleyball practice, or therapy, etc. Sometimes, a caregiver would start the meal and I would finish it when Kristin and I returned from an appointment. Sometimes, I started and finished the meal, with someone else performing intermediate steps. Mostly, I plan the meal, shop for ingredients, and prep and finish the meal by myself, which is my preferred method of cooking. Many times, there may be others in the kitchen, but these occasions tend to be more on the Saturday evening meals, when larger numbers of guests are invited. These menus are suggested for Friday evenings, with family, and perhaps one other couple. This means four to six people at the dinner table.

The menus evolved from simple short notes written to myself to remember what I had planned to serve, or to remember not to forget a side dish in the oven, to longer one-page synopses including ingredients, to one-page litanies for Kate to re-read and enjoy some day. Along the way, after my first trip to Italy, and during my fixation upon learning the Italian language, I began writing them in Italian to increase my vocabulary. I regret that I threw many of them away in the earlier days.

Here are my suggestions when one of your simple meals for four suddenly becomes a meal for seven. Sometimes, you get the phone calls at the last minute; "So-and-so is joining us for dinner." You know that you have only enough food cooking for the four of you. To avoid a trip to the store, asking your added guest to stop at the store, and to reduce the stress of a last minute change of plan, look to your pantry, refrigerator, and freezer. If they have been properly stocked, it should be no trouble to bring out a few other items to complete the meal. The secret is not to make more of what you already were planning to serve, but to add additional courses to the menu. It will look like you planned for the larger group all along, and if you don't tell them they'll never know. So, add a soup. If you don't have something defrostable, put some vegetables in the food processor and add them to some broth, with seasonings, butter, and/or cream. A bag of frozen vegetables and a bottle of cream can make this happen instantly. Try microwaving a potato or two and creating a potato soup course. If you keep frozen bacon or *pancetta*, defrost it, wrap it around something, and stick them under the broiler. Look to your pantry for tins of clams or sardines. Put them on *crostini*, or good toasts, or crackers. Purée whatever you can find in your refrigerator and create extra *antipasti*. Once, I had that call, and I took leftover meat sauce with mushrooms and put it in the food processor. I mixed that with leftover rice, and stuffed and rolled it in frozen grape leaves that had been sitting in my freezer for months. A can of grape leaves kept in the pantry for just this type of evening is a good idea. Once, I had leftover salmon when I got the call that more were coming to dinner. I chopped the salmon, mixed it with mayonnaise, salt, and pepper, and spread it on endive. I have even food-processed corned beef and cabbage (and, another time, pork with sauerkraut) and turned them into a spread for rye bread toasts. Leftover Chinese food can be chopped and put into a defrosted package of egg rolls (or pasta) and steamed or fried. Remember, when you get the "Honey I'm bringing home some extra people tonight" call, don't panic. It's always better to have more people engaged in spirited conversation around the table than it is to have lots of food.

I'm thankful for the flash of inspiration I received while driving one afternoon. At that moment I realized I could pull my menu plans, together with my philosophy, into a book. I hope you enjoy reading these menus and that they provide the impetus for creating many Friday evening meals at your house, too. I may not make it to Oprah's show, but at least my grandchildren will know a little bit more about Grandma and why *their* mother has developed her own idiosyncratic food habits.

L'autunno

CHAPTER 4

I decided to begin the seasonal menus with L'autunno, autumn or fall, because the harvest occurs in this season. I love the fall. The abundance of produce and the need to consume or preserve it combine to give you a good reason to be in your kitchen. The weather begins to get cooler and the days get shorter. Children go back to school and it's a lot easier to hang out in the kitchen. Soups and stews can be simmering on the stove, breads can be baking, and the teapot comes out from its summer hiding place. The teapot reigns supreme on the counter until the longer days of spring banish it away to an out-of-the-way place where it will not get broken. A good place could be behind the margarita glasses, because when spring comes around we know we'll be using them soon enough.

But back to *l'autunno*, as the Italians call it. Today was the first day of rain, and lately the windows have been closing at night. The comforters get pulled up, and it's harder to get out of bed when the mornings are dark. The farmer's market wasn't crowded. The coffee shops were. The artichokes have been getting smaller, asparagus and basil seem to be disappearing, and all of a sudden, there are apples, lots of apples. And squash, pumpkins, turnips, and potatoes. Tomatoes are still in abundance, though I no longer crave them sliced with a little bit of balsamic vinegar drizzled on top. Today it's time to make a thick hearty red sauce. And, since it's Friday and the start of another *Venerdì sera*, let's make meatballs. No one ever turns down a big plate of perfectly cooked spaghetti and meatballs, especially on a dark and dreary day.

So what did I pick up today at the market? Two bunches of the nastiest, thickest, bumpiest carrots I've seen in a long time. One is to be displayed as the vegetable guest of honor and others are to be diced and sautéed with onions for tonight's sauce. Oops, I forgot the celery for the *soffritto* (sautéed aromatic vegetable); *non importa* (it's not important). Let's see if anyone notices, tonight. The meatballs and sauce were cooked earlier today, and are resting comfortably in a large pot in the oven at 140° F, hot enough to keep them safe to eat, and cool enough to allow the flavors to marry without needing to be attended while I take care of all the other day's tasks. Yes, I would leave the house with casseroles in the oven (use your own judgment with respect to fire safety and your oven's reliability), though not today. And yes, the house smells great.

The rest of the meal can simply be a great green salad, though today I had to buy tomatoes. Mine are finished for the year. Some mixed lettuces with some of the purchased parsley, a few leaves of the dwindling live basil plant on my kitchen counter, and some goat cheese. Drizzle all of it with a really good olive oil and get a fresh loaf of bread. A good bottle of red wine for the meal, and an *aperitivo* of

Campari and soda beforehand, and another exciting night is on its way! Of course there are not yet several other courses associated with this meal. I'll probably pull together something for people to munch on when they arrive, and there is some leftover broccoli just begging for a few crumbs to accompany it under the broiler. Kate is running in a jog-a-thon, so I won't get any help from her in the dessert category tonight. Better pull out some decadent chocolate biscuits, and perhaps that last orange. With a little cognac, no one will know....

I took a look at the menus I've saved to include in this book and noticed that there's a preponderance of fall and winter menus, and not a lot of spring and summer. My guess is that even I can get busy in the lazy days of summer and warm weather. It is so easy to be out of the house when it's beautiful, and so easy to cook when it gets colder. It's not called comfort food for nothing, you know.

When you have family members who are coming in from inclement weather, why not greet them with a house full of simmering aromas? You don't need to spend all day cooking. A crock-pot can be a working chef's best friend. Large pots of stews, or large pieces of meat, can simmer all day long in your oven if you cook them at the lowest possible temperature while maintaining kitchen safety rules.

Here in California, it is possible to barbeque late into the year. Many of these autumn menus include the barbeque. As the nights grow longer and colder though, moving to the stove and oven is my preference. Once it starts getting dark, no one seems to want to join the cook outside at the grill.

The menus below, and as listed in the menu index, are somewhat in chronological order, so the foods utilized should progress with the season's offerings.

> *Niente è piccolo di cio che seminiamo con l' amore.*
> (Nothing is small that one sews with love.)

Polpettine e Spaghetti con una Carota Brutta

Meatballs and Spaghetti (with an Ugly Carrot)

- ❖ Vino Rosso della Casa
- ❖ Crostini al Prosciutto
- ❖ Zuppa di Carote
- ❖ Insalata Verde

- ❖ Il Piatto Rosso con un Grande Pomodorone, Pomodoroni Gialli e Piccoli, Prezzemolo, e Condimento di Aceto Balsamico

- ❖ Spaghetti e Polpettine in Marinara
- ❖ Broccoli sotto Pangrattato
- ❖ Un Mandarino condiviso fra tutti

It was Friday the 13th after all, and if a big ugly deformed carrot caught my attention at the farmers' market, it just seemed fitting that he should come home and be a featured item on the menu. Once I got him home with all his friends, I decided he was too unusual to actually cut up and not share, so I put him on a vase and he became the floral (a.k.a. vegetal) table decoration. His friends became the soup. It was one of those nights when things could have gone a little bit better. The carrot was really ugly (see photo) and the paper towel underneath the meatballs caught on fire. Luckily the meatballs were saved. It's very difficult to invite guests when meatballs are being served. They, along with their cousins, the *raviolis*, always seem to be stretched a little thinly. In other words, *we don't like to share them with anyone we don't have to.*

Appunti/Notes

RED WINE OF THE HOUSE ~ Open a bottle and start a glass while you're making the meatballs. You'll want to add some to the sauce, a token offering to the gods of *pomodori*. If the tomatoes are happy, the sauce will be, too.

PROSCIUTTO ON TOAST ~ I rubbed the toast with garlic halves, drizzled some olive oil on top, and placed a bit of prosciutto on top with a bit of *mozzarella di bufala*. Simple. Any cheese would do. Use what you have on hand.

CARROT SOUP ~ Chicken stock made from bones, some onion, celery, a potato, and a big bunch of carrots, seasoned with salt and pepper, a bit of cinnamon, and some cloves, finished with a buzz from the immersion blender, aka the boat motor, and a bit of cream.

GREEN SALAD ~ As always, my favorite greens from the farmer's market that day.

TOMATOES, TOMATOES AND TOMATOES ~ Big heirlooms, small yellow or orange ones from the garden, and green striped ones provide all the flavors, textures and colors for an amazing dish. Display them artfully, and drizzle with olive oil and salt and pepper. Enough said.

SPAGHETTI AND MEATBALLS ~ There's nothing like the taste of mother's meatballs. Even though every mother uses almost exactly the same ingredients, they always seem to taste better when they come from your Mom. I got chastised for using fresh breadcrumbs and herbs because that was not the way Mom made them. It took me a few years to get them right. The truth is that mine are now much better than Mom's ever were. No one will admit it, but it's okay. I know they're good. You can look up any recipe for meatballs and use it, but you need to devote several years of concentrated trial and error before you'll figure out what makes them really good. And no, the recipe is not at the back of the book. Some recipes are never shared.

 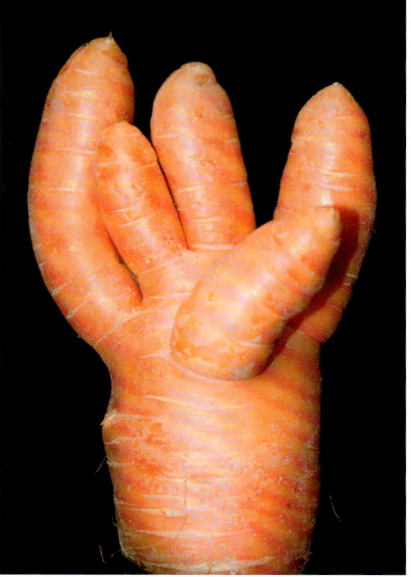

BROCCOLI UNDER BREADCRUMBS ~ This dish is best made with broccoli you've previously steamed and chilled. Add some olive oil to the bottom of a baking dish or gratin pan and layer the broccoli 1–2 deep. Season and sprinkle with breadcrumbs and/or cheese as you add each layer. Cover lightly with breadcrumbs, grated *parmigiano*, dot with butter, and drizzle with olive oil. Bake on high or under broiler until breadcrumbs are toasted and the broccoli is heated throughout.

A TANGERINE ~ Once Kristin, being in a wheelchair, got us kitchen-side seats at Chez Panisse in Berkeley. It was the best experience, because here we were, seated all by ourselves in the dining room at lunchtime, while everyone in the kitchen was preparing that night's dinner. We oohed and aahed over each new item that came out of the giant refrigerator and spent about two hours lingering over each morsel on our own plates. Just when we thought it couldn't get any better, our waiter brought over a small, footed, copper bowl filled with tangerines. How completely elegant, yet simple and unassuming. We stayed another hour just finishing the conversation and the tangerines. Try it!

Bistecca alla Griglia con un Pomodorone

GRILLED STEAK WITH A GIANT HEIRLOOM TOMATO

- ❖ Campari e Acqua di Seltz con Ghiaccio
- ❖ Crostini con Pomodori, Basilico e Mozzarella di Bufala
- ❖ Insalata Mista
- ❖ Un Pomodorone Grande
- ❖ Spaghetti al Burro e all'Olio
- ❖ Bistecca alla Griglia
- ❖ Ciliege, Formaggio con denti

Some Fridays I don't spend the entire day thinking about, buying, or preparing food. This was one of those days. I did make it to the farmers' market, and the tomatoes were outstanding. At the end of the summer and/or start of fall, the tomatoes are gigantic. This is the time to simply slice them and eat them by the plateful. Even Jim, who detests raw tomatoes, agreed to sample from the platter of these amazing beauties. Yes, a simple salad, a grilled steak and whatever else looks good at the market that can be cooked on the grill. The weather is still warm, and the menu should be simply prepared.

Appunti/Notes

CAMPARI AND SODA ~ Over ice. When I have the time I'll get a sprig of mint and use it as the swizzle stick.

TOMATO, BASIL AND MOZZARELLA ON TOAST ~ One or two per person, just to whet the appetite for the tomatoes to come.

MIXED GREENS ~ The greens should be very simple, a couple of leaves from different varieties of lettuce, simply dressed. We are not trying to compete with the tomato tonight. Do not use a bottled dressing.

A BIG HEIRLOOM TOMATO ~ The tomatoes are the featured dish. Get a really big one, and then add a few others for color and textural appeal. Slice thickly, arrange on a plate, drizzle with your very best extra virgin olive oil, some coarse salt, and maybe a drop of balsamic vinegar, but only if it's a really good one. If you can't find a green tomato, put a small amount of parsley or basil onto the plate for color.

SPAGHETTI WITH BUTTER AND OIL ~ Cook the spaghetti, and when finished add a really good oil, some butter, simple seasonings, and serve with a wedge of parmesan and a grater. Add some of the basil or parsley.

GRILLED STEAK ~ A top sirloin, or your favorite steak, rubbed with olive oil and seasoned with salt and pepper and maybe a little garlic. Depending on the number of people, cook one large steak and serve sliced on the platter, or cook several small steaks quickly and arrange them on a platter with garnish. Allow each person to choose their own selection. In the long run, they'll be happier about what they're consuming.

CHERRIES AND A CHEESE WITH SOME BITE ~ A mild cheddar or a havarti would be good. If the cheese has too much bite, like gorgonzola or an aged Asiago, it might compete with the cherries.

Scaloppine di Manzo al Forno
CUTLETS OF TOP SIRLOIN

- ❖ Vino Bianco di Casa Nostra
- ❖ Insalata Verde
- ❖ Lasagne al Forno
- ❖ Scaloppine di Manzo al Forno
- ❖ Pane Rustico Croccante
- ❖ Zucchine, Cotte a Vapore
- ❖ Dolce Semplice

I was too busy to cook this night, so I focused on what I had on hand, a defrosted steak, leftover lasagne, a couple of zucchini on the counter, and reconstituting the previous day's bread. It takes very little time to cut and pound a top sirloin. I believe I did that early in the day and left it in the fridge until it was time to cook dinner. If you take the time to cut and season the meat ahead of time, the flavor will be enhanced. Do the flour dredging part just before browning the meat. Remember to brown each side quickly. At this point the meat is essentially cooked and you are only keeping it warm in the oven until the sauce is finished. Reduce the liquids at high heat. Remember, you can be doing the other steps while the meat is in the oven and the sauce is reducing. It's highly likely that half the white wine in my glass found its way into the sauce, another good reason to have an open bottle of wine around at the start of the meal.

Appunti/Notes

HOUSE WHITE WINE ~ The house white wine will always depend on the house, and can range from $3.50/bottle to infinity.

SIMPLE ANTIPASTO ~ Some olives, a few slices of prosciutto or salami. Something on hand anointed with a little olive oil and vinegar, breadsticks or crackers. Try slicing some French bread and topping with tomato, mozzarella, some French dressing, and a few capers.

GREEN SALAD ~ Simple greens dressed with olive oil and vinegar, perhaps some of the basil or other herbs.

BAKED LASAGNE ~ Left over from Wednesday's dinner, warm it in the same oven. To serve, put individual servings on a plate, drizzle with a very fresh olive oil and grated parmesan. Garnish with the nicer basil leaves.

BAKED BEEF CUTLETS ~ For this dish I used a top sirloin, taken out of the freezer in the morning and allowed to thaw on the counter. Slice the top sirloin into cutlets and pound thin. Season with olive oil, salt and pepper, and coat with flour. Sauté onion slices and garlic together in pan, and remove. Brown the meat and place in baking dish, layered with the onions and garlic. Put in 350°F oven until sauce is ready. For sauce, to pan add 2 cups chicken broth; deglaze and reduce. Add 2 tsp beef bouillon (a leftover), ½ cup chopped tomatoes and juices from baking dish. To serve, pour sauce over cooked beef, add *chiffonade* of the smaller, not as good looking, basil leaves.

CRUSTY RUSTIC BREAD ~ Warm it in the oven, too, until the crust is hard and it steams when sliced open.

STEAMED ZUCCHINI ~ Slice it, drizzle with oil, or dot with some butter and salt and pepper, and microwave it.

SIMPLE DESSERT ~ This is where you can open a tangerine, cut an apple and pull out some of that dark chocolate.

Claire's 85th Birthday:
Bistecca "Tripunta" alla Griglia
A Simple Tri-Tip Dinner

- Prosecco
- Crostini con Mozzarella, Pomodori e Basilico
- Granchio sul Cetriolo
- Insalata Verde
- Il Piatto Rosso con Avocado e Pomodori (Gialli e Rossi)
- Penne con Verdure
- Bistecca Tripunta alla Griglia
- Zucchini Grattate con un Bacio d'Olio Extra Vergine
- Dolce di Mary e Renae

A simple dinner for eleven begs for a large piece of meat. On the central coast of California, when the weather is still warm enough to cook outside, this means only one thing: Tri-tip. The marinade came from Jim's mom, Jemma Eugenia Visitin Carbone. It's likely to have been from a standard cookbook from around the sixties. Once you try this recipe, there's really no reason to marinate a tri-tip any other way. It's just that good. I can't tell you how many times I've rewritten this recipe from the spattered filing card that was originally typed by Jemma. One of the simplest ways I've learned to tell the doneness of a piece of meat is to stick a knife point into the meat, count to ten, then take it out and touch it to your chin. If it's hot, your chin will tell you. If it's not hot, keep cooking it. If you get a little burned point on your chin, you've ruined the meat and you might as well be branded for being stupid. Try again the next time after your chin has healed.

Appunti/Notes

SPARKLING WINE ~ In this family, sparkling wine means one thing to one generation and quite another to the other generation. Some day we of the younger generation will be drinking something other than the one associated with the clinking holiday commercials.

TOMATO, BASIL AND MOZZARELLA ON TOAST ~ This appetizer is as basic as it gets. If you use the very best tomatoes, fresh *mozzarella di bufala*, and large beautiful basil leaves on top of good bread, it is rarely refused.

CRAB ON CUCUMBER ~ I can't claim full credit for this dish, but I do know that a crab salad was placed on top of hollowed out cucumber slices. They looked wonderful. It's important to season them heavily or they can be a bit bland.

GREEN SALAD ~ As usual, try a simple green salad, served lightly dressed.

THE RED PLATE WITH AVOCADO AND TOMATOES (YELLOW AND RED) ~ The Red Plate came out of the "you are special today" mentality, and was originally used for my birthday. Why not have something special every day? Now the Red Plate, affectionately named "*Il Piatto Rosso*," is used on a daily basis. It's usually filled with two to four of the finest salad toppings I can find, or leftover vegetables that have been marinated in oil, vinegar, and herbs. Add cheese and tomato.

PENNE WITH VEGETABLES ~ Although I didn't write down the actual vegetables, they were most likely tomato, zucchini, and red bell peppers. It could be anything from your kitchen. If basil is also featured, I would have added it to the pasta....

GRILLED TRI-TIP STEAK ~ Marinate the steak for an hour, or up to a day. Grill it over hot coals until cooked medium rare. Twenty minutes per side for a large tri-tip. The recipe for this marinade is listed here.

GRATED ZUCCHINI WITH OLIVE OIL ~ I invented this side dish while in Italy in 2003. Letizia had served shredded cabbage as part of her dinner. Days later, while sweltering in Venice, I grated a slightly aged zucchini when it was too hot to cook in our tiny kitchen. With some fresh olive oil and a bit of salt and pepper, it was very well received, and is frequently requested.

DESSERT BY MARY AND RENAE ~ You will very shortly realize that most of my desserts are made or brought by anyone else but me.

Tri-Tip Marinade

INGREDIENTS
soy sauce, California bay laurel, Worcestershire sauce, pepper,
olive oil, cloves, hot red pepper or Tabasco.

PREPARATION
put together and pour over meat.

Stinco di Agnello
Kate wants Moroccan Food (Lamb Shanks)

- Vino Bianco della Casa
- Formaggio Pecorino e Croccantini
- Insalata Mista
- Couscous
- Stinco di Agnello
- Cipolline e Carote in Brodo
- Gelato
- Un Piattino d'Uva

Jim generally refuses to eat anything with the name of shank in its title. Usually, I will buy shanks when he's traveling, or when I just can't pass up a sale. This was one of the sale days. I hoped that if I seasoned them differently, maybe he wouldn't notice that they were shanks. The large bone sticking up out of the pan after I had "frenched" them sort of gave it away. You can always spend more money and do a similar meal with thick-cut lamb chops, leg of lamb or lamb stew meat. The meat roasted on the bone, however, is preferable for flavor. This doesn't sound very Italian, but these spices do show up in Sicily, and in the north along the spice trade routes. I did see couscous on the menu of several restaurants in Sicily. I don't pretend to be a Moroccan cook, but Morocco is very close to Sicily and these flavors could be included in either locale. I added lots of "Italian" style seasonings just to make sure the meal favored the top side of the Mediterranean.

Appunti/Notes

Your Favorite Bottle of White Wine ~ One glass for the cook and one glass for the pot can only improve the entire evening.

Pecorino on Crackers ~ A couple of slices of a sheep's milk cheese that bite back a little and some bread or crackers to put them on.

"Not Enough Lettuce for a Salad" Salad ~ I invented this salad when I opened the refrigerator after coming home from the market and realized that the last head of lettuce wasn't there anymore. The dressing was made from leftover artichoke dip, stretched and embellished to become new. Everyone liked it. The recipe follows.

Couscous ~ This pasta dish should be served with the meat, not before. Cook it in broth, if you have any, unless your children insist on having a bowl in the morning with milk and sugar. They probably won't like the taste of meat in their breakfast cereal. Make a big pot, and take half for this dinner. I like to add currants, diced red and/or yellow pepper, and/or tomatoes and parsley or cilantro for color, just before serving. This is also a good use of frozen or leftover peas.

Dry Rubbed Lamb Shanks ~ If you don't like shanks, you won't like the Italian name for them either: *stinco*. I trimmed off as much of the silver skin and fat from the shanks as I could handle in my time allowed, and "frenched" them so the meat end was about 2-3 inches thick and the rest had been shaved off the bone. Try to keep some of the silver skin around the bottom part of the shank where the meat is still attached to the bone. Cut the shaved meat into cubes. You will brown and use it the same as the shanks. The two different meat types add variety to the dish, and those who are afraid of bones can go for the pieces of meat that resemble stew. Then rub them in olive oil and a dry spice mix of salt, pepper, brown sugar, red chili powder, cinnamon, cumin, and Italian seasoning mix (or oregano) and rosemary. Brown them on all sides and braise in oven with some wine, broth and or/water. (A beer is also good here. Just remember to put some of it into the pot.) Serve the *stinco* in a large, deep platter with the couscous, and pour some of the pan juices on top. Drizzle with a really good olive oil, some lemon zest and lemon juice. Season with fresh parsley, pepper, and coarse sea salt. Grab a shank bone and get dirty.

Onions and Carrots Cooked in the Pan Juices ~ Brown them while you're thickening the gravy so they look better, if they didn't brown while cooking with the meat.

SAVORY GELATO ~ The chutney in this recipe complements the lamb and couscous. If you have an ice cream machine, you can incorporate all the ingredients below into the cream mixture before freezing.

A SMALL PLATE OF GRAPES ~ Two or three types of fresh grapes washed and already cut, so each person can take a set.

I served this meal with a Sangiovese. A spicy young style of Zinfandel would also be good. If you go with a white, make sure it can stand up to the richness of the lamb.

"Not Enough Lettuce for a Salad" Salad

INGREDIENTS

lettuce, cabbage, basil leaves, raisins, tiny orange tomatoes, wedges of small red tomato, artichoke dressing (mayonnaise, vinegar, salt and pepper, lemon, garlic), rice wine vinegar, *mozzarella di bufala*.

PREPARATION

Mix everything together and dress with the wet ingredients, salt and pepper over all.

Jim's Favorite Couscous

INGREDIENTS

1 box or 2 cups couscous, ½ leek, 1 handful of cilantro (chopped), ½ -1 tomato (chopped), roast chicken pan drippings (grease removed), currants, salt and pepper.

PREPARATION

Cook the couscous according to package directions. Add sautéed leek and tomato, currants and cilantro. Season and add pan drippings. Moisten with additional water as necessary when ready to serve.

Savory Gelato

INGREDIENTS

vanilla ice cream, chopped toasted nuts (almonds), toasted coconut (unsweetened), chutney, chopped cilantro, lemon zest, juice and/or syrup.

PREPARATION

Scoop ice cream into dishes and top with nuts, coconut, chutney, cilantro, and lemon zest. Use fresh orange juice or simple syrup, and top with 1 tbsp, just before serving.

Pollo al Forno

BAKED CHICKEN

- ❖ Vino Bianco della Casa
- ❖ Cocktail di Scampi con Salsa Fresca
- ❖ Insalata Mista con Avocado, Gorgonzola, e Noce
- ❖ Zucchini Grattugiati con Un Bacio d'Olio Extra Vergine
- ❖ Peperoni al Forno con Formaggio
- ❖ Penne con Dente di Leone, Peperoncino Rosso, e Prosciutto
- ❖ Pane Fresco
- ❖ Pollo al Forno
- ❖ Sorbetto o Gelati con Cialde Dolci
- ❖ Limoncello del Nonno, 2005

I like chicken. There are so many things you can do with it, it's always delicious, usually inexpensive and goes with just about any wine. What more do you need? A perfectly roasted chicken warms the house with wonderful aromas and should be one of the first holistic foods a beginning cook should try to master. How do you roast a chicken perfectly? That's a good question. If you ask ten different people how to cook one, they will probably give you ten different answers. When people ask me how to cook a chicken I always tell them it depends on how much time you have. An un-stuffed chicken can be rushed at a higher heat, or slow-cooked all day long at a lower heat. How much time do you have? I prefer to slow-cook mine. I usually bring one home from the market, wash and season it, and then put it into a slow oven (somewhere in the 250-275°F range). Then I go about my business for the rest of the day. When I return home or finish whatever else I'm doing, I check the chicken first. If it's finished, I turn it off and let it rest, or keep it warm in a barely heated oven. If it's not cooked, I judge how long I have to finish it before the eaters arrive and turn the heat up accordingly. Do I occasionally overcook a chicken? Yes. Do I occasionally undercook a chicken and have to make everyone wait until it's finished? Yes. That's what the other courses are for. In fact, you can serve a salad at the end of the meal if the chicken is really ready and needs to be eaten right away. Just pretend you planned it that way, and no one has to be the wiser. If they question you about your unusual course sequencing, just say, "I saw it on the Food TV network, and it looked like something I wanted to try. Have some more wine…."

Remember to use your standard cookbook directions on food safety regarding the minimum temperatures and times for slow cooking and holding foods. Practice. You'll eventually figure out what a cooked chicken looks, smells and feels like, and then you won't have to worry about poisoning your family and friends. To my knowledge, I haven't killed anyone yet. The possibilities for using leftover chicken are endless. Take the time to make a gravy or sauce with the pan juices and reserve them for the serving of leftover chicken you conscientiously pick off the bones the next day, or the day after that. Oh, and reward your puppy. He's your best friend after all. He'll become an even better friend if you give him the scraps from the de-boning process. (The chicken carcass does not go into the trash.)

Appunti/Notes

WHITE WINE ~ You'll enjoy cooking more if you start with a glass of wine and take your time with the meal preparation. It's not a chore, it's the winding down part of the weekend….

CHILLED SHRIMP WITH DIPPING SAUCE ~ These shrimp were left over from a chilled seafood salad the day before. They had been sautéed, and then chilled, earlier in that day. The sauce is similar to classic French or Thousand Island dressing and it did not come out of a bottle. Learn to mix your own. One per person, arranged nicely. Try one yourself first, and see if the sauce is light enough to complement, not overpower, the shrimp. Offer the rest of your family/guests a glass of wine, too, when they arrive.

SALAD WITH AVOCADO, GORGONZOLA AND PECANS ~ This salad can be tossed, or composed on or off The Red Plate. Glazed pecans are nice, though not necessary. Toast the nuts lightly.

Grated Zucchini ~ They needed to be eaten, and they were. Coarsely grate them onto waxed paper, and arrange on your serving dish. Anoint with a good olive oil, some lemon if you have it, and salt and pepper. Sometimes I add a dash of vinegar. You cannot make this too far ahead, or the grated zucchini will start to break down.

Baked, Stuffed Anaheim Chiles ~ Slice lengthwise into the top of the pepper (not all of the way through) after you have figured out which side it lies on the best. This way it won't roll around in the dish and let the ingredients leak out. Cut across the top near the stem so you can open it up enough to get the seeds out. Stuff with at least two kinds of complementary cheeses, and anything else that you have lying around. (Some extra *Bolognese*, rice, onion, salami, etc?) Bake it with a little sauce on top. Let it get slightly brown and bubbly. The peppers should hold their form but be somewhat soft. These can also be done on the grill, but it's a little trickier to keep the cheese inside of them.

Penne with Dandelion Greens, Red Bell Pepper and Prosciutto ~ Sauté the prosciutto; let it get crispy, and put aside. Then sauté the onion and bell pepper. Add the dandelion greens and sauté until slightly wilted. Just before it's finished, pour in some of the white wine. Cook the pasta. Mix everything together just before serving, and season with *Parmigiano*, some salt and pepper, and a drizzle of olive oil. Finely dice some of the uncooked greens and red bell pepper, and sprinkle on at the end. A little lemon is nice, and you can even add some of the zest.

ROASTED CHICKEN ~ I like to roast two or more at a time, so everyone can get their favorite parts. The chicken is brought to the table whole, so we can remember that we are eating a bird. Season them inside and out with olive oil and salt and pepper. The olive oil will allow whatever herbs you use to stick to the skin. Fresh herb combinations from your garden are great. You cannot go wrong with *Herb de Provence* or Italian seasoning. I like to put whole garlic, oranges, and lemons, with bunches of fresh herbs, into the cavity. A little wine in the bottom of the pan is great.

Add the innards to the pan. If you don't like to eat them, at least they can flavor the pan juices. Your dog and cat will be your best friend at the end of the evening if you give them the unwanted parts. You might like the necks. I like the livers. While the cooked chicken is resting, deglaze the pan and use the pan juices to make either a gravy or sauce, depending on your side dishes. With this meal, I saved the pan juices for the second night, and served the roasted chicken alone with the above pasta.

FRESH BREAD ~ Put in the oven with the peppers so it can get a crispier crust, then cut into slices.

ICE CREAM WITH SWEET WAFER COOKIES ~ A very rich ice cream or sorbet, with a wafer cookie or *pirouette*, because it'll just seem special. We are, after all, indulging ourselves with simple, delicious foods and the wafer and/or a sprig of mint just shows that you went to extra trouble. It's a little more elegant than eating ice cream with a spoon directly from the carton.

LIMONCELLO ~ Made with Tony's Meyer lemons.

Costole di Maiale con troppo Cavolfiore

Pork Ribs with too much Cauliflower

- ❖ Campari Negronita di Michelina
- ❖ Formaggio Cheddar sopra al Pane di Segale con Condimento di Granturco
- ❖ Zuppa di Cavolfiore
- ❖ Insalata Verde
- ❖ Il Piatto Rosso con un Pomodoro, Aceto Balsamico, e Gorgonzola
- ❖ Risotto ai Funghi, Finocchio, e Porri
- ❖ Costole di Maiale al Forno e alla Griglia
- ❖ Fagiolini con Olio di Oliva Extra Vergine locale
- ❖ Un'altra Storia

It was unseasonably hot after a cold snap, which made it difficult to execute a menu. The markets were filled with fall produce; cauliflower, broccoli, sweet potatoes, fennel, and turnips. The weather had gone back up to the 80s and I was feeling more like eating fish tacos than roasted meats. I arrived home with a cauliflower anyway, figuring I could always use it on Saturday if the weather got cold again. By the time I got to the grocery store for meat, it had gotten quite hot and I leaned towards getting something to barbeque. They obliged by having pork ribs on sale. There I was, then, wondering how to combine cauliflower and ribs, while still keeping the meal Italian. I started pulling out leftovers from the refrigerator and found a large container of roasted mushrooms, and some roasted fennel and leeks from an earlier meal. Then I opened another drawer of the refrigerator to find some leftover barbequed corn, and that I still had a cauliflower from earlier in the week. So, oops, the menu had really better feature cauliflower. The corn became a relish, the mushrooms, fennel, and leeks became a *risotto*, and the cauliflower went into the soup. The ribs were rubbed with a prepared barbeque rub and, feeling guilty, I added Italian seasoning and garlic.

Appunti/Notes

CAMPARI NEGRONITA ~ Campari with soda, vodka and *Triple Sec* served over ice.

CHEDDAR CHEESE ON RYE TOAST WITH CORN RELISH ~ The relish was born of the leftover corn, cut off the cob and mixed with chopped celery, red pepper, and fennel tips. I added lemon, caraway, fennel greens and Tabasco until it had enough heat, and then finished with salt and pepper and olive oil to bring it all together. This was spooned onto toasts with olive oil and melted cheddar. They were great!

CAULIFLOWER SOUP ~ I started with onion and leeks, added some leftover roasted garlic, and then cut up a potato and the cauliflower. Chicken broth and cream were used as liquid. It was partially blended before serving.

GREEN SALAD ~ There was so much going for this meal that the greens were simple. I don't think I even mixed different varieties of lettuce.

THE RED PLATE WITH TOMATOES, GORGONZOLA, AND BALSAMIC VINEGAR ~ Tomatoes, gorgonzola and balsamic sauce. Again simple, there's more to come.

RISOTTO WITH MUSHROOMS, FENNEL, AND LEEK ~ Having used all of my chicken broth in the soup, I started the *risotto* with fresh leeks and garlic to get some flavor into the oil, since I knew I would have to use water for the rice. After sautéing these, I browned the rice and added my liquids. I finished it with finely diced leftover mushrooms, fennel, and leek, some wine and cream, with parmesan on top.

SLOW ROASTED PORK RIBS FINISHED ON THE GRILL ~ I roasted the ribs, covered in the oven, for several hours at a low temperature and then finished them on the grill so they would pick up some caramelization.

GREEN BEANS ANOINTED WITH OLIVE OIL ~ Steamed, served *al dente* with a fresh, local olive oil purchased that morning at the farmers' market.

WE'RE TOO FULL FOR DESSERT ~ But we'll eat a half cartoon of Ben and Jerry's NY Super Fudge Chunk later that evening.

Another recipe for using leftover corn on the cob can be prepared as follows:

Succotash

INGREDIENTS
1 cup fresh roasted corn taken off the cob, ½ cup peas, fresh or frozen defrosted, ⅛ onion diced, 1 avocado cubed, oil and vinegar, salt and pepper, 1 tsp cumin, 1 pinch clove.

PREPARATION
Mix and serve with *crostini*, bread or crackers. You can even use succotash as one of the ingredients on *Il Piatto Rosso*.

Gamberoni con Pesto e Prosciutto

Shrimp with Pesto and Prosciutto

- Vino Bianco della Casa o Cocktails "Bellini"
- Patate, Formaggio, Salsa e Olive Nere
- Insalata Mista
- Il Piatto Rosso di Avocado, Pomodori, e Formaggio Pecorino
- Zucchini Gratinati
- Riso con Verdure
- Gamberoni con Pesto e Prosciutto
- Mandorle di Spagna e Mandarini

Sometimes the shrimp are so large that they look like little lobsters. This was one of those times. Now of course, here in the United States we don't find shrimp with heads very often. When you can find them (try looking at the Santa Barbara farmers' market!), forego the *pesto* and prosciutto and just pan fry or grill them with a little lemon oil and seasoning. They will have a lot of flavor by themselves, and will not need this preparation. This dish assumes that the shrimp are uncooked, headless and have had their shells and the intestine removed. This meal is all about the shrimp, so the other dishes should complement, not compete for your attention.

Appunti/Notes

WHITE WINE OF THE HOUSE OR BELLINIS ~ Some for the cook, some for your friends and family ... Bellinis are made with Prosecco (Italian sparkling wine, pureed peach and a dash of Martini Rosso (sweet vermouth).

POTATOES WITH CHEESE, SALSA AND BLACK OLIVES ~ This dish started with a leftover potato. It was sliced, covered with shredded cheese and sliced olives (taken off the pit, not from a jar or can) and a spoonful of red sauce. I may have used salsa. Put under a broiler until brown and bubbly. Finish with some olive oil, coarse salt, and either chopped parsley or cilantro.

THE UBIQUITOUS GREEN SALAD ~ Two or three different types of lettuce, carefully picked over and torn into bite size pieces. Never cut the lettuce because you slice through cell membranes and the lettuce will rust more quickly.

THE RED PLATE WITH AVOCADO, TOMATOES AND SHEEP'S MILK FETA ~ Sheep's milk feta is usually milder than goat's milk feta. An Italian Pecorino cheese would be good here, too. The combination of a mild feta with avocado is sublime. All these items can also be chopped and mixed together as a chutney and served in lettuce cups.

BAKED ZUCCHINI ~ Sliced fresh or leftover can be used. Drizzle a little olive oil into a flat baking dish and layer zucchini with multiple cheeses and salt and pepper. Some cream can be added. Top with your homemade bread crumbs and cook until the top browns. A little onion and bacon or goose fat can be added for additional flavor.

RICE WITH VEGETABLES ~ Knowing me, this was a simple embellishment to last night's steamed white rice. It was not a *risotto*. In a skillet, sauté some onion and a little red and/or yellow bell pepper. I probably added some of the zucchini to get the green color. Mix in the cooked white rice and stir to combine.

LARGE SHRIMP WITH PESTO AND PROSCIUTTO ~ Slice into the shrimp along the length to make a pocket to hold the *pesto*. Use a thick *pesto* so it stays in place. Carefully wrap with long slices of prosciutto, overlapping as you wrap so there are no leaks. Fasten with toothpicks. I prefer to grill these but they can be done in a pan. Brown them first, and finish in a hot oven. You want to get the prosciutto somewhat crisp without cooking the shrimp to death. If done in a pan, deglaze it with some white wine and pour over the shrimp. Top with fresh lime or lemon juice to cut the richness.

SPANISH ALMONDS AND TANGERINES ~ Spanish almonds are glazed and are therefore somewhat sweet. They go very well with the tanginess of the tangerine. *Croccantini* (or other glazed nuts) can be used. So can oranges, though a bowl of fresh tangerines with the stem and leaves still attached makes a wonderful presentation. A blood orange is slightly sweeter, so match it with a stronger nut, like a walnut or a spiced nut mixture.

Zuppa di Pesce
Sea Bass and Watercress

- Vongole in Brodo
- Torta di Granchio
- Insalata Verde
- Il Piatto Rosso di Avocado, Mozzarella, e Cetriolo
- Zuppa di Pesce
- Pane Fresco
- Biscotti

This is a variation of a recipe I found in *Gourmet Magazine* that called for halibut placed into a broth with baby lima beans. I tried it and it was very good. There was leftover broth, but not fish and lima beans. I had watercress and some sea bass, so I tried it again. It was better, because the sea bass had a much sweeter and more delicate flavor. The fish stock came from the smiling whole snapper dinner. The carcass had been patiently waiting in the freezer for just the right moment. It went into the stockpot, smiling head and all, along with shrimp shells, crab, and lobster shells. The broth contained mostly the snapper flavor, which was good, because the shellfish could have overpowered the red snapper. I wasn't sure if Jim would like the fish soup, so I made sure there were plenty of other delicious dishes leading up to the simple main *zuppa*. This meal almost qualifies as spa cuisine. Everyone loved it.

Appunti/Notes

STEAMED CLAMS ~ The steamed clams were served in their shells in a bowl with broth and chopped parsley.

CRAB CAKES ~ A small one for each person made with lump crab meat, some celery, onion, parsley, breadcrumbs and just enough mayonnaise to hold it together. The secret is to sauté it slowly without turning until one side is browned, then carefully turn it to finish.

GREEN SALAD ~ As usual, simple greens, although this time it can be several whole leaves lightly dressed, with the crab cake on top. The Red Plate can be passed at the same time, or afterwards.

THE RED PLATE WITH AVOCADO, MOZZARELLA, AND CUCUMBER ~ If the tomatoes look wonderful, slice them into big rounds. If they aren't so great or have bad spots, cut them into wedges or smaller pieces. Sometimes a mélange of multiple colors and sizes can be enticing. Stripe the cucumber before slicing to make it look more interesting.

FISH SOUP ~ This is a composed soup. All the ingredients are cooked separately, and then added to the hot broth when served. It was amazing. The tomatoes were slowly roasted in the oven with chopped garlic and olive oil on them. The fish can be grilled or broiled. It's good to get some color and caramelization on it. The flavor will be better. This can also be done with leftover fish, as long as you can still reheat it without it becoming overdone. Ladle some of the hot broth into a decorative bowl and place one roasted tomato next to a small serving of the fish. Add watercress, drizzle with a really good extra virgin olive oil and some lemon. I tried it with salmon also, but the sea bass had the sweetest flavor. All of them were delicious, yet different. Try multiple combinations and see which you prefer.

TODAY'S BREAD ~ This meal begs for a simple French baguette. Anything heartier would overpower the delicate soup.

BISCOTTI ~ Dessert doesn't need to be full of sugar. A simple *biscotti* or small plate of assorted cookies becomes no trouble and completes the meal. Iced *biscottini* are excellent; however, be aware that you're increasing the amount of sugar per bite, and it's way too easy to eat several hundred if you have no will power. Fortune cookies would be fun here because they mimic the opening of the clams at the beginning of the meal. Cookies are an excellent segue into tea....

" *Il pesce nasce nell'acqua e affoga nell' olio.*
(A fish is born in water and drowns in oil.) "

Agnello alla Griglia
GRILLED LAMB

- Tempranillo 2001
- Insalata di Spinaci e Lattuga "Piccola Gemma"
- Spinaci alla Panna

- Spiedini di Verdure con una sorpresa per "tutti i coraggiosi"
- Agnello alla Griglia
- Pane Fresco

- Uva, Mandorle e Taleggio
- Cioccolatini
- Un po' di Passito di Pantelleria

This was a day where the greens were particularly catching my eye at the farmers' market. The lettuces all looked great, there was an abundance of fresh spinach (the spinach scare of 2006 had not yet occurred) and the fall vegetables looked young and delicious. The Brussels sprouts came to the market still attached to their long stalks. How could I not go home without one cradled in my arms like a newborn babe? The beets were in small attractive bunches. The larger beets, which usually occur later in the year, are another story. On this day they were still tiny, almost like large radishes. Small potatoes and tiny onions were available. The weather, still warm, convinced me to stay outside for the cooking. With all of these wonderfully bite-sized items, it just seemed natural to try putting them on skewers to see what would happen. The scotch bonnets were of course for "all the brave ones" because it's always fun to have an experimental food for conversation purposes, if for no other reason.

Appunti/Notes

RED WINE ~ Your favorite to go with lamb. I picked the Tempranillo because it is not so rich that it would compete with the lamb.

SPINACH AND BABY LETTUCE SALAD ~ Baby spinach leaves mixed with baby lettuce leaves plus large shavings of parmesan and thinly sliced mushrooms. Dress it lightly.

CREAMED SPINACH ~ Baby spinach leaves sautéed in olive oil, with salt and pepper and some cream which came from the plug at the top of the bottle of organic milk. I save them each time I open a bottle of milk. With two or three, used quickly before they spoil, you have enough to cream a vegetable or add to pasta.

VEGETABLE SKEWERS ~ Potatoes, onions, Brussels sprouts, beets, and a scotch bonnet pepper. I par-boiled all but the pepper, put them on the skewers, and brushed them liberally with olive oil. A little salt and pepper is a good idea, too.

GRILLED LAMB ~ I used racks of lamb, having found them on sale and kept them in the freezer until the time was right. Butterflied leg of lamb or chops would be great, too. I made a paste with olive oil and lots of salt, pepper, rosemary, garlic and a little mustard, and then marinated them all day.

FRESH BREAD ~ Warmed until the crust has some teeth.

GRAPES, ALMONDS, AND CHEESE ~ Dark red juicy grapes, Spanish almonds—slightly sweetened, and a Taleggio cheese for a smooth finish.

CHOCOLATES ~ Small squares of dark chocolate, or if you're lucky someone may make a *ricotta* cheese tart with an almond crust.

SWEET SICILIAN WINE ~ Pantelleria is an island which is closer to Africa than Italy, but we found the wine in Sicily and loved it. Your local dessert wine, served chilled and in tiny glasses, is wonderful here, and helps you to linger at the table having conversation just a little bit longer before everyone disappears into their own little worlds in front of the TV.

L'inverno

CHAPTER 5

In many places in the United States, the winter weather comes on at a predictable time of year. Some time before November, the leaves will fall from the trees and the wind begins to blow, followed by rain and snow. Here, in Santa Barbara, we're lucky if we get some rain, and the weather will occasionally drop below 40°F at night. We'll stop wearing our sandals and put on our sheepskin boots, sometimes with shorts. Hats and scarves will be seen around the holidays, because we get them as gifts and they're festive. They're rarely worn for warmth. After Thanksgiving, the holiday season is in full swing. Leisurely Friday evenings are often replaced with trips to the shopping mall, and cocktail parties, recitals, sports, and school performances. These evening events can make it stressful for the person who prepares the meals. If you're not eating out before an event, the time you have to prepare, serve, and clean up after the meal can be abbreviated. If you dash out of the house without finishing, you arrive home late to a kitchen full of congealing dishes and food which sat out of the refrigerator too long. I've found that I examine my Friday evening events with a critical eye, these days. "Would I rather rush the evening or skip the event and enjoy my *Venerdì Sera?*" Where the old me would never be home on a Friday evening if I could avoid it, the current me looks forward to *Venerdì Sera*, and I jealously guard our private time. Saturdays are for entertaining, Fridays are for dining and relaxing with family and very close friends.

During this holiday season, you may, at some point, actually get a quiet evening at home on a Friday. Cherish it. Surround yourself with a small group of people who understand the concept of dining. Everyone should come to the table prepared to give of him or herself. This can be a bottle of wine, bread, flowers, an anecdote, a dessert item, especially chocolates, a poem or a story. We frequently read each others' astrological forecast during the lull while dessert is being served or afterwards. It's a great conversation starter. Part of the lost art of dining in the American household is the loss of meaningful conversation. It is a time to reconnect with your family members and find out what their week has been about. It's also a good time to talk about upcoming commitments that may involve everyone else's time. Try listening to music; dinner music. It's background for what's happening at the table, a communion of people who love each other and break bread. We've been known to break a wine glass or two. Encourage your fellow diners to converse about other things than their problems. Problems are not conducive to dining or digestion. Leave them, and the people who bring them to your dinner table, behind. Turn the TV off for awhile.

Some of the meals that follow are simple. Others require a bit more time to prepare. Most of these meals involve a concerted effort for the main or a particular side dish. If you are not into spending your entire Friday preparing an evening dinner, focus on one signature item and take shortcuts for the others. Many of my side dishes come from existing items in the refrigerator. If you prepare a larger quantity of a particular item for your Thursday meal, you can usually re-invent it as a side dish the next night. One of the pleasant side effects of developing a holistic kitchen is that you don't have to constantly prepare every dish from scratch at every meal. Things evolve, especially in a kitchen.

Remember dorm food? Turkey *tetrazzini* was a classic example of a reasonable use of *avanzi* (previously prepared food), aka leftovers. I still maintain,

" *Il tempo ben speso è un gran guadagno.*
(Time well spent is a big gain.) "

contrary to popular belief, that given good ingredients and with proper preparation, even turkey *tetrazzini* can be delicious.

But, back to *L'inverno*; light some candles, open a good bottle or two of your favorite wine, wash out that teapot and enjoy the season in your kitchen, not at the local food court. Your body and your wallet will thank you. As an aside, it does get a little cold and wet for grilling. However, you may suddenly find you have an excellent source of grill lighting from 3-foot-high flames from that barbequed duck that you experimented with. Just scrape off the black part, add a bit more sauce and open another bottle of wine. You won't be the first one to set a dinner on fire.

Cotolette di Manzo
SHORT RIBS ON POLENTA

- ❖ Zuppa di Puré di Verdure
- ❖ Lattuga Romana con Funghi e Parmigiano
- ❖ Cotolette di Manzo con Intingolo di Carne
- ❖ Polenta
- ❖ Piselle
- ❖ Birra o Vino Rosso
- ❖ Mandarino o Persimmon

Short ribs are one of my all-time favorite comfort foods. Yes, I know, they can be fatty. If you know how to cook them, they're delicious. Like all fattier foods, you have to slow-cook them to render the fat away. Some people who own restaurants are reported to serve them off the bone. I think this is a crime. Even if they have fallen off the bone, which they should while cooking, you should still cozy those bones back up to the meat and put them back on the platter. Sucking the end of the bones to get that little bit of caramelized flavor should not be missed. This is a drawback of restaurant eating. You're not supposed to pick up the bones. (What bones? When was the last time you even saw a bone in a restaurant meal? What's with that, Mario?) Our Italian cousin was mortified when one of us (I won't say who, but you know who you are) picked up a pork chop by the bone and began to nibble on it. She will really be in for a shock when she comes to eat short ribs at my house! Short ribs (with gravy, noodles, and peas, covered with parmesan) are totally a Michele meal. Kristin, as a speaking child, coined the phrase "Pasta, peas, cheese please!" to go along with short ribs. Since then, I have learned about *polenta*. It's now my new favorite. Jim's mom used to laugh and laugh and laugh whenever she saw *polenta* on the menu at a fancy restaurant. *Polenta* was what they ate because they were poor and couldn't afford anything else. I like it. Whatever the cost, it's good, so eat it.

Appunti/Notes

PURÉED VEGETABLE SOUP ~ I've noticed that people will frequently dip into a pot of new soup in the refrigerator and have a bowl, but after it's been there for a while, they stop serving themselves, even if the soup got rave reviews two or three days before. Sometimes minestrone or another vegetable soup gets puréed, and a dollop of butter and/or cream is added, with a few new herbs, and passed off as new. Nothing gets thrown away in our house if it still has life in it.

ROMAINE LEAVES WITH PARMESAN AND MUSHROOMS ~ I created this salad while on a vacation where there weren't a lot of choices at the market or in the refrigerator. I arranged whole romaine heart leaves on a platter, sliced the raw mushrooms very thin, and shaved parmesan over the top with a vegetable peeler. A good drizzle of extra virgin olive oil, fresh black pepper—coarsely ground, and coarse sea salt finished the dish. It was easy, well received, and was placed on the "You Can Make This Again List."

SHORT RIBS AND BROWN GRAVY ~ Short ribs were a mainstay for me in my working days. I'd put them, still frozen, into my crock-pot and come home later, thicken the gravy, and serve them over noodles. Since then, I've had the opportunity to be at home while they are slow cooking. Taking the time to brown them first makes all the difference in flavor, though I wouldn't turn them away if they were cooked in the busy career woman style of my youth. Now I brown them well on all sides and put them in a braising pot with all manner of things I find in my refrigerator. Onion, garlic, a little *marinara*, herbs, wine, beer or whiskey, broth or water. Simmer them in a good pot with the lid off, in lots of liquid. The liquid will reduce (don't let it boil off) and the ribs will brown nicely as the level of the liquid recedes. A strainer and a gravy separator are essential here because you'll want to get as much of the fat off them as possible. They can be real artery cloggers if you let them. Another way to remove the fat is to refrigerate them overnight and then break off the hardened fat. They're delicious either way. Your proximity to a former life as an animal will be evidenced by how big the pile of unwanted scraps is that's left on your plate. By the way, those strips of cartilage are not edible, but the other parts are. My dog knows better than to beg for scraps off of my plate on nights when short ribs are served. If you hear the coyotes howling on a Friday night with a full moon, beware. It may just be me eating short ribs!

POLENTA ~ All it takes is hot water or broth, salt and pepper, cornmeal, and butter. Put it under the meat; smother with gravy, and perhaps parmesan. I started with 2 cups of coarse *polenta* and 8 cups of hot water. Instant *polenta* you say? Prepared *polenta* in a tube you say? Look at the prices. It's your choice, just don't tell me about it. Thicken the pan juices from the meat with flour and re-season.

PEAS ~ Green peas look and taste great with short ribs. Frozen ones are my favorite. One of these days I'll have to try fresh peas....

BEER OR WINE ~ Short ribs lend themselves to beer, especially if you use a bottle of it as part of the braising liquid. Red wine, however, seems to keep the blood flowing more smoothly through your veins.

TANGERINES OR PERSIMMONS ~ The citrus or persimmon will help clean your palate after consuming this "stick to your ribs" meal of ribs.

Okay, more about *polenta*: Bill Buford, in his book, *Heat*, talks about his quest for understanding *polenta*. He comments that probably no one would be as interested in the details as he was. Well, Bill, I'm interested in the details. I, too, had *polenta* cooked in Italy by a *cugina*, and noticed that no matter how hard I tried or how long I stirred, it never tasted the same. I also had the privilege of using an unlined copper pot sent to me by *a cugina*. I felt morally obligated to figure this one out. So, when I read Bill's discourse it started me thinking. You're right! You don't have to stir it. And you especially don't have to stir it with a whisk. Come on now, I don't think whisks were available before the 19th century, at least. So there I was, standing at the counter preparing another set of courses for that *Venerdì sera*, when it suddenly occurred to me, too. Those old Italian women weren't in a restaurant with seventeen other people available to give a stir now and then. They were in their kitchens doing a whole lot of other things besides stirring. So, like the meats and vegetables that are slow roasting in the oven, why wouldn't the *polenta* be on the back of the stove bubbling at the lowest possible heat? I didn't stir my oatmeal. I didn't stir my rice. I didn't stir a lot of things. I knew that my cousin had left a pot emptied of *polenta* on the back porch of her house with soapy water in it overnight. I had photographed it. Come to think of it, the pot had a black crust at the bottom. Certainly it was very dark brown. I knew Mario had told us that the *polenta* needed to be toasted to get that certain flavor. How could it sit long enough on the copper sides and bottom of the pot if we were stirring it constantly?

I always tell people that many foods were invented by a starving Italian woman who was trying to feed her family. It was certainly true of *cardone*. But back to *polenta*. Could it be possible that that same starving Italian woman had to leave the pot unattended? Perhaps, she left it unattended for a little too long. The liquid ran out, and lo and behold, the *polenta* at the bottom of the pot burned. There it is, then. The toastiness of the perfectly prepared *polenta* was originally an accident! Or perhaps the wood fire was a bit too hot. Or she forgot to start the *polenta* and tried to rush it over a very hot fire? Either way, we now knew that it could be cooked all day long without constant attention. Well, we would see. So I tried it. I started the *polenta* at 12:45 PM. I stirred it now and then and tasted it as the day wore on. After the first hour, I poured in some extra hot water and left the kitchen to write this passage. I took a bath.

I plucked a few gray hairs. I rechecked the *polenta*. It was doing fine on its own. The revelation I had was that the scenario of having everyone wait for the big *polenta* pour when the *polenta* was finally ready was really untrue. The *polenta* could wait until we were ready for it! Clearly, the *polenta* could be served when those who were ready to eat it were around the table. How long could the *polenta* be held? I finished this passage. I dried my hair. I put on makeup. At 3:00 PM, it was still moist and doing well on its own. I noticed that some cornmeal was stuck to the sides of the pot. Scraping some off, I began to taste the hint of toasted corn. Okay, let's keep going. We finally served the *polenta* at 6:30 PM. I added water around 4, and let it continue by itself. At the very end, instead of stirring it vigorously I put the heat on high and deliberately let it get a toast on the bottom of the pot. We liked it. It tasted as if it had finished its day and was relaxed and ready for a quiet evening. It did not taste like it was in a hurry to get into your mouth. It did not cry out to be scraped into a leftover dish and put into the refrigerator. It tasted like it was happy to be there, next to the big pot of short ribs. Whatever happened next, it could handle it. It had, after all, spent the last 4 hours sitting on top of a fire. Where could it go from there?

> *The peas? Who cares about the peas! The "Polenta Rapture" was happening here!*

La Cena per Federico, Tami e Verni

Rollini di Vitello Brasati

Rolled, Braised Veal (almost)

- Antipasto di Salame e Formaggio
- Insalata Mista
- Il Piatto Rosso con Zucchini, Funghi, e Cavoli di Bruxelles Marinati
- Peperoncini Ripieni con Risotto e Funghi
- Rollini di Vitello Brasati
- Spaghetti
- Dolce di Katerina con Banana Soffritta, Gelato di Cioccolato, e Frutti di Bosco
- Espresso
- Passito di Pantelleria e Liquore

We wanted to get this group together for a long time. Someone was always out of the country (mostly Vern or Jim), or it just got put onto the back burner. We had a lot to celebrate. Tami had successfully survived a bout of chemotherapy, Fred had announced his retirement, and both Jim and Vern were in the USA at the same time. I felt like cooking, something Italian, of course. Fred and Tami had been to Italy, and were trying to live *La Dolce Vita*, as I was. Vern had dropped off the fast track a few years before, suddenly, like myself, and was managing to live the good life with a foot in the Philippines and a foot in California. My plan for the evening was to roll out veal cutlets and stuff them with *mozzarella di bufala*, sun dried tomatoes, and basil. The day got away from me, and someone else wasn't available to help with Kristin, so the meal quickly took a turn towards simplicity. I really wanted to roll those cutlets, so I'll tell you how easy it is to do, and then tell you what I wound up preparing after all. Veal cutlets are frequently available in the markets and at your local butcher shop. They are usually cut thin by the butcher and pounded thin, so you don't have to do it yourself. I've bought a whole veal shoulder and leg, and have sliced it very thin myself. It's not easy to do. You can save some money by doing it yourself. Veal is not inexpensive. In our family, it's reserved for special occasions. I've found veal cutlets at a local wholesale meat supplier, which helps to make them a little more

affordable. They're usually frozen and vacuum packed. Forethought to buy them ahead of time is required, so they're defrosted and ready when you need them. The nice part about the blister packs is that you can pound them while they're still in the pack (defrosted of course) and it's not so messy. Taking each thin slice and placing a basil leaf or two, a couple of sun dried tomatoes, and some mozzarella is very easy, and really not too time consuming. I do it early in the day, secure them with a toothpick and leave them wrapped between sheets of waxed paper in the refrigerator until they're ready to be browned with some shallot, and then braised in some broth and/or white wine. Well, this procedure did not happen on this day. So....

Appunti/Notes

CHEESE AND SALAMI ~ Jim did agree to get some fresh bread, and that's what we had, with a couple of different cheeses and salami.

MIXED GREEN SALAD ~ It came out of a bag and was personalized with some additional greens from the farmer's market.

THE RED PLATE WITH MARINATED ZUCCHINI, MUSHROOMS, AND BRUSSELS SPROUTS ~ Occasionally, when I have too much of a particular vegetable, I will put it either raw or par-boiled into a jar with some olive oil and vinegar on top of it. The zucchini was cubed beforehand, the mushrooms were whole small ones, and the Brussels sprouts were halved. Luckily, I had done this in the past week, so out of the refrigerator they came. The unused mozzarella went onto The Red Plate, all covered with Italian herb and a very fresh olive oil, with salt and pepper.

ANAHEIM CHILES STUFFED WITH MUSHROOM RISOTTO ~ We had had a mushroom *risotto* earlier in the week and I'd bought chilies, but they hadn't made it onto the grill. I stuffed the chilies with the *risotto*, put some cheese on top, added a couple of spoonfuls of *marinara* sauce, and put them in the oven to cook slowly.

ROLLED, BRAISED VEAL ~ So ... It became a *scaloppine*. I chopped up some onion, celery, and mushrooms, and sautéed them with the sliced cutlets. I added wine and cream, and let the whole thing simmer in a slow oven until ready to serve after the guests arrived. I finished it with fresh lemon juice, lemon zest, and parsley. They loved it. Now, my secret is out!

SPAGHETTI ~ Finished with butter, olive oil, and parsley, and served in a big bowl alongside the *scaloppine*.

BERRIES WITH CHOCOLATE ICE CREAM AND SAUTÉED BANANAS ~ My darling Katerina sautéed some bananas with whatever it is she does to them to taste so delicious. (I did see her getting down off the counter after putting back some bottle of alcohol.) She arranged them in small glass bowls with defrosted berries and a very good chocolate ice cream. I believe there were sprigs of mint.

COFFEE ~ We loaded up the *moka* and poured everyone a robust, though short, coffee for the road.

SWEET SICILIAN WINE ~ Fred started telling stories, so we opened the wine, brought out the liqueurs, and kept talking. We spent another hour at the table, so I brought out some nuts and chocolates.

We started talking about this book and how much we loved Italy. Fred told this story about their experiences in Venice. I wanted to be there, too. You may be glad you weren't. He and Tami were having a drink near the Rialto Bridge on a very wet afternoon. Some old Italian men came into the bar to get drinks, also. One of the men had a large heavy brown bag under his arm. They went to an outside table under the covered patio. From out of the bag came a cooked pig's head. They proceeded to sit around the table, and while talking among themselves they began to slowly devour the entire thing. Fred and Tami were astounded, of course, and lingered in the bar just to visually partake of this extraordinary experience. After quite a long time, it became apparent to the Italians that they were being observed, probably because Fred and Tami were the only other people in the bar. They began to talk and were invited to join the men with their culinary conversation piece. This is not an experience you're likely to have in the United States. Fred and Tami will remember it for the rest of their lives. For one afternoon, they truly lived *La Dolce Vita* in Italy, with Italians. I have yet to cook an entire pig, or its head, but someday....

> "*Se vuoi vivere bene, prendi il mondo come viene.*
> (If you want to live well, take the world as it comes.)"

Cioppino
FISHERMAN'S SOUP

- *Crostini con Prosciutto Crudo e Asparagi*
- *Assortimento di Pane con Pâté di Anatra, Salumi, Olive, e Melanzane*
- *Insalata Mista con Gorgonzola, Prosciutto Fritto, e Avocado*
- *Condimento di Crescione, Barbabietola e Sugo di Arancia*
- *Cioppino di Michelina*
- *Ancora Pane*
- *Torta di Ricotta*
- *Caffè*

Many months earlier, we had gone to Mexico to spend a week on the beach. I wanted to go to the fish market. Jim and Kate didn't want to go. Rudy wanted to go, too, which was a good thing because I don't speak Spanish. Jim did not want to take care of Kristin because he and Kate were planning to swim. It's not easy to swim when you're in a wheelchair. Kristin did not really want to go to the fish market, but Rudy and I couldn't go without her.

"Kris, do you want to go to the fish market?" She shook her head "No."

"Kris, do you want to go to the fish market?" She shook her head "No."

We took a vote and she was outnumbered. "Kris, we're going to the fish market."

Now, a fish market in Ensenada is another story all by itself. Needless to say, it was wet, smelly, and the fish come in whole sizes only. We couldn't even recognize fish we ate regularly in the States. We got a lot of stares, me with my blond hair, Kristin in her wheelchair, obviously mine, and Rudy? What was that guy doing with those gringas? We came home with crab claws, some whitefish for ceviche, and lobsters (contraband at that time of year but we didn't figure it out at the time). It was our last day before coming home. We steamed the shellfish, melted a lot of butter, and finished off the beans, rice, and tortillas while sitting in our dining room on the sand. The meal for six cost less than $30. "How does this relate to

cioppino?" you ask. It does. Read on. Never one to throw away any food, I took the empty crab and lobster shells, along with everything else left in the refrigerator (onion, carrot, cilantro, parsley, tomatoes, etc.) and boiled them all evening on the stove. Before I went to bed, I filled two large plastic containers and put them in the freezer. They became the ice blocks for cooling the drinks and fresh tortillas we brought back with us across the border. I had been saving these incredibly rich stocks for just the right cold stormy evening.

Today was the day!

I put the frozen stock on the counter and drove to the fish market. It's good to make *cioppino* when you have a large group of people, because it takes a large variety of fish to make it very tasty. I try to count each piece per person when buying the fish. The flavors are delicious the next day, but the fish can get overcooked if you reheat it, so it's better to buy small amounts of each fish. This will usually drive your fishmonger mad, not to mention all the people who are in line behind you. If you go shopping early, they will remain your friends.

> *Contadino scarpe grosse cervello fino.*
> (A peasant's shoes are heavy and his brain is fine.)

my more formal friends, too, because it insists they become peasants, like me. I've been making *cioppino* for many years, but the best one occurred the time I kept the stock and fish separate until the very end. I created the soup by sautéing the standard *soffritto* (finely diced onion, carrot and celery), and adding parsley and herbs from my garden at the end. I added some whole tomatoes, cubed potatoes, and larger pieces of carrot and celery to simmer with the defrosted stock all afternoon. Now the stock was more concentrated, and the vegetables were fork tender. I turned it off and let it sit until dinner time, making sure it did not get cool. I flash fried the shellfish on medium high heat with more onion and a little garlic, starting with the biggest pieces first. As soon as each piece took on a little bit of color I took it off the fire and added it to the soup, where it continued to cook very slowly. After the last piece of fish went into the pot, the *cioppino* was just about ready to serve.

MORE BREAD ~ Serve it piping hot with lots of butter.

CHEESECAKE AND COFFEE ~ Who needs it after several bowls of *cioppino* on a cold Friday evening?

It's much simpler to cook the fish directly in the pot of simmering stock, and I have done this many times. The flavor, however, if you take the time to fry the vegetables and fish first, is much more intense, because their natural sugars will caramelize. Start slowly, get the cooking order down first, and then "Kick it up a notch."

> *"Il caffé deve essere nero come la notte, caldo come l'inferno.*
> (Coffee must be black like the night, hot like an inferno.)"

Tournedos di Bistecca

INDIVIDUAL "BEEF WELLINGTON" FILET MIGNON

- ❖ Un Piattino di Avocado e Insalata di Granchio
- ❖ Insalata Verde Semplice
- ❖ Zucchini in Marinara con Cipolle e Peperoni Rossi e Gialli
- ❖ Tournedos di Bistecca
- ❖ Patate e Cipolle al Forno
- ❖ Torta di Fichi
- ❖ Fette di Persimmon
- ❖ Tuaca

Beef Wellington has always been one of the ultimate culinary challenges I've kept for myself. In my mind, it represents the luxurious lifestyle of my parents' generation, and should be coupled with Manhattans and metallic gold *palazzo* pants cocktail outfits. It is basically a whole filet mignon covered with mushrooms and wrapped in a pastry shell. Although it sounds simple enough, I've always been afraid of it, until today. I had sautéed mushrooms and onions from the night before and, with the addition of cream, I felt I was adequately armed for the mushroom *duxuelles* required by the dish. I splurged and bought a whole filet mignon. I had inherited a box of puff pastry from a friend who moved away. I got out the recipe from James Beard's book and read it. Then I read it again. Then I put the book back on the shelf and proceeded to cut the whole filet mignon into individual steaks. Yes, I was going to accept the challenge, but in my own way. Individual Beef Wellington would be less daunting and the level of doneness would be easier for me to control.

Appunti/Notes

A SMALL PLATE OF CRAB SALAD WITH AVOCADO ~ Being a Cancerian, I really do not like to cook crabs. I love to eat crabs, however, and when not given one as a gift, I will resort to occasionally buying crab legs, claws or canned crabmeat.

Crab salad, like any salad, involves mayonnaise, onion, and or celery or peppers to give it crunch, and flavor from salt, pepper, lemon, vinegar, or whatever suits you that day. Crumbled saltines added at the last minute can also provide crunch. I put a small spoonful on a plate with a slice of avocado next to it. These *antipasti* were eaten standing up before the dinner was served.

Simple Green Salad ~ By now you may have noticed that salads are a necessary but not a particularly inventive part of my meals.

Sautéed Zucchini, Onion with Red & Yellow Peppers, in Marinara ~ This tasty vegetable dish can always be pulled together at our house. Zucchini is available year round, and when sautéed with peppers and onion, and finished with a little bit of leftover sauce, they become a tasty and colorful dish.

Individual Beef Wellington ~ Okay, I chopped the leftover mushrooms, re-seasoned them, and added cream. I left the whole thing on the stove simmering slowly so the cream could reduce while I browned the individual filet mignons. I cooled them down in the refrigerator until just before dinner hour. Then each filet was placed on a piece of puff pastry big enough to fold onto itself and make a tight package. I had visions of cutting little leaf pieces out of the excess dough but there wasn't any. Slits on top to let the air escape was all they were going to get. I cooked them in a hot oven until the thermometer registered the right temperature for rare beef. They didn't look like they would have if they had been served at a restaurant, but they tasted great. I'm not afraid of them any more.

Potato Baked with Onion & Cheese ~ I microwaved several potatoes, and, when cool enough to touch, sliced them into ½ inch rounds. With a little olive oil in the bottom of the shallow casserole, I layered the slices with previously barbequed onion slices, oil, butter, and salt and pepper. I finished them with two or three different types of cheese and a little bit of breadcrumb. They went into the oven with the Beef Wellington.

FIG GALETTE ~ I didn't have extra pastry dough, because I had put it aside for a crust to go underneath fig tarts. Since Kate is the baker, not I, she came home and pulled together a galette after school. From the pantry and into the crust she put chopped figs, apple, almonds, cranberry sauce, raspberry jam, *Triple Sec*, rum, and honey. An egg wash and some sugar went on last, and it went into the oven as the beef came out.

PERSIMMON SLICES ~ Much later in the evening, a persimmon was sliced and passed around. This got me out of my reading chair, and the next thing I knew I was reaching for a nip of something good from the liquor cabinet.

TUACA ~ TV and Tuaca are not a bad combination. Tuaca is a *liquore Italiano* (Italian liqueur), medium amber in color and, as the back of the bottle tells you, with "hints of vanilla and orange flavors." It does have the fruitiness of a *Grand Marnier*, but only a hint, as advertised. *Grand Marnier* is big and fruity, and hits you right in the kisser. Tuaca is more reserved, like an Italian you haven't been introduced to. The vanilla flavors are subtle and provide a smoothness on the tongue that you won't find with *Grand Marnier*. The bottle tells you to enjoy it "as a chilled shot or mixed in your favorite cocktail." It's one of those liquors that you can add to a dessert, coffee or chilled cream, though I prefer it poured directly into a snifter. What's on TV? How about watching an engaging film like *The Godfather, Big Night* or a classic Italian film such as *La Strada, Cinema Paradiso, Mediterraneo* or *La Dolce Vita*? Or perhaps try a newer film, like *La Meglio Gioventù*? If you choose the latter, start with a full bottle of Tuaca, and perhaps some fresh-squeezed orange juice, because it's highly likely you'll still be watching the movie when the sun comes up.

> "*Il tempo vince tutto.*
>   (Times wins over all.)"

Una Celebrazione di Frutta di Canale
Stufato di Melanzane (AKA Ratatouille)
Eggplant Stew

- ❖ Vino rosso
- ❖ Formaggio e Pane, Salsa e Olio
- ❖ Insalata Verde
- ❖ Stufato di Melanzane
- ❖ Riso Bianco
- ❖ Cioccolatini

This meal required another fast preparation and easy cleanup. Rudy was not available to help with Kristin, and Kate had a volleyball game across town. A one-pot meal or a one-pot main seemed like a good idea. It's actually a two-pot meal/main, unless you had the foresight to serve rice the previous evening, and to make extra. I always make extra rice; it either gets used in lunches or served within a couple of days for another dinner. It can also be put into a shallow casserole, either alone or with vegetables, and covered with cheese, *bésciamella*, and crumbs. *Melanzane stufato* is one of the fastest meals you can make. It holds well and can be served as a main course or can be paired with meat. It can serve a large group of people and is very inexpensive to make. It can be made without meat. This version uses a ground meat. I have prepared it with beef, lamb, and turkey. I usually use turkey. It's lean and flavorful, and makes a great alternative to the other meats, which we tend to eat a lot of. It can be made with or without eggplant, and must have zucchini and red sauce in it. Mushrooms can be added. Jim does not like eggplant. He will eat it in this recipe because it is cleverly hidden among all of the other vegetables.

We were eating lunch at a canal-side table in Venice. It was a weekday and many boats were passing by, filled with products required by the citizens of the island. I did not see a brown

UPS or a FEDEX boat pass by, but we did see all manner of items that were being taken into or out of the small boats used by the locals. All of a sudden we spied something bobbing toward us in the water. It turned out to be an eggplant, recently rolled or dropped from a boat or dock. Since that time, if has been affectionately dubbed "*La Frutta di Canale*" by Jim. He never liked it anyway, and will always grab the opportunity to tell you that eggplants originated in the polluted canals of Venice. This dish, to me, is one of the Italian equivalents to pea soup. It's comfort food. It's always welcomed during cold and wet weather.

> *L'acqua fa male e il vino fa cantare.*
> (Water makes you feel bad and wine makes you sing.)

Appunti/Notes

RED WINE ~ I choose my wine to accompany this meal depending on the weather. If it's really cold or wet, a cabernet, merlot, or pinot noir is excellent. If it's not so cold, pick something spicier, like a sangiovese or a zinfandel.

BREAD AND CHEESE, SALSA AND OIL ~ With all of the coming and going, it's better to serve an *antipasto* that can sit out, doesn't need refrigeration, and can still be tasty when the diners arrive. Sometimes Kate runs in, grabs the *antipasto* and runs out the door. Fresh bread and a good cheese are the ultimate in simplicity when it comes to the appetizers. They make a smaller mess than crackers in your car, if you're driving. Salsa and oil are also simple to prepare, though not recommended for consumption while driving.

GREEN SALAD ~ Simple greens, undressed, with a fresh dressing on the side, so it doesn't wilt while waiting for the later arrivees.

EGGPLANT STEW ~ Brown the meat and hold. Chop onion, bell pepper, zucchini, mushrooms, and eggplant into bite-sized similarly sized pieces. Sauté in order, so that at the end all the vegetables and the meat are in the pan. Add garlic, and immediately add red wine and tomatoes. Tomatoes can be whole, chopped or crushed. You could even use a jar of prepared sauce, although I prefer chopped or crushed tomatoes, as they will retain some of their individual character. Add herbs to your taste, usually Italian seasoning. Once browned and beginning to simmer, you can keep it on the stovetop, if eating soon, or put it into a slow oven and leave it alone. Cover or not cover it, depending on how juicy you like it and how long it's going to simmer. This dish can hold a really long time, and works well if people are coming and going.

WHITE RICE ~ Make a pot of rice that can be microwaved when your diners return to the house.

CHOCOLATE ~ If you're leaving the house, a small cookie or chocolate is a great accompaniment to that last swallow of red wine.

La Prima Sera di Bill Maher al teatro Arlington
Cotolette di Agnello alla Griglia
Grilled Lamb Chops

- Vino Rosso della Casa
- Vongole Affumicate su Crostini
- Lattuga Romana con Parmigiano
- Il Piatto Rosso con Pomodori, Gorgonzola, e Broccoli Marinati
- Calzone dalla Ricetta di "Chez Panisse"
- Cotolette di Agnello alla Griglia
- Verdure al Forno (Carote, Cipolle, Finocchio, Barbabietole, e Patate)
- Mandarini

I love Bill Maher. Not in the biblical sense, but definitely in the political sense. He can be really abrupt, as can I. Even if I don't always agree with his approach, I love the fact that he gets right into his guests' faces and puts them on the spot. I used to really like to do that too, but my list of friends began to dwindle. The list of friends who would entrust a secret to me is quite small. I have since changed my ways and decided that some secrets are better kept, especially mine. In California, Bill's show comes on at 8:00 PM on Friday night. In the beginning of the official days of recording the *Venerdì Sera* meals, we would hurry to finish and watch the show promptly. I'm sorry, Bill, but thanks to digital video recording it is now possible to linger at the dinner table a little longer and then watch the show. Not on this night, however. On this night Bill was coming to town, and we were definitely going to see him *alle otto in punto* (at eight on the nose)! The meal needed to be great to commemorate this rare event, but also speedy because Bill waits for no Carbone.

The farmers' market had the usual winter supply of vegetables, and I remember that the weather was quite nice, so I did want to cook. It just had to all be ready to eat quickly in sequence and be easy to clean up afterwards.

Appunti/Notes

RED WINE OF THE HOUSE ~ The bottle was opened early so we could have a glass or two before needing to drive across town.

SMOKED CLAMS ON CRACKERS ~ Yes, I opened a can of smoked clams and put them on crackers, good crackers, but crackers nonetheless. There was no word in my Italian dictionary for cracker. It sounds so much nicer as *crostini*, don't you think?

ROMAINE LETTUCE WITH PARMESAN ~ On this night the salad should have come out of a bag, but I had been to the farmer's market. I served whole washed romaine leaves with shaved *parmigiano* lightly dressed with a great olive oil, seasoned rice vinegar, and salt and pepper. It's one of the fastest fresh salads you can make. Mushrooms or other thinly sliced vegetables can be added easily.

THE RED PLATE WITH TOMATO, GORGONZOLA AND MARINATED BROCCOLI ~ You can almost always do this plate ahead of time. The broccoli stems from another meal were put into a jar with oil and vinegar for a couple of days before using them here. By now you should be able to tell that I really love gorgonzola. It bites back when you bite into it, sort of like Bill Maher.

CALZONE ~ Alice Water's recipe is so good that we never make *calzone* any other way in our house. Yes, you can fill a *calzone* with anything you want, but here, when we get a picture of *calzone* in our head, it always has the white cheese combination oozing out of it. We call it "The Flow." A *calzone* is graded by the quality of the flow, then the crust. My family can be very forgiving on the doneness of the crust as long as what's inside of it never changes. The *calzone* was cooked in the afternoon so I could clean up the mess before dinner.

GRILLED LAMB CHOPS ~ The chops were the only menu item that needed attending to at the last minute. They were rubbed with olive oil, salt and pepper, and probably a little bit of garlic and rosemary. They were on the grill when everyone walked in the door for dinner.

Roasted Vegetables (Carrots, Onions, Fennel, Beets, and Potatoes) ~ The vegetables were rubbed with olive oil, salt and pepper, and roasted whole or cut into large chunks (fennel and potatoes). I prepared them as soon as I got home from the market and slow-roasted them all afternoon. The pan went directly into the dishwasher.

Tangerines ~ I don't think they were eaten in the car but they could have been.

A good substitution for the roasted vegetables could be *Patate Dolce al Forno*, Baked Yams.

Patate Dolci Al Forno/Baked Yams

INGREDIENTS
fresh yams, olive oil, salt, pepper, butter, brown sugar, parmesan, pine nuts.

PREPARATION
Wash the yams and remove any bad spots with the end of your knife. While unpeeled, slice the yams into ¼ inch or smaller disks. In a metal pie pan or braising pan, cover bottom with some extra virgin olive oil and begin arranging the disks in any overlapping pattern. While doing this, sprinkle with olive oil, salt and pepper, and brown sugar as you build up several layers in the pan. Add 1/3 cup water, cover and simmer on medium high for about 10 minutes. Uncover, dot with butter and more oil and salt and pepper. Cover with grated parmesan cheese and ½ cup pine nuts. Finish in 425 degree oven until browned. Serve while hot.

"Osso Buco" di Vitello

VEAL OSSO BUCO

- Trota Affumicata con Crostini, Asiago e Basilico
- Minestra di Verdure, Foglia Verdi di Cavolfiore, e Fagioli Bianchi
- Lattuga Mista con Contorni a Sorpresa
- Foglia Verdi di Dente di Leone
- Polenta
- "Osso Buco" di Vitello
- Assaggi di vari Vini Rossi
- Varietà di Cioccolatini di Katerina

It's finally getting cold here, cold enough that I had to convince myself that I really did want to go to the farmers' market today. The sun was shining, and I was reasonably well dressed for warmth, so I really didn't have any excuse not to head over to the market, after a very brisk walk with friends, both female and canine. The market was smaller than usual. Not everyone wanted to brave the cold either. Now of course we are still in Santa Barbara, so when I say cold, I'm talking about the mid-forties. Most people from the more northern parts of the world will laugh. For once, I was ready to buy Brussels sprouts, think about meals cooked on the stove, and actually make a hearty soup that people would be interested in eating when they came in the door. It's been hard to write this winter section of the book, because the effects of global warming are being felt in our already warm part of California. Today, at least, it felt like winter.

Last week I went to our local Santa Ynez Valley to do a little wine tasting, and it was quite chilly. For about an hour and a half it looked like it might rain. A few drops fell. That was all. Further north it rained quite a bit. We're just not seeing it here this year. By the time we left our third winery, Jim remarked to our friend Nick, "Well, that was winter!"

Appunti/Notes

SMOKED TROUT WITH CRACKERS, ASIAGO CHEESE AND BASIL ~ There have been a few complaints that we are eating too much food. My reply is that you are eating too much food. The rest of us are nibbling our way through courses. So, as a post holiday reminder to me and you and everyone else who wants to live the good life, remember to not heap large portions of food on your plate, even if it tastes good. There will be other things to eat next, and by the end of the meal you should be full, but not stuffed. Don't eat your entire evening's calories at the first plate. The *antipasto* can be just a taste to get the mouth waters flowing. This course should have one or two pieces of a couple of choices for each person. Don't feel like you have to put out the entire package of crackers, slice a whole loaf of bread, or put out an entire wedge of cheese. Just a taste. For this meal, I put out 2-4 oz of smoked trout, 2 *crostini* (about 2-3 inches roughly in diameter) and about five small slices of asiago cheese. Jim could easily eat the entire wedge, but that's not the point. As soon as people are starting to look frantically around for more snacks, move them to the table for the next course, which is a soup.

SOUP WITH WHITE BEANS AND BRUSSELS SPROUTS GREENS ~ I was originally going to sauté the greens from the top of the stalk of Brussels sprouts. I cut them off the stalk and realized that the stem portion would probably need to be trimmed. As I began trimming off the leaves, I realized that rather than throw them into the compost bucket, I could actually create an entire course around the stem tips. The frying pan went back in the cupboard, and out came the soup pot. I quickly got some small white beans soaking in hot water and began to build the soup. The last of the reserved bacon fat that I always keep in the pantry, and a little olive oil, went into the pan, with a *soffritto* of onion, carrot, and celery, finely diced. The day before, I had made a stock using a hambone. Half of that stock went into yesterday's lentil soup; today I used the rest here. I added several sprigs of fresh thyme, stems and all. (It's very easy to get the stems out later in the cooking process.) I added a few bay leaves (California bay laurel picked from our local forest), a diced tomato, some diced Anaheim chile (for heat), and seasoned it aggressively with salt and pepper. It's simmering slowly now, while I write, and by dinner time the beans (which were not adequately hydrated) will be ready to consume. If a bigger bean was used for

this soup, it would have to simmer much longer, and would probably not be ready in time for a same-night dinner. Next time, Michele, plan ahead when you're making a bean soup. It doesn't take a whole lot of forethought or action to soak a cup or two of beans overnight, or while you do some marketing.

MIXED GREEN SALAD WITH A SIDE OF SURPRISES ~ At this time of year, the local heads of lettuce usually get a little bit smaller, and I find that I don't crave green salads as much as I do at other times of the year. My family would be just as happy having only a soup before the main course, and sometimes only a soup as the main course. I still cling to the green salad as an aid to digestion (and regular you know what), so even a small one, served plain without the ubiquitous Red Plate, starts looking good to me in the late winter. The side of surprises is just that: I will probably surprise even myself and maybe not have the accompaniments to the greens at all tonight.

POLENTA ~ The "*Polenta* Rapture" has already been discussed. This one was made with water and finished with a bit of butter. I did not stir it constantly.

VEAL OSSO BUCO ~ Most of my braised meals start out pretty much the same way.

Get the best meat you can find for the number of people you're serving that evening. A true *osso buco* uses the small part of the hind leg towards the shank, but without the knuckle; the part of the leg bone with the hole, as opposed to the bottom with the knuckle still attached. A good butcher knows how to prepare this cut for you and will keep the silver skin properly attached to help hold the meat together while it cooks. Use the appropriately-sized braising pan and brown the meat. Season the meat before browning with olive oil, salt and pepper, and a small amount of herbs, to your taste. This version used shallots, one carrot each for four people, and one each stalk of celery. If you're going to make *osso buco*, you should, after all, taste the veal. You can add tomatoes and garlic if you want to give it a truly Italian flavor. Make sure it does not become a red sauce. You can use white wine, and/or chicken or veal stock, as your braising liquid. Either or both is great. Water will work, too, but it will be harder to develop the richness of flavor which is usually associated with *osso buco*. When it's finished cooking, remove the meat from the pan, and bring the braising liquid to a boil to reduce to a gravy or sauce-like consistency. Some amount of acid, either the lemon, a small amount of vinegar, or white wine at the end will provide balance. Serve it with a squeeze of lemon, some zest, and lots of fresh parsley, and it should be delicious as its falls off the bone and onto your fork.

A Tasting of a Variety of Local Red Wines ~ Since this meal will be cooking itself in the oven for quite awhile, why not open a couple of nice red wines and try sampling for what your palate believes is the perfect match for this meal. Of course you can also have a white wine with your veal. The old adage "red meat red wine, and white meat white wine," comes in and out of favor. Drink whichever one you like best, though you may have an opened bottle of white wine left over if you didn't put it all into either the braising liquid or your mouth!

A Variety of Kate's Handmade Chocolates ~ Kate has designed her own delicious truffles, using a basic recipe for *ganache* and melted chocolate to coat them. We enjoyed peppermint (a hint of peppermint schnapps added to the *ganache*, then coated with dark chocolate and rolled in crushed peppermint candies), orange (a hint of *Triple Sec* added to *ganache* and rolled in chocolate after being coated in my homemade candied orange peel), and almond (a hint of amaretto added to the *ganache* and then coated and rolled in chopped, toasted almonds). I am so lucky to have such a talented daughter! (My friend, Merrily, will vouch for their delicious decadence.)

TGIF/GDEV*
Galline Farcite
STUFFED CORNISH GAME HENS

- Zuppa di Verdure d'inverno
- Insalata "Cesare"
- Il Piatto Rosso di Pomodori e Mozzarella nella Salsa Pesto
- Gnocchi di Zucca
- Fagiolini
- Galline Farcite di Ciliege, Mandorle, Sedano, Cipolline, Finocchio, e Pangrattato
- Cioccolatini di T.J.s

Cornish game hens were on sale, so I bought some. There's always leftover bread in our house. My housekeeper constantly hides the extra loaves in the pantry, because of course they don't look good on the counter if you're used to having a clean, as opposed to a working, kitchen. Every week, I take them back out of the pantry and put them on the counter so I'll remember to turn them into *crostini*, bread crumbs, or in this case bread stuffing. I dug into the pantry and pulled out packages of dried cherries and nuts, opened the refrigerator, and grabbed some onion, celery, and fennel. Into the food processor went some rather stiff pieces of "day old" bread and a couple of eggs with seasonings.

*Thank God it's Friday/*Grazia Dio è Venerdì*

I turned on the TV, and Mario was making *Gnocchi di Zucca*. Well, I could do that. I just scraped the roasted squashes from the Thanksgiving cornucopia display into a container. And, yes, I did have eggs and flour, too. But, I had a pot of broth that needed to be soup-i-fied, so what the heck; I put the arborio rice back in the pantry, put away the eggs, and decided to make *Risotto di Zucca* instead. Out came the pot of broth. I opened the lid and took a whiff. Whew! The smell was awful. The stock had spoiled before I could get around to using it. We wouldn't be making *risotto* after all. I went back to the pantry, got the flour, brought the eggs back out of the fridge, and yes, *Gnocchi di Zucca* it would be tonight, after all.

Appunti/Notes

ROASTED WINTER VEGETABLE SOUP ~ The soup had been made previously, so it was very easy to warm and serve a small bowl as a starter. It became a lifesaver later on....

CAESAR SALAD ~ Small romaine heart leaves, left in large pieces and drizzled with parmesan shavings, topped with diced anchovy.

THE RED PLATE WITH MOZZARELLA AND TOMATOES UNDER PESTO ~ There was a little bit of *pesto* in a jar, covered with olive oil to keep it from browning, so I placed a couple of spoonfuls in the center of the plate so people could take it or not, depending on how they felt.

ROASTED SQUASH GNOCCHI ~ It takes about ten minutes to make *gnocchi* if you have the main ingredient, in this case squash, ready to put through a potato ricer. I recommend thinking a few days ahead if you want to make *gnocchi*, so an extra potato, squash or other vegetable is already cooked and waiting. Boil the *gnocchi* until they float for awhile and then put into a pan with some sautéed shallot, melted gorgonzola and butter.

GREEN BEANS ~ From the farmer's market that morning, and looking good enough to eat raw. Some were reserved for those of us (Kate) who did.

CORNISH GAME HENS ~ I bought four for six of us, stuffed them loosely, and roasted them slowly in the oven. Then I took the pan juices, added a little flour, and then wine to finish. I cut three of them in half, trying to keep the stuffing inside, spooned the sauce oven them and brought them to the table on a large platter. The fourth was reserved in case anyone wanted it. It wasn't eaten, so I put the whole thing in a freezer bag and froze it for an emergency meal for one or two of us, to be consumed at a later date.

CHOCOLATES ~ Out of a box and put on a small pedestal. It was elegant enough to follow this comfort food meal without needing to be a job unto itself.

It was a wonderful meal, although Tony arrived late and gave us all a scare when he didn't answer our telephone call. We didn't know it at the time, but it was the last meal we all had together before the Great Flu of Christmas 2005. Shortly thereafter each of us got sick in sequence, and our plans for a relaxing holiday season were supplanted with spending up to a month in front of the television, accompanied by multiple boxes of tissues. Luckily, days earlier I had made a lot of winter vegetable soup. It kept us going for awhile.

> *Chi vivrà, vedrá.* (If you live, you'll see.)

Minestrone

MINESTRONE

- ❖ *Pane con Burro*
- ❖ *Minestrone*
- ❖ *Tè*
- ❖ *Medicine per il Raffreddore*
- ❖ *Stasera non ci sentiamo italiani*

At some point when everyone is or has been sick, one person will tend to feel better ahead of the others and eventually get hungry. By this time, all the food resources in the house have usually been exhausted, and this person will volunteer to go to the market. This time it was Jim, who decided minestrone would be just the right thing to fix everyone up. The only problem was I had to cook it, and I really wasn't feeling all that great. Luckily, at some point earlier in the week I'd crawled to the freezer and taken out two of the chicken carcasses waiting for just such a moment. They'd been boiled and cooled, and Jim had taken the bones out.

My dictionary describes minestrone as a thick vegetable and pasta soup. What it doesn't say is that there are as many recipes for minestrone as there are people in Italy (or Italian-Americans elsewhere). Everyone believes theirs or their mamma's is the best. Mine is much better than my mamma's. It is different every time I make it, because there's really no recipe for minestrone. I owe it to my brother-in-law Frank, who showed me that if I quadrupled the amount of herbs I put into my soup it would have much better flavor. I thought he was nuts when he emptied about four spice jars into my large pot of soup. It was so much better than before. So this is our family secret. You need to add a lot of herbs to the pot. Beyond that, add all the vegetables you can think of or have around, or could buy that week at the market. Zucchini is a must, as are carrots, celery, and onion. Sometimes I add cabbage. Always put in tomatoes in some form. Little tiny pasta in the shapes of balls, stars or even dolphins, can be added. I would not use a noodle or *spago* (string) shape in this soup.

Appunti/Notes

BREAD WITH BUTTER ~ Thank God Jim went to the store and had the foresight to stock up on fresh food items so we could hang in there for another couple of days.

MINESTRONE ~ The broth was heated. Into it went, each in its allotted time slot, onions, celery (especially the leaves), carrots, green beans, zucchini, a can of chopped tomatoes, entire branches of herbs from the garden (stems to be fished out later), and the rind of parmesan. It simmered while we coughed and hacked and sneezed. It was delicious. After we ate the soup, the whole pot went back into the refrigerator and the bowls went into the dishwasher. Anything else would have to wait.

TEA ~ A large pot of chamomile tea was just what the doctor ordered.

COLD MEDICINE ~ Plop, plop, fizz, fizz, and off to bed we went.

WE WEREN'T FEELING LIKE ITALIANS THIS NIGHT ~ We weren't feeling much like Americans, either.

We were all feeling a little bit better the next morning.

> *"Non ha il sapore delle due cipolle quell che in re al pentola bolle.*
> (It doesn't have the flavor of two onions that are
> boiling in a royal pot.)"

La Festa di San Martino e Il Compleanno di Nicholas Sluchevsky

Oca al Forno con Ripieno di Frutta Secca

Roast Goose with Dried Fruit Stuffing

- *Insalata Mista con Pomodoro, Salame, e Formaggio*
- *Zucca con Zucchero Marrone*
- *Fagiolini*
- *Oca al Forno con Ripieno di Frutta Secca*
- *Purè di Patate con Un Bacio di Lardo*
- *Cavolo Rosso con Aceto e Mela*
- *Torta di Mela*
- *Porto*

Roast goose. Goose. Roast goose. Goose. As with turkey, there are a million ways to complicate a goose. If you wanted to, you could probably figure out a way to brine it with a salt brine that had been infused with the soaking liquid from partially digested wild cherries that had been chewed by Himalayan yaks. In the case of this meal, it would have to be Hungarian yaks, if such an animal existed. I've always wanted to cook a goose, and after spending an entire weekend eating goose in Budapest during the festival of *San Martino*, now was the time. Since that first event, which was highly successful, a new tradition has been born in our house. Saint Martin's feast day just happens to be November 11, which corresponds with the birth of our good friend Nick, one week later. Nick usually tries to come to Santa Barbara for a visit, and happened to be visiting on the actual feast day, when I cooked my first goose. One thing for certain when Nick is around is that there will be plenty of cooking and plenty of drinking. There will also be plenty of stimulating conversation around the dinner table, or sitting around a computer while sipping tea. Taking a step back now, I must also tell the embarrassing story of my first night in Budapest.

Jim was there on business and was engaged for the evening when I arrived. I was on my own. Not wanting to venture far from the hotel, I dressed nicely and headed for the hotel dining room. When I arrived, the maitre d' asked me if I wanted the buffet or the winemakers' dinner. Well, it was obviously an easy decision for me to make, and there I was in a room full of wine connoisseurs listening to a wine maker and a chef describe their pairings in Hungarian! The waiter was kind enough to occasionally come to my booth and provide some whispered translations. I soon realized that the gentleman at the table next to me was also an American who was dining alone. He was looking equally distressed, so I asked the waiter to ask him if he wanted to join me. Now we had two strangers together who had interests in wine and food. Tonight's featured menu was goose. Goose liver chunks in a broth served in an espresso cup, crispy goose pieces on top of salad, and quite frankly, after the waiter delivered three bottles of the wine we had tasted to our table I don't really remember what kinds of goose we had after that. I do remember weaving toward the restroom several times and that the aforementioned gentleman ordered a martini at the end of the meal (God, how could he even think about drinking after all the wine we consumed?). I still had my wits about me and managed to get back to my hotel room just as Jim was getting ready to call out the Hungarian National Guard to find me.

I have been in love with goose ever since that evening. I have also been in love with down comforters after that evening, particularly since I spent most of the next 14 hours in that lovely bed in Hungary. There is nothing like a wonderful down comforter to help you through a major hangover. So, at the end of this trip I returned home armed with an additional suitcase filled with down comforters, and a love of goose.

The following year, Saint Martin's feast day happened to be on Friday evening, Nick was in town, and there you have it. I was compelled to master the beast, if only to prove to myself that it was not going to be my master. Now I will admit that I was sorely defeated by the Hungarian wines. If you're interested, look up the story of the Bull's Blood. My experience

> "*A male estremi, estremi rimedi.*
> (A bad extreme, extreme remedies.)"

with Hungarian wine is perhaps not as historically significant, but I will respect anyone who can master three bottles of their wine and still order a martini as a *digestivo*.

So, back to goose. Roast goose. Goose. From the standpoint of cooking, a goose is not too much different to prepare than what you would do for a chicken or a turkey. Like duck, however, a goose is a very fatty animal. Some of the world's best down comes from Hungary, where it gets really cold. Along the way, the geese must have figured out that the Hungarians were stealing all of their feathers, so in defense against the cold, they began to develop a thick layer of fat just underneath their skin, particularly on their thighs. (Sound familiar?) If only we could prick our thighs ever so gently with a meat fork and slowly watch the fat melt away while resting in a cozy warm room....

> *Amici e vino devono essere vecchi.*
> (Friends and wine must be old.)

Appunti/Notes

MIXED GREEN SALAD WITH TOMATO, SALAMI AND CHEESE ~ The main part of the evening would be about the goose, so I didn't spend a lot of time on the salad course. We had just enough greens to make this course worth getting the plates dirty, and The Red Plate with the requisite three things as a minimum to create a selection.

SQUASH WITH BROWN SUGAR ~ Winter squash is such a comfort food, and as it gets later in the year, many of the other vegetables become scarce. I like to roast vegetables while I am also roasting the meats. The oven is on anyway, so why not use it if you have the space. The goose was not as tall as a turkey, so there was plenty of room to put a low dish of cubed squash on the top shelf towards the end of the cooking time. This squash was cooked previously, so I just had to cut it up, and add some butter and olive oil, with salt and pepper. I sprinkled pine nuts in among the pieces of squash and gave it a light dusting of bread crumbs, and another sprinkle of olive oil to help it brown.

GREEN BEANS ~ Nick has recommended that green beans be always cut on the diagonal to facilitate cooking. He insists on boiling his, and they were delicious. I have always steamed mine and then finished them with a bit of olive oil and salt and pepper. When Jim is not around, we'll sprinkle them with lemon juice, too. In a pinch, I have even just microwaved them, but they're never as good. Don't let them get overcooked, and take the time to stop the cooking in an ice water bath, especially if you're not going to eat them immediately. I definitely prefer cold, properly cooked vegetables to hot ones that have been cooked to death.

ROAST GOOSE WITH FRUIT STUFFING ~ I had to order the goose ahead of time, so my butcher could bring it in for me at great expense. Goose is a lot more expensive that a turkey, primarily because American's don't eat enough of them, which is a shame. I think they are a lot tastier. A goose has no white meat, so if you're a dark meat lover like I am, this is the bird for you! If everyone who reads this book goes out and tries goose and loves it, perhaps we can create a demand and the prices could come down. Plus, if we all render the goose fat and use it for flavoring and cooking

throughout the season, our food will be tastier, too. Forget about your cholesterol. If you use it sparingly; drink plenty of red wine to keep that grease moving through your system and get exercise, too, you'll probably not die of a coronary because of the goose. But how do I cook it? Start with a 350 degree oven and allow approximately 20 minutes per pound. The times and temperatures are not rocket science. Look those details up in any cookbook and adjust for your oven and tastes. Use a meat thermometer to verify it is food-safe before eating. What will really make the difference is how you personalize it. I pre-soaked most of the dried fruit in my pantry (apricots, cherries, currants) in water, and added some nuts to my usual turkey stuffing recipe. I cut up the stale French bread that was on the counter, added onion and sage, and egg and broth, until it looked like a stuffing. Add plenty of salt, because the bird will suck some of it out of the stuffing. Stick it inside the bird. Prick only as deep as you need to get through the skin and fat layers particularly around those pesky thighs (the bird's, not yours!), rub with olive oil, and season with salt and pepper and whatever else interests you, and put the whole thing in the oven. Cook it until the meat thermometer registers the correct temperature (around 185°F for poultry). By now you have probably realized that I'm the type of cook who likes to season lightly and not use a lot of obscure spices. I do like spicy foods, too, but I really prefer to taste the meat. Heavy seasonings can be used for disguising the taste of bad meats, and are frequently used to mask bad cooking. If you cook it properly, you will not need to overpower it with spices.

MASHED POTATOES WITH A KISS OF GOOSE FAT ~ For God's sakes, keep the garlic out of the potatoes! Garlic is a flavoring, not a main ingredient. Used in excess, it will ruin your taste buds if any other menu item has a delicate flavor. Potatoes are delicious all by themselves, and need only to be lightly dressed with salt and pepper, a bit of butter or goose fat, and maybe a dusting of an accent like paprika or chives. Mashed potatoes are easy to make, and go well with roasted birds and gravy. The potatoes can be steamed and mashed earlier in the day, and held in the refrigerator for a last-minute warm-up. If you prep all of your sides earlier in the day, or the day before, the goose alone will not seem so daunting. If you can cook a chicken, you can cook a goose. Strain the pan juices and brown some flour in the roasting pan. Add broth or water and re-season. The gravy will be rich and delicious. Add a touch of white wine or vinegar to give it some acid, and it won't appear so flabby on your tongue.

RED CABBAGE WITH VINEGAR AND APPLE ~ You can sometimes find pickled red cabbage in a jar or can. I bought a whole cabbage and cut it up as if for making slaw. I sautéed an onion, and at the last minute decided to add an apple for sweetness. I rough-cut the apple and sautéed it until it was partially cooked, then added the cabbage and sautéed them until the cabbage was starting to get soft. I added about a cup of vinegar and let the whole thing boil on high until the cabbage was fully cooked. Then I added some sugar until the right balance of sweet and sour was achieved. I prefer it to be on the sour side, particularly with goose, which is very rich on its own.

APPLE TART ~ Something with apples will continue the theme, especially if you added any to the stuffing. I defrosted sheets of puff pastry and docked (pricked with a fork) the center part. I then placed slices of a mild white cheese (Jack is acceptable) and placed slices of apples that had been tossed with lemon juice on top. I left the edges un-docked so that they could puff up and a serve as a crust. I sprinkled sugar on top plus a tiny pinch of salt and cooked it in the hot oven while we were eating the goose.

PORT ~ A final sip of a fortified red wine would be another excuse to linger at the table....

You may be asking, what does the feast of *San Martino* have to do with eating geese? Well, it is said that when a lowly fourth century guy was searched out to become the Bishop of Tours in 371 AD, he hid in the goose barn. The geese made so much noise that Martin was found out. In revenge for them contributing to getting him caught, he caught one of the geese and ate it for dinner. Whether or not he started the tradition is up for speculation, but people have been eating goose during his feast day ever since. I suspect that we were eating goose before *San Martino* came around, but it's a good story, so why mess with it? To me this feast will always be remembered as the feast of the down comforters. Kate remembers it as the season of mom's obsession with down. I also remember it as one of the best gatherings of old friends.

La Primavera

CHAPTER 6

All of a sudden your feet are not cold, you forget to close the window before going to bed, and realize you were not freezing during the night. "Hey, it's not dark during dinner any more!" It's a good time of year. If you live in Santa Barbara, you can begin riding your bike, or taking the dog for a walk in the evenings, either before or after dinner. And it's possible to take a walk on the pier or breakwater without freezing. If you live in other places, I'm guessing the piles of snow may be beginning to melt. Small bright green things begin to poke up all over the place, especially at the farmers' markets. The boxes of holiday chocolates have been consumed, or, if not, you no longer hoard them selfishly and begin to share them with your close friends and family members. Bathing suit weather is coming, and if your winter was anything like mine, there was a lot of chocolate consumption this past holiday season.

Our family holidays were broken up into six weeks of celebrations. Yes, the tree was up for six weeks and one day, a new Carbone holiday tree record, hopefully never to be repeated. Several of the therapists walked in the door and sort of gave me the look: She still has her tree up? What day is this? Is there really something weird about her, after all? (That kind of look.) I could see it in their eyes, and immediately proceeded to say, "We still have one family member who hasn't arrived yet, and we're planning one more Christmas dinner next Saturday. Honest, I'm not that kind of a nut...." But now the tree is out of the house, and the neighbors who drive by give me that kind of look, and hopefully the garbage collectors, or the people who take the trees away will come and remove it soon.

> *Anno nuovo, vita nuova.*
> (New year, new life.)

Meanwhile, it's a good day to go to the farmers' market and see what spring has to offer. Now for me, at this moment, it's late in January. Where you live, it may not yet look like spring. Technically, it's not spring yet, if you follow the equinoxes. When I cook, I follow the weather, so for me, today it's spring. If the weather turns cold again, I'll go back to warm and fuzzy comfort foods. I made the mistake of weighing myself (something I rarely do and do not recommend). For now, I need to lighten things up a bit, and look to a more spa-cuisine approach to dining. So how can the first menu for the *nuoveau*, or perhaps it should be *nuova stagione* (new season), be duck? Well, unlike the heavy stuffed goose with all of the winter trimmings, this duck will be cut up and barbequed. If you do it just right, it will not be fatty, and can be crispy and delicious. Just don't do what I did that night and think that the other person was watching the barbeque while we were having the soup course. It's amazing that a burning duck smells exactly like an electrical fire. Two of us recognized the smell....

CHAPTER 6 — LA PRIMAVERA | 129

Burnt Offerings
Anatra alla Griglia
Barbequed Duck

- Cocktail: La Dama Bianca
- Assortimento di Salumi, Formaggi e Pane
- Insalata di Crescione e Foglie Verdi di Dente di Leone
- Risotto con Funghi Selvaggi
- Asparagi con Olio di Olivo
- Anatra alla Griglia
- Torta di Cioccolato di Pietro
- Frutti di Bosco con Panna

Jim had never seen flames shooting out of the sides of the barbeque quite like he did that evening. I'd made the mistake of experimenting with a new menu with guests. They always tell you to never do that, and here I was getting burned, really burned, in front of guests who had never been to the house before. What did we do? We scraped the black part off the big pieces, and threw the little bits of charred meat away. We poured more wine, lots of it. We laughed and had a great time in spite of the duck. I will have to try it again, just to make sure that the duck doesn't remain the winner.

Ducks don't have a lot of meat on them, as chickens do. But what's there is delicious, if cooked properly. A test of any chef's skills is whether he or she can cook a duck so that the skin is crispy, the meat is juicy and not dry, and the fat has been properly rendered away. Once you've had a perfectly cooked duck, you will be forever critical of anything less. Writing this reminds me that I have more work to do on mastering this one. Unlike the goose, this one is currently duck 1, me 0.

I knew how to grill, so I decided that a recipe using a cut up duck would be easier for a first time attempt. I almost succeeded, because the flavor was good, and if the grill had been attended to, I could have pulled off a succulent fowl (or parts thereof). In James Beard's *American Cookery*, he states, "Game, and especially wild duck, flamed with gin,

is so agreeable that it is astonishing that it is not done more generally." Gin can make anyone agreeable, so why not a duck? He also mentions that the flavors of sage, thyme, and juniper berries complement a duck well.

Alice Waters, in the *Chez: Panisse Menu Cookbook*, marinates a duck for grilling in red wine. You can use gin, red wine or vermouth in combination with these herbs and/or bring in the flavors of orange juice, onion, and tart cherry or current jelly. It can only be bad if you undercook it or flame it a little too aggressively.

Appunti/Notes

WHITE LADY ~ There may already be a drink named the White Lady, but Kate and I invented this drink while thinking about *Cointreau* and gin, both flavors purported to be good with duck. So for this spring *aperitivo*, we mixed four parts gin to one part orange juice, and added a whiff of *Cointreau*. We added ice to a shaker, put in orange zest and juniper berries, and served it in a martini glass with a zest. Hence the name *La Dama Bianca* (Kate's middle name is Bianca).

DELI MEATS, CHEESE, AND BREADS ~ If the main course is very special, prepare a simple starter that challenges the palate, but doesn't overwhelm it, for the flavors ahead. For me, picking out two to three really good deli meats that are sliced that day and not brought out from an anonymous plastic package are my favorites. Just having to make a special trip to a good deli is worth the extra time and travel. Look for something you haven't tried before, and expand your horizons beyond *Salame di Genova* and Prosciutto. If you serve a spicy *Capocollo*, you may just need some gin to wash it down. Toast or grill some good bread, and put out a mild cheese to go with them.

SALAD OF WATERCRESS AND DANDELION GREENS ~ Watercress and dandelion greens are sharper tasting than the usual lettuces, and look exotic when

paired. I prepared a creamy *vinaigrette*, the usual oil and vinegar dressing, with a little citrus and yogurt mixed into it. Season it well, especially after mixing in the yogurt.

WILD MUSHROOM RISOTTO ~ Use what you can find to give it a more exotic taste. You can use the plain old ordinary white or brown button mushrooms; just embellish them with some of the harder to find and tastier fungi. It would be better to add a few dehydrated *chanterelle*, porcini, cloud ear or even shitake, than to use just the button variety. Portobello mushrooms will give you a variation in the color and texture, but the flavor is basically the same. Chop the mushrooms roughly. I like to be able to distinguish the individual pieces within a *risotto*. Some people prefer a homogeneous, almost minced texture to their *risotto*. Choose whatever you prefer. Start the *risotto* with some onion family items and just a touch of garlic. I prefer to cook the mushrooms apart from the *risotto*, and add them toward the finish. You can do it either way. Fry the rice in a bit of oil, then add the broth bit by bit as the rice cooks. Toward the end, add some white wine (or perhaps gin?), the mushrooms, and a bit of cream or butter to bring it all together. The amount of cream and butter is directly dependent on how much chocolate you consumed over the winter and

how soon you will have to appear in public wearing a bathing suit. If you're like me, use the phrase "I have fair skin," forget the bathing suit, and enjoy the *risotto*! Walk a little faster with the dog the next time.

ASPARAGUS ~ Rubbing asparagus with a very good olive oil and grilling it is my favorite. You can also do it in the broiler. Steaming works, too. Be sure to finish it with a good coarse sea salt (this is when I would use the more expensive *Fleur di Sel*), freshly ground black pepper, and perhaps a squeeze of fresh citrus. Orange could be nice if you're using orange juice with the duck or in the *aperitivi*. Add some zest.

GRILLED DUCK ~ So now let's cut the duck into pieces. It has basically the same parts as a chicken. Just look for the joints and insert knife. My first attempt at cutting a duck was successful, though I must admit the parts were a bit obscure. We ate them anyway. The marinade consists of carrot, onion, peppercorns, herbs, bay leaves, and salt and pepper. Alice Waters adds a whole bottle of red wine, pricks the fat all around, and precooks it in a hot oven before finishing it on the grill. If you have a grill with selectable burners, you can go hotter on the temperature; just keep the flame away from the side where you place the duck. Either way, you'll want to have your fire hose ready. Don't try to sit in the dining room while the grill is on. Pause the meal and refresh the drinks or open a good bottle of a young red wine to go with the duck after it comes off the grill. Make sure you get the skin crispy. I don't eat chitlins, but I'm guessing they're a close rival of crispy duck skin.

CHOCOLATE CAKE WITH BERRIES AND CREAM ~ Pietro has his own bakery, so the dessert course was definitely on him. The dark chocolate of the cake was a perfect match to the blackened duck. We added berries and cream, and by the time we finished it and the bottle of wine, no one cared about the duck anymore.

> "*Sbaglia solo chi lavora.*
> (Only those who work make mistakes.)"

Una Piccola Pasqua
Salsicce e Agnello alla Griglia
Grilled Lamb & Sausages

- ❖ Pinot Grigio
- ❖ Carciofini Stufati

- ❖ Insalata Verde
- ❖ Cardone
- ❖ Lasagne

- ❖ Salsicce e Agnello alla Griglia
- ❖ Sorbetto al Limone

Piccola Pasqua means Little Easter. This meal is not for a real Easter, which for me requires many more courses and a lot more people. At our house, Easter comes with twenty or more friends and relatives, and involves a lot of cooking. In the past, our Easter meals have ranged from a total repeat of the Thanksgiving traditions, to ham with meatballs, to stew made with goat, and most recently to my favorite, which is barbequed lamb and Italian sausages, complemented with stuffed baby artichokes and cardoons, harvested from our own backyard.

Now about cardones, or cardoons as the Italian-American side of the family prefers to call them. I had heard about the magnificence of cardoons for years after I married into this family of mine. Whenever they were spoken about, the speaker would get all misty-eyed and would speak oh so reverently about the many virtues of a properly cooked *cardone*. If only I could have had the ones prepared by Aunt Nancy! I had never heard of them, never seen one, and soon figured out that most Italians I spoke with had never heard of them either. I was beginning to think they were related to unicorns.

> "*Natale con i tuoi e Pasqua con chi vuoi.*
> (Christmas with your relatives, Easter with whomever you want.)"

"Are you sure they're not a variety of artichoke? Do you really eat the stem? Is that thistle growing there by the trail really a wild *cardone*?"

"No, no, no!" was all I heard. I figured out that when harvested they looked like gigantic silvery stalks of celery with leaves that came out from the sides of the ribs. The bush was believed to look like an artichoke plant.

One day, I was walking past one of the familiar booths at the farmer's market, and lo and behold, I stopped dead in my tracks. "Are those cardoons?" I recognized them immediately because they truly do not look like any other vegetable that I had seen.

The vendor said, "Yes, do you know them?" I said, "Not really, give me all you have," and promptly took them home to show off my prize. Jim arrived home late that Friday evening, and when I proudly showed him the cardoons and asked him if we could make them tonight, he said "Hell, no! Cardoons take a sh___load of work!" and that was the end of it, until Saturday.

Now I know why so many people do not know about cardoons. Only a starving Sicilian woman would have figured out that these things are edible and would have the patience to cook them. In our family, the entire bush is trimmed at the dirt level, each stalk must be sliced along both its edges to take off the leaves (and yes, they do have thorns), the tops must be tipped, and the strings removed. Then, if you haven't died from exhaustion, you can begin the first part of the cooking. Yes, I said first part. They must be sliced into six-inch pieces, parboiled, not once, but twice, or until the bitterness and a lot of green oily juice is leached out of them. Then you get to do the second cooking. Once drained, you coat them in egg and seasoned flour, and then you fry them until they're crispy and golden brown. If you do not use extra virgin olive oil for the frying, you will be shot.

Do they taste good? They are *fantastico*! They taste like artichoke hearts with the crunch of celery added in. They're delicious, and worth every ounce of work to make them several times a year. Because they're so much work and so tasty, they're a delicacy in this family, and are synonymous with Easter. Making an entire bush of cardoons is quite a job, and it takes a

> "*A casa sua, ciascuno è re.* (At one's house, each is a king.)"

big family to eat them all. Most family members will not help you make them, but if you get them wrong, they will surely tell you about it. I asked once why I couldn't just take a couple of the outer stalks off the bush and cook a smaller amount, and was told it just couldn't be done. We have matching photos of cousin Joe and Jim, each holding an entire bush of cardoons, as if to say, "See, mine is the biggest!"

We traveled to Sicily to visit the town of Jim's grandparents' birth, and as we neared the town we saw what looked like wild cardoons growing alongside the road. "Stop the car!" Jim shouted, "We must be getting close!" We took pictures of the *cardone* plant. The town was literally around the next bend.

Jim hunted down a seed supplier and promptly planted twelve plants. They grow like weeds and restart themselves every year. I have secretly taken only a few outer stalks and prepared them in small batches. Surely this *Piccola Pasqua* was one of those times. I also sneaked them into a soup. Other than that, they must always be prepared only in the described manner. Once, Jim actually ordered them prepared differently in a restaurant. He has seen other chefs' preparations on TV, and has taken our own cardoons into one of our local Italian restaurants. He went into their kitchen to show them how to prepare cardoons. In every case, there was something profoundly wrong with their preparation: they didn't make them like Aunt Nancy.

If you do find an occasional stalk of cardoons at the market, by all means buy them. Think of me while you are eating them. Even though I try to never water the many plants, hoping some of them will die, they always spring back, and someone will eventually say, "Hey, isn't it time for some cardoons?" If no one is looking, you can serve them with a little red sauce or a squeeze of lemon.

> *Se vuoi vivere lieto, guarda davanti, e non guardare indietro.*
> (If you want to live happily, look ahead, and don't look behind.)

Appunti/Notes

Your Favorite White Wine for Aperitivo ~ A really good pinot grigio is perfect with the beginnings of this meal. I recommend segueing into a heartier white or red wine with the meat.

Stuffed Baby Artichokes ~ I am not allowed to change the preparation of baby artichokes in any way. In this family, if you want to remain a member of it, you must follow Nana's recipe. They can only be made when the artichokes are at their peak. Buy only the smallest artichokes you can find, take off all the outer leaves, and cut off the tops and stems. Pry them open gently and wiggle them around until they open up and allow you to fill them. Stuff them with seasoned bread crumbs, mixed with grated *parmigiano*. Arrange in a steamer, drizzle with olive oil, and steam until tender. If you do not take off enough of the outer leaves, you will know it as soon as you bite into one. If done properly, they can be eaten in one bite. If prepared inadequately, you will get pieces of leaves that cannot be chewed, and you'll have to figure out how to dispose of the nasty partially chewed leaves that remain in your mouth. Again, they are delicious. Both these and cardoons are an acquired taste. The artichokes

can be prepared a day ahead. Steam them until almost soft and then re-steam when you're ready to eat them so they get hot and tender.

Green Salad ~ A simple salad or even a plate of sliced cucumbers and peppers would be good. Make it easier, because the rest of the meal takes some effort.

Cardone or Cardoons ~ Like artichokes, they will rust when cut edges are exposed to air, so work quickly and hold them in acidulated water until you get to the cooking part.

Lasagne ~ On this night it was not cooked from scratch. Left over lasagne makes a great side dish on the second night. My family does eat it as a main course, but only for the first night. After that any leftovers make their way into lunches and sides. Our Italian cousin made her lasagne with veal and a *béchamelle* sauce. Her red sauce included rosemary, and not the more familiar oregano and Italian seasoning mix. The flavor was delicious. She used very little garlic and only a slight amount of mozzarella and *parmigiano* on top. We loved it, and I hope you try it, too.

Grilled Lamb and Sausages ~ I grew up on roast lamb. Once you've tasted grilled lamb, there's no going back. The mix of olive oil, garlic, rosemary, mint, and any other herbs you prefer, with the char of the grill is just heavenly. Tony likes to stand by the grill and spoon additional garlic and oil over the meat as it cooks. This particular night, I used a butterflied leg of lamb. Your butcher can do it, or try it yourself. You may also find a boneless leg of lamb rolled up and held inside a string basket. Take this basket off, because for grilling you want the meat to be thin so it will cook more evenly. I'm one step away from making my own sausages. Jim has rejected any Italian sausages available in Santa Barbara, and I usually travel to Los Angeles to get the ones that have the peculiar flavor that he remembers from his youth. Grill the lamb until it's medium, and the sausages until the temperature is at your safe point for pork.

Lemon Sorbet ~ Serve a spoonful to refresh the palate (and complete the meal).

ALICE DOESN'T LIVE HERE ANYMORE
Capesante su Fettuccine
SCALLOPS ON FETTUCCINE

- ❖ Vino Bianco
- ❖ Il Piatto Rosso di Cetriolo, Pomodori, e Feta con Aceto Balsamico
- ❖ Capesante su Fettuccine
- ❖ Fragole con Aceto Balsamico e Pepe
- ❖ Vino Dolce

The worse part is I don't really remember why we called this meal "Alice Doesn't Live Here Anymore," except that Alice did live next door, and may have moved around this time. It's more than likely from the song lyrics, "You can get anything you want…" and it definitely was not from the traditional Thanksgiving radio play of *Alice's Restaurant* by Arlo Guthrie. "Whatever," I say, or in Italian, "*Boh, non importa!*" It was written on a scrap of paper from 2001, and I do remember that the dish was quite tasty. There was probably a lot of cooking and drinking and eating earlier in the day, so that by the time we moved into dinner not much more had to be prepared. This meal is one of those "Take everything from your refrigerator and defrost some of the scallops you keep on hand for nights like these," or else someone very special came over with a cache of fresh scallops earlier in the day.

> "*A caval donato non si guarda in bocca.*
> (Don't look a gift horse in the mouth.)"

Appunti/Notes

HOUSE WHITE WINE ~ Pick one with enough body to stand up to the richness of the pasta.

THE RED PLATE OF CUCUMBER, TOMATO, AND FETA WITH BALSAMIC VINEGAR ~ A nice change from the ubiquitous green salad is to just do a platter of the things that usually go into the salad and leave out the lettuce altogether. A heaping plate of cubed cucumber, diced tomato, and cubed feta, with or without some shaved onion, is delicious by itself. Add the dressing at the very end because the balsamic vinegar will color the cheese. If it sits too long in anticipation of its turn at the table, the cheese will begin to look like something you've had in the fridge for way too many nights.

SCALLOPS ON FETTUCCINE ~ The toppings were sautéed one at a time in a pan large enough to hold all the ingredients below, plus the cooked pasta at the end. Cook the pasta at the last minute while allowing the sauce to thicken. Begin by sautéing the leeks, scallions, garlic, and prosciutto (previously chopped), then add parsley. Allow the parsley to sauté for a few minutes, and then take them out of the pan while you sear the scallops. (A good place to hold them is in the upside-down pan lid balanced on top of the pasta pot, or held by an unused burner, or on top of a nearby drawer so that it will not tip over.) Make sure the scallops are adequately spaced, so they sear and don't steam before adding the tomato (either fresh or canned), with its liquid and the held ingredients. When the pasta is almost cooked, add the spinach leaves to the skillet and let them wilt. Then add *ricotta* with milk. Allow to thicken before adding the cooked pasta. Remember that the pasta will soak up some of the sauce, so don't let it get too thick. Eat it right away, or you'll need to add more milk (and seasonings if you do). Season with salt and pepper as you add each ingredient, and finish with more salt and pepper, chopped fresh parsley, a squeeze of lemon, and a drizzle of your best extra virgin olive oil.

STRAWBERRIES WITH PEPPER AND BALSAMIC VINEGAR ~ Fresh strawberries sliced in half and lightly dusted with pepper and a drop or two of silver or gold label *aceto balsamico* would be a refreshing counter to the creamy sauce of the *fettuccine*. Try a

squeeze of lemon and/or salt with some of the zest of any citrus you have on hand. (I once heard that if the bottle says *balsamico*, and it's from Italy, you will know you're getting a controlled product and are not subject to the misrepresentation that sometimes comes with products made and marketed in the USA.) I would always want to add *a biscotto* or wafer to the bowl of strawberries. A mint leaf would complete it visually.

SWEET DESSERT WINE ~ A liqueur would probably overpower the strawberries. A dessert wine or sparkling wine such as a Prosecco would be a great finish. It would also make a great start to this meal.

Little Green Things
Spaghetti con Verdure Verdi in Padella
Spaghetti with Sautéed Greens

- ❖ Funghi con Ripieno di Pesto e Formaggio
- ❖ Insalata Capricciosa
- ❖ Spaghetti con Verdure Verdi in Padella
- ❖ Un Piatto di Carne Fredda Assortita per L'Uomo che ha fame, per favore
- ❖ Torta di Cioccolato con Fragole

Sometimes, when the weather is really beautiful and the chill has left the morning air, you can get up really early and get to the farmers' markets before most people have beaten you to the very best produce. My favorite tomato supplier will have seconds for half the price of the usual tomatoes. When I know that I am going to be using a lot of them in the next few days, or I plan on chopping them for a salsa, sauce, or soup, I don't really care if there's a blemish or cut in the skin of the tomato. On this morning the tomato pickings were excellent. What I wasn't expecting was an excellent selection of fresh spring greens. Every vendor had his or her best spring greens, dandelion, Brussels sprouts, small young cabbages, colored chard, arugula and even basil. They all looked good, and I bought several different types. When I arrived home, I realized that I'd bought way too much in the greens category. Jim will eat some greens, though usually under duress. If it's raw, and is arugula, he will notice it every time and complain. A perfectly sautéed platter of greens is definitely not something he will look forward to or request. He will very likely pass on the entire course. If I occasionally add it to pasta, it can be delicious. He will eat it (not too often), although he once told me that adding greens to pasta was just a good way to ruin a perfectly good plate of pasta. Never mind that greens contain huge amounts of anti-oxidants and other great nutritional elements, he'd rather just have the pasta, and "Skip the greens, please!"

Appunti/Notes

MUSHROOMS STUFFED WITH PESTO AND CHEESE ~ I can usually put basil into anything, and it is well received. After a long winter, the sight of basil is a welcome thing. I made a quick *pesto*, most of it to be used for another evening. Pull the stems out of the mushrooms, and, as a minimum, put a little cube of a light cheese into each, followed by a dollop of *pesto*. A coating of breadcrumbs (you made them yourself, right?), salt and pepper, herb and olive oil, and into the oven or broiler. They can be cooked ahead, and reheated just before serving if you're pressed for time at the dinner hour.

CHOPPED RAW VEGETABLE SALAD ~ Not only were the greens wonderful, but the sugar snap peas and small green beans had arrived on the scene. This salad can be made by keeping the vegetables whole or chopped into very large pieces. For variety I like to finely chop the green beans, sugar snap peas in their pods, and pieces of colored bell peppers, and combine them with the chopped stems from the chard, parsley or dandelion greens, and even julienned cabbage leaves. You can dress the mixture with either oil and vinegar or a coleslaw-like dressing involving the addition of some mayonnaise or yogurt. Season it well; add some of the herbs and perhaps a bit of lemon zest and juice.

SPAGHETTI WITH SAUTÉED GREENS ~ Now for the greens: You can do this dish in a vegetarian manner; however, I prefer the flavor of pork or poultry. (Did you know that if you get a yellow layer of fat off the top of a pot of chicken broth that does not get hard, it's actually called the *schmaltz*?) Start sautéing your onion, leek or shallot in a little bit of *schmaltz*, bacon fat or goose fat with your olive oil. You can sauté bacon, ham, and *pancetta* with the greens, also. I like to sauté the meat until it's crispy and then reserve it on some paper towels and use it at the very end as a garnish. Sauté any of the greens, including spinach (for those wary of the more unusual greens), and finish with some form of acid; either lemon juice, a bit of wine or vinegar. Add your favorite cooked pasta to the pan. Add some of the reserved pasta water so it's not too dry. Toss together, add grated *Parmigiano* or Romano cheese, and finish with chopped parsley or basil.

A Plate of Assorted Cold Meats for the Hungry Man, Please ~ Now, while the rest of us can be content with a great plate of pasta for the main course, especially if some crispy meat pieces are included, my man loves meat! So, as homage to his inner beast, and as a diversion from the greens, which cannot be so cleverly concealed when tossed with pasta, I added a plate of whatever meat happened to be around from the night before. A leftover steak, chops or roast, sliced and artfully displayed with some crumbled gorgonzola or herbs, allows him to decide to eat them cold, or microwave them at will. Either way, a meat eater can be empowered and not have to succumb to the "girl food" pasta preparation. My husband will count the number of pieces of meat and the number of people, and, if the number of meat is not vastly greater than the number of people, he will state, "There's not enough food!" in a voice of panic. I will tell him calmly that "The women are not having meat tonight, dear," even if it's not true. There's usually plenty of meat for all, as necessary, the rest of us requiring far less than his "fear of insufficient meat" obsession allows.

Chocolate Cake with Strawberries ~ Whenever we have an entire cake for someone's birthday or other event, it's usually pawned off on an outgoing guest with, "*Please*, take home some cake!" No one else will eat it, except me. Nowadays, I try to only eat really good dark chocolate pieces for dessert, so even I will be willing to let a cake go home with someone else. This cake was a very good bakery-made seven layer chocolate torte. I couldn't let it go, but knew I needed to limit our (meaning my) consumption, so I had quartered it and frozen each piece. It had gotten a little banged up in the freezer, so I sliced it into the size of lady fingers while still frozen. I placed them along the bottom and sides of a trifle dish and added lots of frozen strawberries and boysenberries to fill the spaces between. The dessert became about the berries, not the chocolate. The whole dish went back into the refrigerator to stay chilled until time to serve. Once everyone was seated at the table, I pulled out the dish, drizzled some orange liqueur over it, and left a container of vanilla ice cream on the counter to soften. Some of the ice cream was spooned on top, and in this case a few birthday candles were added. It made a delicious dessert, and I did not have to dilute my available time with baking or driving to the bakery that day.

Experimenting with More Little Green Things
Costole di Maiale alla Griglia e Orecchiette con Fave
Grilled Ribs and Pasta with Fava Beans

- ❖ Crostini con Purè di Fave
- ❖ Zuppa di Pane in Brodo
- ❖ Insalata di Cavolo Verde

- ❖ Costole di Maiale alla Griglia
- ❖ Orecchiette con Fave

- ❖ Birra Italiana o Microbrew, Vino della Casa
- ❖ Fragole con Aceto Balsamico e un Biscotto

Fava beans start arriving at the farmers' markets in the late spring. You will see the small pods of tender green favas, no larger than a lima bean, or sometimes you will see the beans themselves, resembling the lima, though darker in color. They usually show up again later in the summer as larger pods or very large individual beans. They're all tasty. They're not the most popular food item in my family, so I try them only occasionally when they first show up and again when they're gigantic. When they initially arrive at the farmers' markets, they're so young and tender you can almost eat them raw. On this day, I parboiled the beans in the husks and then, when cooled, opened the pods and pulled out each of the beans. Later in the day, I retrieved them from the refrigerator and sat down with paper towels in front of me to perform the delightful task of pulling each bean out of the membrane which surrounds it. You can eat this membrane. It is slightly gray in color, and is not nearly as appetizing as the color of the bean when it has been squeezed ever so gently out of the membrane. Now you have a much smaller bowl of brightly colored, delicious fava beans. I tend to eat many of them at this stage of the preparation, and, if Kate is around, watch out, because the bowl will be even smaller if she arrives on the scene during this part of the process. They are delicious simply anointed with a very fresh olive oil and a little bit of

salt and pepper. Some were puréed for the *antipasto* and the rest were added to the pasta, its shape chosen to approximate the size of the fava beans themselves. When mixed, the favas will snuggle up to the *Orecchiette*, or are the *Orecchiette* embracing the favas? Either way, it's *un matrimonio favorevole* (a favorable marriage).

Appunti/Notes

PURÉED FAVA BEANS ON TOAST ~ If you haven't eaten all of them by the time you get around to making the *antipasto*, you were lucky enough to purchase the correct amount. If they were fully cooked at the initial stage of removing the husk, you will not need to re-steam them now. It's just a function of how much they cooked the first time and how well you like them cooked. I like them *al dente*, similar to pasta: not mushy and not too hard to the tooth. Make a *pesto* out of them by putting them into your food processor (or chop and mash) with some garlic, salt and pepper, and enough olive oil to develop a spreadable consistency, similar to homemade peanut butter. You can add a bit of lemon or vinegar and some form of heat (hot sauce, white pepper or hot pepper). Taste it and season until it pops in your mouth. Spread it on your favorite toast or cracker, or serve in a bowl, under olive oil, with a spreader and bread nearby.

BREAD SOUP ~ This soup is a simple, delicious, and an easy way to get rid of the extra fresh bread you've been buying and not having time to make into breadcrumbs. You can make it with water, which is the original poverty food style. If you've had meat the previous few days and still have the bones (you're keeping the bones, right?), use the stock to make a richer soup. Start with sautéing the usual onion, carrot, and celery, add any tomatoes, herbs, and water/stock you have on hand and simmer until reduced. Add the bread just before serving, allowing enough time for the bread to fall apart and thicken the soup. Ladle into bowls, top with olive oil, grated cheese, and a slice of toast; or melt the cheese onto the toast and float it in the soup. Finish with chopped parsley and extra salt, as needed.

SALAD OF SHAVED GREEN CABBAGE ~ Our cousin Letizia served this simple salad on our first night in Italy. She simply grated or shaved a head of green cabbage and piled it onto a platter with a drizzle of very good olive oil and salt. Sometimes I like to add just a touch of vinegar or lemon and some pepper. You can slice the cabbage ahead of time but don't add the other ingredients until just before serving. This Italian style of coleslaw is fresh and less fattening than our mayonnaise version and won't spoil if taken to a party.

GRILLED PORK RIBS ~ Ribs are one of my favorite foods, and "Pork and Beans" just go together well. Using fava beans instead of American baked beans lightens the meal up a bit. When you serve it with the *Orecchiette* instead of french fries, you might as well put on your favorite Italian music and pull out a nice bottle of red wine.

EAR-SHAPED PASTA WITH FAVA BEANS ~ This pasta is not served with a thick sauce, as you might expect with a shape like *Orecchiette*. The thickness of the dried pasta shape will tell you how much sauce you need to have with them. If they're reasonably thin, you can make this dish with just oil, butter, and a little pasta water to give it some starch. If the *Orecchiette* are very thick, I suggest not using them in this preparation. Try small shell-shaped pasta instead. The idea is to have a shape consistent with the fava beans. I started with some oil and butter in the pan and sautéed some shallots. After that, I added diced red and yellow bell pepper (again paying attention to the homogeneous shapes). If you did happen to eat too many of your fava beans during the preparation, you should add something green here, like zucchini or diced asparagus, though I wouldn't mix the two together if the amount of favas is not sufficient for the amount of guests. A small amount of fresh tomato, either red or yellow or both, is okay, too. Don't let it overtake the dish. The dish is about the favas, after all, so the amount of other ingredients should complement and not compete for your attention and taste. When these ingredients are softened but not mushy, add the favas and pasta water, but do not cook them any more than is necessary to warm the favas. Serve over your cooked pasta and pass the grated *Parmigiano*!

ITALIAN BEER OR MICROBREW OR HOUSE RED WINE ~ Although ribs go very well with beer, and you can find Italian beers in the United States, a good local microbrew or lighter American wine complements the ribs nicely. I would pick a Sangiovese or Chianti.

STRAWBERRIES WITH BALSAMIC VINEGAR AND A COOKIE ~
The strawberries are beginning to catch my eye, yet they are still not fully ripe and as luscious as they will be in a few months. A drop or two of a very good balsamic vinegar or balsamic syrup, if you can find one that's not full of corn oil, and *un biscotto* or a single cookie on the side is a refreshing end to a warm spring evening meal. *Buon appetito!*

Cucina di Stazione Termale
Medaglioni di Pescecane
Medallions of Shark

- Vino Bianco della Casa
- Asparagi, Bianchi e Verdi, Arrostiti
- Insalata Mista con Varie Cose
- Contorni di Pepe, Funghi, e Cipolle
- Medaglioni di Pescecane con Salsa di Piselli e Pomodoro
- Spaghettini
- Grappoli di Uva e Biscotti
- Tè di Erbe

The weather has definitely not been cooperating with the writing of this book. Each time I sit down to write about a meal I've planned or consumed, the weather has impudently changed into a different persona. This spa cuisine meal was put together on the hottest day we've had so far. I had pulled out my white capris for the first time this year. The evening was warm, and we debated about eating *all'aperto* (in the open). No one was quite ready for that, so we opened the windows and pretended we were dining outside. Now, when I am actually writing this, low-lying clouds are on the mountains, and I've closed the windows to keep the chill away.

Appunti/Notes

HOUSE WHITE WINE ~ We opened a bottle of our favorite chardonnay.

GRILLED WHITE AND GREEN ASPARAGUS ~ I don't usually buy white asparagus because I'm cheap and hate to pay all that extra money so someone can periodically cover an already wonderful vegetable with dirt so that it has to struggle to grow

without the sun's natural rays. It just seems wrong, like keeping a tiny calf in a pen so it cannot get exercise, becomes anemic and unhealthy. However, I had looked at them longingly a few days before, remembering how my mother treated them as a luxury food. Then I looked at the price and said to myself "*Basta*, I'm a no gonna buy them now." Three days later, I found them in the marked down bin of the same store for a fraction of the cost. Obviously, no one else wanted to pay that high price for them either. I checked them over and they still looked pretty good to me, so I bought a bunch for the much more reasonable price. Since I had already put two bunches of the small green asparagus in my shopping basket, I decided to do a taste test with them, and see if the white asparagus were really all that much better than the green ones. I washed, snapped and olive-oiled the stalks and sprinkled them with salt and pepper. Onto the grill they went, the big white ones near the back where the grill was hotter; the thin green ones onto the front of the grill where the flame was lower. Both were turned once, and removed back into the same dish with the marinating oil and seasonings.

Chopped Salad with Various Things ~ This was another occasion where I didn't have enough lettuce for the amount of people I was planning to feed. Oops. I emptied my refrigerator of anything I could find that could be added to the lettuce: red and yellow bell pepper, Spanish almonds, and sugar snap peas. All were chopped and put into the salad. The Red Plate remained in the cupboard alone.

Sautéed Red and Yellow Bell Peppers with Mushrooms and Onions ~ My plan for the meal was to grill the fish and serve them on top of the spaghetti with the sautéed peppers and mushrooms; the whole dish was then to be drizzled with the red and green sauces. I started with slicing the peppers and onions to be similarly shaped to the mushrooms, so the entire *contorno* would be homogeneous.

Medallions of Thresher Shark with Sauces of Pureed Peas and Roasted Tomatoes ~ Shark has a wonderful meaty texture, although I really don't know if it is currently on the endangered species list or not. You can use whatever fish you find freshest at your market, as long is it can be cut into 1 to 2 inch thick

medallions. I microwaved a bunch of small scallions just until they became pliable, and then I wrapped them whole around each medallion, securing them with a toothpick. I added the requisite olive oil and salt and pepper. These were refrigerated while I played with the purées. Previously roasted tomatoes (olive oil, garlic, and salt and pepper) were put into the food processor and puréed until smooth. The work bowl was rinsed and then I played with the sugar snap peas. I carefully opened each one and separated the peas from the shells. Normally we eat them whole, raw and occasionally steamed. After I had a small bowl of the shelled peas, I puréed them. There wasn't enough and they didn't actually become sauce-like at this point. I probably should have parboiled them, but I hadn't. So, frustrated and wondering what the proverbial Italian grandmother would have done with the discarded shells, I put them into the food processor too and gave it another whirl. Oops, now I had an even coarser purée with little bits of shell and strings sticking out of it. So the smoothing function was employed. I added lemon juice, olive oil, and salt and pepper. It got better, but still needed something to bind it together. If only I had some potatoes.... Well I did have a cooked potato and in it went. This was much better. I added more oil and seasoning, put the whole thing through a screen, and funneled it into a squeeze bottle. It actually tasted pretty good. I grilled the fish on high to get nice grill marks on each side and then held them in a hot oven until the *spaghettini* was cooked.

THIN SPAGHETTI ~ *Spaghettini* is thinner than spaghetti, and yet thicker than *capellini*. It holds up better than *capellini*, which would have been too delicate for the peppers and mushrooms, which really didn't have much of a sauce with them. The pasta was cooked according to the manufacturer's instructions, and then I added just enough butter to keep it from sticking. On each person's plate I placed some *spaghettini*, spooned the pepper-mushroom mixture, and placed a shark medallion on top. I decorated the whole thing with the two different sauces, and *Ecco!* They were served.

BUNCHES OF GRAPES AND COOKIES ~ Grapes encourage you to sit at the table a little while longer. When purchasing grapes, get them only when they are just fantastic. If the bunches have any grapes missing (as evidenced by the visible stems) don't buy them. You eat first with your eyes, and there is nothing appetizing about a picked over or, worse yet, old bunch of grapes. If they are sold in a bag, and you can

see grapes lying on the bottom of the bag, they're no longer fresh or have been mishandled. When they come to your market and look gorgeous, buy them and eat them quickly. I like to serve them either in large bunches on a platter, with a small scissors (to encourage you to take a few and not graze across the entire bunch), or cut them into individual bunches. By all means cut off any empty stems and arrange them so the most attractive side of the bunch is out.

HERB TEA ~ A simple plate of small cookies or *biscotti* served after the grapes, with a light herb tea, completes the meal, but hopefully not the conversation.

When Life Hands You Eggs
La Colazione di Sera
An Evening Breakfast

- Prosecco
- Insalata con Pomodori, Avocado, e Mozzarella
- Uova Quasi Strapazzate/ Quasi Omelette
- Pancetta non Affumicata
- Fegatini di Pollo alla Casalinga
- Pane o Toast
- Frutta

Sometimes you have one entire meal planned for the evening and life throws you a curve ball (or in this case seven eggs that were laid that morning by happy organically fed chickens) which necessitates a complete change of plan. Good eggs can be found at various specialty stores and at many a local farmers' market. Eggs from chickens who have names and personalities known to you or your loved ones should be eaten with reverence and

rightfully demand accompanying dishes that bow before them in homage. The American style of eating eggs has evolved into the practice of the made-to-order omelet. Anything that can be put into eggs, is, and in whatever combination or quantity. The egg itself has become merely a vehicle for holding other ingredients. Perhaps this has occurred because our mass-produced eggs no longer have much flavor. Taking a step back, and thinking of where our food comes from, remember that once again, a being is giving up its life for our consumption. Be a vegetarian if you want; or respect that you are eating another creature and do your best to prepare it well and consume it in respectable quantities.

The mass production of eggs for American consumption has degenerated into huge chicken and egg factories which promote deplorable conditions for the animals unfortunate enough to be part of this food chain of American over-consumption. We would all be better off, and would probably do more for our planet, if our eggs traveled to our kitchen from the backyard instead of halfway across the state or country in a large gas-guzzling truck. Eat local. Buy local. Eggs should be one of those items you can get locally. Wouldn't you rather support your local organic chicken and egg farmer instead of some Abu Ghraib prison for chickens?

Now, let's get back to Anna's eggs. Anna is my friend. She's not one of the egg-laying chickens. As this was the first time she had given me what I had hoped were the start of many fresh eggs, I knew I had to do something amazing with them, and that it was a perfect thing to write about. If you have ever seen the film *Big Night* you should remember the closing scene where Stanley Tucci's character cooks eggs for Cristiano, his only restaurant employee, played by Marc Anthony, and his brother, played by Tony Shalhoob. This scene epitomizes everything you should know about cooking eggs. The eggs in that movie were cooked and served with love, and nothing more, except for a little olive oil and salt. It's also interesting to note that the eggs were taken from the bottom shelf in that kitchen, not from a refrigerator! "Un-refrigerated eggs?" we Americans gasp! Although the movie is set in the States, clearly the Italians have a different attitude about the storage of their eggs. The message here is to start with eggs that you know are fresh (there's that relationship with your food thing again) and prepare them simply. Taste the eggs, not the filling. If the eggs are fresh, they'll taste good all by themselves. If they're not good, don't eat them. If you don't like eggs ("You don't like eggs?"), eat something else.

Anna's chickens are named after the queens of England. I think they should be given their own American names and be properly crowned as the queens of Montecito; perhaps Barbara, Michele, Merrily and Louise?

Appunti/Notes

SPARKLING WINE ~ There is nothing like Sparkling wine, Champagne or Prosecco to lift your spirits and your evening breakfast to new heights. Sparkling wines tend to be reserved for special occasions only in America. I believe that we should explore pairing them with less noble occasions, like eating the queens' eggs. Sparkling wines are light, vivacious and mood elevating. Why wouldn't we want to drink them at the start of a wonderful weekend? And if there's any left over, cork those bottles well and do it again on Sunday morning!

EGGS SORT OF SCRAMBLED/SORT OF AN OMELET ~ I do admit I don't always make plain eggs. I love to make *frittate*, and have been practicing with getting the flip of the pan for a perfect omelet. For these eggs, though, I started with a mix of olive oil and butter. Make sure that the pan is hot but not smoking when you put the eggs into it. These were lightly scrambled and seasoned with salt and pepper only. Wolfgang Puck will tell you to whisk the eggs while they're cooking. He likes to keep them moving. I like to do a combination of both styles, which is to move them shortly after they're in the pan and then leave them alone until ready to flip or re-stir. When the eggs come out of the pan you can top with a tiny bit of herb or grated cheese as a garnish. I like to put something green, and a slice of tomato on the plate with the eggs for color. Play with them. Eggs are a simple, somewhat forgiving food to begin your culinary adventures.

PANCETTA OR BACON ~ Although *pancetta* is the national bacon of Italy, we do live here in the USA after all. So, sticking with the living local theme, we should be consuming our own local natural bacon, cut thickly and slowly fried until light brown and crispy. The secret here is to fry it slowly. If you start bacon on high heat

it will burn before the entire slice is cooked. Then you will not have the crisp slices which have had most of the fat rendered into the pan (and not your bloodstream). Don't throw the fat away. Use it sparingly as a flavoring for the rest of the weeks' meals Cook the entire package of bacon and then try making some into a spinach salad, or use it in pasta.

CHICKEN LIVERS ~ I grew up with chicken livers coming only when there was a roasted chicken. It usually went into the bottom of the roasting pan with the other unmentionable parts. They would be roasted until almost hard and you had to scrape them off of the bottom of the pan to eat them. Yet when you bit into one it would still be creamy, almost of the consistency of fudge. I loved them, and would have to fight my mother to see who got it first. Hearts and gizzards were never my favorites; it just seemed wrong to eat the animal's heart and gizzards are like chewing on boot leather. The dog, however never seemed to mind, having the ability to swallow them whole. In college, it was at the dorm "commons room" where I discovered that chicken livers could be really delicious. They were dusted with flour and deep fried. You could eat as many as you wanted to until the head serving person started giving you the evil eye. It was the memory of college eggs and chicken livers which inspired this preparation. Wash them carefully and pat dry with paper towels. Coat them in well-seasoned flour, and pan fry in the bacon fat on high heat until browned but not cooked through. Add some onion slices and some bacon fat to a baking dish. Spread thinly sliced red onion and garlic, and then put the livers on top. Cover them lightly with sprigs of herbs and tangerine or mandarin orange slices and roast in the oven until cooked through. Season with more salt and pepper, lemon zest, and juice before serving.

TOAST ~ We used English muffins, though any bread you prefer is obviously usable here. Yesterday's bread always makes good toast today.

FRUIT ~ A shared orange peeled at the table and sectioned into waiting hands is a perfect ending to an evening's breakfast.

Non Fa Bel Tempo, Oggi
Minestra di Piselli
Pea Soup

- *Indivia con Purè di Qualcosa*
- *Pane Fresco*

- *Minestra di Piselli*
- *Zucca al Forno*

- *Pollo, Patate, e Carote al Forno*
- *Mousse di Cioccolato di Katerina*

Just when I thought spring had really sprung and that we weren't going to have a winter after all, a real rain finally came to Santa Barbara. Today's weather forecast was projecting a full day of rain *(non fa bel tempo, piove)*. It had started in the night and then, blessedly, had given a pause so all good puppies could get in their days' exercise without getting their paws too wet. After the exit of children and husbands and before running out of the door with leash in hand, I initiated the main item for tonight's meal: Pea soup.

Pea soup is just a great part of a rainy day meal, no matter which season the rain comes. I did not have a spring meal planned for today; it was my plan to go shopping after the *passeggiata con il cane*. This was one of those days where a properly stocked kitchen comes in handy. I pulled out my stockpot, filled it halfway with water, and threw in leeks (they needed to be used before the onions), a couple of carrots, and a frozen ham hock. I checked to see if I had dried peas, and then ran out the door. We finished the walk without getting drenched, and then on to the rest of the shopping. I bought the celery, which is a necessary part of a good pea soup, and wandered around the market looking for inspiration on what would go well with the soup. You can make an entire meal out of a soup, but I like to serve smaller bowls of it as a first course (to warm the wet returning family members) and then move onto the rest of the meal. I was leaning toward a pasta dish with scallops or something, as we had been consuming a lot of rice dishes lately. The potatoes were very small and fresh, and "Oh, how

could I sneak them into a meal when my husband always prefers pasta to potatoes…" and then I got the call. "Can you run down to Ventura (about an hour away from where I was at the time) and do a small errand for me?"

Well so much for having time to prepare anything at the last minute. Tonight would have to be a "pull it all out of the oven meal." I turned the corner from the fish counter to the meat counter and asked for the biggest chicken they had. So, along with the soup, there will be roast chicken, carrots, (you guessed it) small red and white potatoes, and (who would have guessed) a butternut squash. I went home, unpacked the groceries, pulled the ham hock and vegetables out of the stock, sliced up the celery, more carrot and leek, added the dried peas and left the house again. Several hours later, when I returned, I seasoned the entire chicken, put a tangerine, lemon half, and the leek tops into the chicken cavity, added carrots and the unpeeled potatoes to the bottom of the pan, and then got to the computer to take care of everything else I had planned. Oh, yes, I forgot about the squash, so today I pierced it with a knife and put it into a baking dish whole. I'll season it at the plating stage, if it gets served tonight at all. If not, we'll have it tomorrow. The chicken is happily roasting below the squash in the oven, and I get to write. It's a good day so far.

Appunti/Notes

ENDIVE WITH SOMETHING PURÉED ~ A Belgian endive will last for a week or
> more in the refrigerator. I like to buy two at a time and start taking the outer leaves off each, and use them instead of crackers or *crostini* as a vehicle for serving puréed things. Sometimes the puréed thing is a leftover piece of meat or vegetable, re-seasoned and/or mixed with some cream cheese or yogurt. Once, I found a piece of steak from an earlier dinner. I put it into the food processor with some onion, a clove of garlic, salt and pepper, and goat cheese. It needed something else, so I added parsley and basil and a touch of sun-dried tomato. I spread it onto the endive and topped it with some *parmigiano*, lemon, and toasted pine nuts. Another way to do it is to purée ham and mix in chopped *cornichon* pickles and capers.

TODAY'S BREAD ~ Fresh hot bread is the best with pea soup, but if you forget to buy some, toast what you've got or revive it with some water and warm inside foil in the oven. Forgetting the bread is another good reason to keep a box of breadsticks on hand in your pantry. Don't tell everyone you forgot the bread. Wrap some prosciutto around it and pretend you planned it that way.

PEA SOUP ~ After I added the chopped leek, carrot, celery, and dried peas, I simmered it uncovered so it would reduce while it cooked all afternoon and not be too thin. I like pea soup with bay leaves and thyme, and enough salt and pepper so it isn't bland. Pea soup is a great place to use the celery leaves, too.

BAKED SQUASH ~ You know what? It's a lot easier to cut a whole butternut squash after it is partially cooked than it is to cut it when it's raw. I recommend trying it. I waited until it had cooked in a 350°F oven about an hour and then sliced it open, scraped the seeds and threads out with a serrated-edge, grapefruit spoon, seasoned and sprinkled some brown sugar on it, and put it back into the oven with the chicken and its vegetable friends.

ROASTED CHICKEN, POTATOES AND CARROTS ~ I like roast chickens in every season. Sometimes it can make the kitchen hot, if the weather is really hot, but most of the year the extra warmth is welcome. The kitchen just seems cozier if something is roasting in the oven and something else is bubbling on the stove. Today I got to have both. The soup simmered all afternoon, and around 3:00 PM I started the chicken. I like to season the bird inside and out. I won't be upset if a prepared spice rub is used here. Put olive oil or butter all over the outside and rub some into the cavity. Then season with coarse salt and pepper, and roll the whole thing in spices. You can use a large plastic bag here if the bird will fit. You can even cut the chicken up yourself if you're pressed for time, although I think the chicken is tastier if it's cooked whole. Put any aromatic vegetable pieces or citrus into the cavity, as I mentioned above. Place small whole or cut up potatoes, slightly oiled and seasoned, into the bottom of the pan so they can brown in the pan juices and add their own discarded juices to the mix.

KATE'S CHOCOLATE MOUSSE ~ I was trying to clean out the pantry and found several packages of various dark chocolates, one a single origin 100% cocoa bar from Panama, and another big brand 86% dark chocolate bar and a small half eaten bag of semi-sweet chocolate chips. I had just pulled out the double boiler and had turned on the flame when Kate walked in the door. Luckily for me she took over, got out some cream and a whisk and produced a delicious dessert, topped with pecans and coconut.

If You Can Grill A Big Pizza...
Pizzette alla Griglia
SMALL GRILLED PIZZAS

- *Vino Rosso*
- *Sedano con Bolognese*
- *Minestra di Pollo*
- *Pizzette*
- *Cotolette di Maiale alla Griglia*
- *Asparagi o Zucchine alla Griglia*
- *Fette di Pera con Noci*
- *Acqua Minerale Frizzante*

I tend to obsess about things. At this moment it's writing about food, eating food, and speaking Italian. A while ago, it was about making the perfect pizza. My quest for understanding and producing the perfect pizza has taken me over five years. No pizza, pizza article or pizza stone was left unturned. I tasted every pizza I could get my hands on in Italy and tried many different recipes at home. I bought sea salt from Sicily, tomatoes from San Marzano, and herbs from my local farmers' market. I bought double zero flour, pizza starters, and pizza flavoring mixes. I tried different types of pizza stones, all of which cracked. I tried making my own sauce. I tried pizza sauces out of a jar. I tried fresh tomatoes.

I tried different yeasts. I tried different cheeses. I watched every show I could on the making or eating of pizza. I read articles about excellent restaurant pizzas around the world. My pizzas were occasionally good, they were often tasty, but they were never perfect and were definitely not repeatable. In despair, I went into what I think is the best pizzeria in Santa Barbara and talked to the Sicilian man who runs it. I explained my dilemma and begged him to share the secrets of his dough with me.

He didn't.

He didn't tell me the secrets of his dough, but told me something much more valuable. He confirmed the one nagging suspicion that had been forming a crust in my brain. This is what he said. "You know I can make a pizza here at my shop and take it home to cook and it won't be any good. It's probably not your dough; it's probably your oven."

Of course he was right. I had seen several shows about the making of pizza, and I remembered that one pizzeria had stated that their pizzas would cook in about five minutes because their ovens went up to 750°F, or higher. I came home and promptly requested a new oven. Okay, that didn't work. I was determined to get that wood burning pizza oven someday, but it would have to wait until a full kitchen remodel was facilitated by a winning lottery ticket. Not wanting to wait until my next trip to Italy for a good pizza, I wracked my brains about how I could get the right amount of heat. Maybe I could take the pizza stone out of the oven and put it in the fireplace? And then the light bulb went off. I had seen Michael Chiarello cook bread like pizzas in his barbeque. He put his directly onto the grill which probably produced a good eat, but didn't technically count in my book. Why not put the pizza stone directly on the grill? I did. I cranked that BBQ up as high as it could go and then took my next pizza and slid it onto the stone. Most of it made it onto the stone. Part of it missed the stone and hit the grill, sticking there and anchoring my near perfect preparation, thereby ensuring it would be part briquette. The good news was that the part that wasn't briquette was eventually cut away from the grilled portion. It was fantastic! It took a little while to get the hang of the shake to slide the pizza onto the stone, but I did it. You can too. If you don't want to invest in a pizza peel, I have found that a pizza pan with little to no lip on the edge works just fine and may fit into your kitchen better than a peel would.

On the next trip to Italy, however ... do you think a peel can fit into a suitcase any better?

Appunti/Notes

HOUSE RED WINE ~We actually tried a bottle of homemade red wine, and it was pretty darn good. A fine Brunello? No, but perhaps a drinkable Sangiovese, which complements pizza pretty well.

CELERY WITH MEAT SAUCE ~Always looking for a new way to put out a nice *antipasto*, I tried putting celery ribs filled with meat sauce into a casserole dish. A bit

of grated cheese on top and some breadcrumbs, olive oil, and salt and pepper is all it took. Put them on the top shelf of a hot oven, and make sure they are heated through but still firm enough to hold up to being eaten by hand.

CHICKEN SOUP WITH PASTA ~ Someone I know makes an excellent simple chicken soup. Concentrate the broth and add just enough sautéed carrot, celery, and onion to give it a little bit of visual interest and flavor. Broken vermicelli or *capellini* pasta can be added. This soup always cheered me up and I hope it will you, too. I like to hit it with a bit of fresh parsley just before serving.

PIZZETTE ~ Homemade pizza is easier than you think if you break down the components and attack each one separately during the day. Start the dough up to two days ahead of time, if necessary. You can find pizza dough recipes in most Italian cookbooks. They are usually similar, containing yeast, flour, salt, water, olive oil and sometimes honey or sugar. The ingredients for traditional Margherita pizza dough are controlled in Italy and consist of only flour, yeast, water and salt. Put in enough salt, or no matter what you do, the flavor will be flat. The trick is to make enough pizzas so that you understand the consistency of the dough you need to get a perfect crust. It has to be kneaded to get the glutens to relax, so that the dough is stretchy and not cake-like. This will yield a chewy as opposed to crumbly crust. It has to be dry enough that you can keep it moving on the pan or peel so it will slide onto the pizza stone. The stone has to be hot, hot, hot, so the dough instantly sears when put onto the stone. This is what gets the crust crisp. Your ingredients must be dry enough and sized properly so they will cook in the same amount of time as the crust. The hotter the oven, the thinner the crust and toppings need to be so the bottom is not burning while the toppings are lagging. The fire will give it the smoky flavor you remember tasting in Italy. And burning or smoking a piece of wood at the same time can help too. Start with just cheese (try Gorgonzola as a top note of flavor) and when you've mastered that, move on to one or two other ingredients. The sauce should not be runny, and it must be jam-packed with flavor, including enough salt and herbs so that it pops when combined with the bread. Make pizza after you already have a *marinara* sauce from a few days before. Make sure each topping ingredient is perfect unto itself and

a perfect complement to the next and don't load up your pizza with garbage and too much cheese. When it comes out of the oven, drizzle a bit of your best olive oil on top, some extra coarse salt and pepper, and more fresh herbs. Wait 5 minutes for it to set up, and then cut it. Taste it and analyze each attempt until you understand what works and what doesn't. Resist the temptation to pick up that phone and dial that take-out number. A delivered pizza will never be as good as one you've perfected that has just come out of your oven or barbeque. On this night I made dough for two large pizzas and split them up into five small *pizzette*, serving them as *secondi* before a *piatto pricipale*. Similarly, when they come off the grill, drizzle some olive oil on top, add a bit more coarse salt, freshly ground pepper, and another handful of fresh chopped herbs (or Italian seasoning mix).

GRILLED PORK CHOPS ~ The barbeque was already hot, so I carefully removed the pizza stone (hold it with two hands or it could break in half) and seared thinly (thin is important here because of the high temperature of the grill) cut pork chops while the *pizzette* were being consumed outside, near the grill. Bone-in pork chops (oiled lightly and seasoned) will always have better flavor than boneless ones. Boneless pork chops along with boneless chicken breasts are just a shame when grilled.

GRILLED ASPARAGUS OR ZUCCHINI ~ The grill is hot, so why not throw a vegetable on it alongside the meat? Finish with lemon and coarse salt.

SLICED PEARS AND PECANS ~ If you can still get good pears at your market, try them with a simple bowl of nuts. Sometimes we just bring in a clean plate and one person cuts the slices and hands them directly to each person at the table. Use any fruit that looks good that day. We tried and love crispy Asian pears. I haven't put any fruit on the grill just yet, but I'm getting a hankering to try it. Perhaps pineapple....

CARBONATED MINERAL WATER ~ A bit of the bubbly without more alcohol, *perchè no?* Many of us grew up on bad American pizzas washed down with loads of brown carbonated soda. This lighter version preserves the urge for carbonated beverages with a pizza but leaves out all the sugar.

Salmone alla Griglia
Grilled Salmon

- Prosecco
- Insalata Verde con Gamberetti

- Il Piatto Rosso di Pomodori Gialli e Rossi, Ravanelli, e Formaggio Stilton
- Spinaci alla Panna

- Salmone alla Griglia
- Riso Bianco con Aneto
- Ananas alla Griglia
- Acqua Minerale Naturale

A while ago, I purchased an entire side of salmon for a dinner party of 6 people. I was thanking one of several groups of friends who had been instrumental in helping me during the early part of Kristin's recovery. A large side of salmon barbequed, dressed, and brought to the table, is just a beautiful sight to behold. It was a delicious meal, although I think we consumed less than one quarter of the amount of fish. Needless to say, we ate leftover salmon for almost two weeks. I produced approximately 27 person meals which made the cost of it affordable, if you calculate it as dollars per serving. One week after finishing the salmon, Tony brought over another large piece of salmon. Jim rolled his eyes and I set about finding even more things to do with leftover salmon.

After about two years, we were ready to try salmon again.

Appunti/Notes

SPARKLING WINE ~ You can have any *aperitivo* you desire before this meal. I don't need to be adventurous when I'm at home making dinner for the family. I usually stick with white wine, because it may be open and available. If there are enough people present to make it worth opening a bottle of sparkling wine, do so. You can usually invent some special reason to celebrate. How about, "It's Friday, let's celebrate that we don't have to go to work in the morning!"

GREEN SALAD WITH SHRIMP ~ For this meal I combined the shrimp, which could have been served alone as an *antipasto*, into the salad course. Toss the greens with a light oil and vinegar dressing, and then add a couple of shrimp per person around the side of the bowl, either on the greens or on the edge. Squeeze a bit of lemon on the shrimp and put the lemon zest in with the greens. Follow with The Red Plate for other things that can be eaten with or after the shrimp.

THE RED PLATE WITH YELLOW AND RED TOMATOES, RADISHES, AND STILTON ~ If you can get locally grown organic tomatoes in the spring, by all means use them. Sometimes you can find smaller varieties, and that's okay, too. The radishes have been really catching my eye in the markets lately, so I've been using them on The Red Plate when I can't get tomatoes. Red and yellow pepper rings with zucchini sliced very thin can also be used. I tried Stilton in place of the ubiquitous feta or gorgonzola, and everyone liked it.

CREAMED SPINACH ~ Sauté the washed spinach (use your salad spinner four to five times to ensure the sand is rinsed out, or many sink loads of clean water) with a little onion or shallot. Finish with several tablespoons of cream or half and half. There's not a lot of fat in the rest of the meal, so you can afford a few tablespoons here. If you decide to substitute *risotto* for the rice, then put the cream there and leave it out of the spinach.

GRILLED SALMON ~ I still maintain that the best way to cook salmon is to grill it simply. This means just marinating it in just a little bit of olive oil, perhaps some vermouth, and salt and pepper. I like to add fresh dill all over the fish before cooking, and more at the end, with olive oil and finishing salt just before serving. Some people will add a lot of spices and herbs and garlic to the salmon.... It can stand up to it because it is a strong-flavored fish. If you like the taste of salmon, though, why not enjoy it simply prepared? The fish has to be fresh in order to eat it without smothering it with other flavors. Use more seasoning if you can't get fresh fish. If you can't get fresh fish, though, you shouldn't be buying it at all! If it has had dye added to it to make it look colorful enough to eat, perhaps you should eat another type of fish instead.

I like to grill it with the skin on, so that the skin gets burnt, but not the salmon itself. Start with the skin side down, and do most of the cooking while it's on that side. Flip it once and remove the skin at the grill while you're just getting a bit of brown on the top side. Serve with the removed skin side down. Garnish with a bit of lemon and fresh dill. The colors together are marvelous, not to mention the flavors.

WHITE RICE WITH DILL ~ The only time I put dill in rice is when it's being served with salmon. I don't know why; they just go together well. You don't need to use Arborio rice here, although a *risotto* with salmon does kick it up a notch. Just prepare your favorite brand of white rice according to the manufacturer's directions. Add seasoned salt and dill, with a little olive oil or butter. Fresh dill will be more flavorful, but dried dill can also be used. You could try any herb you can find fresh, and use it with both the salmon and the rice.

GRILLED PINEAPPLE ~ Slice the pineapple into rounds and grill it before you put the fish onto the grill. Don't move it around, or you will lose the nice straight grill marks. Once you've mastered straight grill marks, try getting an X on both sides by moving it at 90° angles once before flipping onto second side.

MINERAL WATER ~ Bring a bottle to the table and use a champagne bucket, if you had one out for the Prosecco earlier. The water with the pineapple will leave your palate clean, refreshed, and ready for scientific or political banter.

So, what can you do with leftover salmon? Well for starters, if you thought ahead and got bagels and cream cheese, you are on your way, especially if your guests spent the night. The next night you can eat it with the leftover rice, but by the second night you'll have to either get creative or freeze some for later. Salmon and cream cheese with spinach goes really well in an omelet. You could make it into a soup with cucumber; put it into cooked pasta with the red and yellow bell peppers. When all else fails, purée it with some yogurt or sour cream, and make a dip to be eaten with *crostini* or chips. Put it into a soufflé or get some frozen puff pastry and make it into tarts. Put some cooked mushroom *duxelles* on top of it, wrap the whole thing in pastry, and re-present it as Salmon Wellington. Serve it as part of a different course in later meals, and make a meat for your *piatto principale*.

L'estate

CHAPTER 7

I spent most of my childhood summers in southern California. I thought I knew what heat was. We had occasional heat waves where the thermometer would reach 102 to 104°F. Most of the summer days would be at or near 100°F. On those days we lived in or around the pool, or stayed inside with our air-conditioners blazing. We didn't worry about electric bills due to excessive air-conditioning, and thought nothing of using an indoor gas grill on the hottest days of the year. Climate control prevailed thoughout the summer.

Then I came to Santa Barbara for college and decided to spend the rest of my life here. It's much cooler in Santa Barbara, and our summers are usually plagued with an early morning fog. So, while we think of Santa Barbara (and the tiny community of Summerland) as idyllic sandy beach communities with palm trees and abundant sunshine, the truth is that our springs and autumns are much nicer than our summers. We complain if the temperature gets above 87°F. Most people don't have pools and air conditioning, so we're forced to go to the movies or go shopping at an air conditioned mall on the really hot days. Mostly we just put on our shorts, spaghetti strap camisoles (if we are women), and thong sandals. (In fact, this is the style of dress for most of the year in Santa Barbara.) Over the years, my tolerance for hot weather diminished.

We happened to be in Italy during the great European heat spell of the summer of 2003. Daily temperatures ranged from 90° to 99°F throughout July. The 2003 average global temperature ranked as second warmest on record, and 14,000 people were reported to have died of heat-related causes. 90° to 99°F hardly seems like it would be a problem, but most of Europe is not air conditioned, and the big cities were sweltering. God knows what the humidity levels were, but based on my personal experience, they were high. Shorts, thongs, and spaghetti straps were way too much clothes for me. On this trip, I surmised why so many of the high fashion European styles of dress have cut-outs and vents in them. It's just too hot to wear clothes for much of the summer. But, society dictates that you must, and in some of the smaller towns showing a lot of skin is not fashionable. If you tour the churches and cathedrals, you will have to wear a scarf to cover up your nakedness in front of the Lord. (Incidentally, the churches and cathedrals are some of the coolest places to be at high noon when in Italy, a fact that I'm convinced is responsible for the high rate of Catholicism there. Leave it to the Italians to find a great place to cool off on a hot summers' day, and they serve you wine, too.)

While we were visiting our relatives in Northern Italy, one of them asked Jim if there was a particular food that he really liked. He commented that he had never really had good *polenta*. His cousin Martha said she would make it for him. No one ever rolled their eyes and said, "Hey, don't you know it's a thousand degrees outside and we don't eat *polenta* in the summer?"

After a day of touring, we arrived at Martha's house and she had a pot of bubbling *polenta* cooking on her wood-burning stove. Her house probably didn't cool back down to a normal temperature for the rest of that summer. To this day I wonder if she curses Jim's name every time she gets out the *polenta* pot. It would start something like, "Those crazy American cousins...."

So how does all this relate to *Venerdì Sera*, and living *La Dolce Vita* in America? It does, eventually. The point is that summers are generally hot and you may have to modify your evening meal plans to accommodate the weather. It doesn't do anyone any good if one person is sweltering over a hot stove to cook your dinner that evening. The cook will be in a bad mood. It is never a good idea to anger the cook. Allow her/him to choose an appropriate meal for the day's weather, and eat seasonally. Now is the time to fire up the grill and do as much cooking as you can outside. While in Italy, we ate our large meal at the middle of the day, in an air-conditioned restaurant whenever possible. I tried to cook one or two nights, and the apartments were so hot that we quickly abandoned the idea of a hot meal in the evening. Besides, if you had meat and pasta at lunch, you surely didn't need to be eating it again later that evening. Two good reasons for the big meal at noon are, 1. You can do your marketing early in the day while the food is fresh and the air is still cool. 2. You can prepare hot foods before the house gets too hot to cook in.

The American lifestyle does not follow the big meal at noon premise, partly because most of us work during the day and we do not follow the *riposo* philosophy of taking the hours of 1:00 PM through 4:00 PM off for eating and resting. It is unlikely that this tradition would be adopted here, but if it could, it would certainly contribute to a change in attitude resulting in better adjusted and healthier Americans.

Since we continue with our cocktails and dinner at 6:00 PM or later lifestyle, here are a few summer menus that utilize the ever-present American barbeque, with side dishes that can either be cooked on the grill or quickly prepared on the stove or in the oven.

> *Quel che mangia e non riposa non fa ben nessuna cosa.*
> (Who eats and doesn't rest won't do anything well.)

Devo Andare Via (I've Gotta Go)
Insalata di Gamberetti
Shrimp Salad

- Vino Bianco
- Grissini con Prosciutto
- Insalata di Gamberetti
- Salsa per Gamberetti
- Fragole
- Vin Santo

It's not often that I'm not home for dinner on a Friday evening, and it's even rarer if I go out without Jim, but it does happen, occasionally. This was one of those rare occasions. It was hot and I didn't want to spend the entire day cooking, especially because I wasn't going to be there to eat it anyway. I had to leave something for my family to eat. It had to be good or I would definitely get the, "So, you go out to dinner and leave the rest of us with cr—p for dinner..." conversation. It's disappointing to cook a really great meal, and then go out and pay money for something that's not as good as what I left behind. Also, I don't get motivated to go to the farmers' market when I know I won't be able to play with the produce all day long. So what to "cook" when I'm not motivated, it's hot and there isn't a lot of fresh produce around? Well, let's see....

Appunti/Notes

WHITE WINE ~ Finding a nicely chilled and re-corked bottle of the current favorite white wine that we're drinking in the refrigerator, or in an ice bucket next to your place at the dinner table, is always welcome after a long day at work. Put out a nice glass that doesn't have any water spots on it. The lack of water spots usually is not noticed, but the water spots themselves frequently are noticed.

BREAD STICKS WITH PROSCIUTTO ~ Make one or two per person of the thin *grissini* (with a good prosciutto wrapped around the top half). Displayed on a nice plate, or standing in a vase or water glass next to the wine bucket, they will act as a mood enhancer and will help to keep hunger at bay. If left out moments before the first person arrives, it should not spoil.

SHRIMP SALAD ~ I had planned ahead for this meal, so some of the items had been purchased earlier in the week; others came from that properly stocked pantry. I defrosted the shrimp while I walked the dog, and then I sautéed them with garlic, scallion, and red pepper flakes when I returned. I finished them with some white wine (which is why the bottle was re-corked), and chilled them in the refrigerator. I washed and dried the lettuce and placed it on a large platter. To this I added tomato rounds, hard boiled eggs (cooked properly with no gray ring around the yokes), julienned carrot, julienned red and yellow bell pepper, cucumber rings (edges sliced with garnishing tool), and *cornichons*. I diced the end pieces of the tomatoes and cilantro, and scattered them across the top of the platter. I arranged the chilled shrimp (tails still on for color, and to act as a handle) around the edge. I poured the reserved pan juices (from when I sautéed the shrimp) over the top and squeezed lime juice over everything. The filled platter was covered and returned to the refrigerator.

SEAFOOD SALAD DRESSING ~ This is my rendition of a seafood Louie dressing, or thousand island dressing. It comes together from things you should already have in your kitchen for nights like this. The main ingredients are mayonnaise or yogurt, Worcestershire sauce, and either lemon or lime. On this day I used lime. Add a little bit of something red, like ketchup or cocktail sauce. I had leftover *bruschetta* topping, so I used it. I also had leftover artichoke dip, so I added it to the mix, too. A little bit of vinegar can come from pickle relish or pickles. I finely diced some of the *cornichons* and added a little of the juice to the mixing bowl. Whisk it all together, add some hot sauce if you like it tangy, and put it in an attractive bowl with a nice sauce spoon, if you have one. Since this salad gets dressed by the eater, make it as pleasurable an experience you can for them.

STRAWBERRIES ~ Wash and dry them and put a bit of sugar on top. I like to leave the leaves on to act as a handle and to make the dish look fresher and more colorful.

SAINTS WINE ~ A second smaller wine glass, and a taste of the sweet dessert wine you have on hand for just this type of evening, pairs well with a bowl of fresh strawberries. My family knows just where to find the box of *biscotti* or dark chocolates if they're craving a really sweet finish....

DINNER WITH THE NEIGHBORS
Pesce al Forno
WHOLE BAKED SNAPPER

- ❖ Antipasta del Giorno
- ❖ Insalata di Lattuga Nuova
- ❖ Il Piatto Rosso di Mozzarella, Trota Affumicata, Zucchine Grattugiate, e Olive
- ❖ Capellini con Verdure Verdi, Pomodorini, e Cipolle
- ❖ Pesce al Forno Contro Pesce alla Griglia
- ❖ Biscotti di Katerina e Gelato
- ❖ Acqua con Frutta

I wanted to try cooking an entire fish. Not some measly trout that will fit into a small frying pan, but a big whole fish that any fisherman would be proud to be standing next to in a photo. Not a swordfish or a marlin, of course, because no one has a frying pan big enough for one of those puppies, but a nice one (like a shrubbery), not too big. In Santa Barbara your average market will not have a whole fish, but I talked to my fish monger, and he agreed to get one for me. I ordered a red snapper because it was reasonably inexpensive, considering that I wasn't really sure what I was doing and didn't want to break the bank on a costly food mistake. We were having some neighbors over for dinner this night, and to be safe, I also got some yellowtail for the barbeque in case the snapper turned out to be a disaster. The snapper was not so large that I thought it would feed eight people so I decided that dueling *pesce* would be the way to go. Those who wanted to eat the whole fish could, and those who preferred to not have their fish looking back at them could choose the barbequed yellowtail. It was warm enough to eat outside in the twilight, and I think everyone preferred to not have to see the snapper looking back at them.

Appunti/Notes

TODAY'S ANTIPASTO ~ The meal was becoming somewhat elaborate, so this course was simplified. I sliced about eight pieces of cheese (one for each person) and put out an equal number of *crostini*.

SALAD OF BABY LETTUCES ~ One of the farmers' stands had really nice looking bags of fresh baby lettuces, so I opted to not buy several large heads and mix them myself. This is a time-saving luxury for me, as I prefer to buy local heads of lettuce and wash and tear off leaves as I need them, mixing them, depending on who is at the meal and what their lettuce preferences (or aversion to arugula) may be. Since I was busy worrying about the whole fish adventure, I tried to simplify the other courses.

THE RED PLATE WITH MOZZARELLA, SMOKED TROUT, AND OLIVES ~ Fresh mozzarella, a package of trout, since it was an evening of seafood experimentation, and, oh, here are some olives (let's put them on the plate, too). Drizzle with a great olive oil (there are guests tonight), and finish with the best salt on hand. And, of course, a "scritch" of pepper.

ANGEL HAIR PASTA WITH DANDELION GREENS, LITTLE ORANGE TOMATOES, AND ONION ~ The best looking of the greens at today's market were the

dandelions. I washed them, chopped them up a bit, and added them, with the little orange tomatoes from my garden, after sautéing the onion and mixing in the cooked pasta. The colors are wonderful together. Finish with olive oil, lemon, and salt and pepper.

WHOLE BAKED SNAPPER VERSUS GRILLED YELLOWTAIL ~ I haven't had a lot of meals of whole fish, but it looks easy when it's done on TV so I had to try it at least once. The snapper was not that big, but he was a little bigger than my largest pan. I had a bit of trouble figuring out how to fit him into my oven, and finally opted to let him hang over the sides of the pan with some aluminum foil underneath the overlapped parts. This didn't work too well, as it made a mess in the bottom of the oven and the foil stuck at the end of the cooking. Somehow, I managed to get it out of the pan and onto a serving plate. He didn't remain completely whole, but he was delicious, even for a snapper. And boy, did he snap! The mouth actually opened slightly during the cooking process. So, he looked quite fierce when I brought him to the table. It was as if he wanted us to know that his larger friends would be waiting for us the next time we chose to swim in the ocean. How did I prepare him? I washed out the inside and filled him full of herbs, slices of lemon and onion, and seasoned him liberally with salt, pepper, and olive oil. Then I put him in the oven to bake until the thermometer registered that he was safe to eat. After you master snapper, try branzini!

The yellowtail was rubbed with olive oil and then covered with Cajun blackening spices. It was grilled medium rare, and arranged around the big guy on his platter, with parsley to fill in the spaces between.

KATE'S BISCOTTI WITH ICE CREAM ~ A small lovely glass bowl of vanilla ice cream with a homemade almond and orange *biscotto* and a sprig of freshly picked mint completed the meal. Kate used homemade candied orange peel in the *biscotti* recipe, and added a bit of *Triple Sec* to accompany the freshly roasted almonds I'd purchased earlier in the week. The *biscotti* were made ahead of time, which made the preparation of this dessert very easy. It's another good reason to always have a very good vanilla ice cream or *gelato* in your refrigerator at all times, and mint growing in your kitchen garden.

FRUITED WATER ~ I have been wanting to try one of those big recycled green glass Italian water jugs with the little brass spout, but always choked at the expense. Where would I put it anyway? My friend Kathy had put out a splendid spread for an afternoon cocktail event for *Le Italianucce*, and I fell in love with the concept. Imagine my surprise when, within a week after falling in love with her jug of citrus-infused water, I spied one in an antique store I was walking past. It was much smaller, and had the name of a very well-known vodka company pressed into the glass, but it was $3.00! Sold! The price made the experiment totally worthwhile, and since it's smaller than most of the similar containers, it actually fits on my windowsill, so I find I'm using it all the time. I sliced a lemon from my tree, and added the slices to the jug. Lemon-infused water is delicious to drink.

Pollo al Marsala

CHICKEN MARSALA

- Vino Bianco della Casa
- Formaggi e Noci
- Zuppa di Pesce
- Insalata di Romana e Frissè
- Il Piatto Rosso con Pomodoro, Basilico, Avocado, e Mozzarella di Bufala
- Fettuccine Alfredo
- Pollo al Marsala con Funghi
- Verdure Verdi sotto Pangrattato
- Caffellatte con Cioccolatini
- Acqua alla Menta

This is a meal that has a few very easy courses; courses that can be started well ahead of time, and courses that get finished at the very last minute. Much of it can be done ahead, thereby minimizing your time in a hot kitchen on a hot day. The *antipasto* requires no cooking, and the soup is composed from leftovers and a pot of broth that can simmer on low at the last minute. The salad can be prepared early in the day and left in the refrigerator until ready to serve. The pasta, and even the chicken, can be done a day ahead if necessary. If cooked in sufficient quantity, the greens can be served sautéed one night and then re-presented the next day with the topping of crumbs. Although I prefer to make all my chicken dishes with a whole chicken, and include pieces of chicken both on and off the bone, others in my family prefer all boneless white meat. The boneless chicken breasts were on sale, so I cringed, looked around to make sure no one would see me buying them, and put on my sunglasses before hurrying out of the store. I was breaking my code, but the rest of the family would be happy tonight.

> *Le piccole spese vuotano la borsa.*
> (The little expenditures empty the purse.)

Appunti/Notes

HOUSE WHITE WINE ~ Chill a bottle of your favorite, or hope that your guest brings over a better one.

CHEESE AND NUTS ~ Depending on how many people, or how long your meal/evening is anticipated to be, this can be several different cheeses or just a couple of slices with a small bowl of nuts. I like to put out three cheeses (not the entire wedge, or everyone will be full before you get to the next course), preferably a mild white, a strong yellow cheese, and something with a mold in it, like gorgonzola, blue or Roquefort. Cut the wedges into smaller wedges and save the rest in the refrigerator for another meal. Put them on a nice plate, and include a cheese knife. The act of cutting the cheese burns off a minute amount of calories and requires the eater to develop a relationship with the food. If you find you're still cutting after four or five slices of cheese, you're eating too much.

FISH SOUP ~ The outer leaves of the frissè are too tough to put into a salad, so I used them in the soup. We had made a broth from a previously eaten sea bass, and to each bowl of hot broth I added the frissè, a bit of roasted tomato with garlic and olive oil on it, and a small piece of the leftover sea bass. All these items had been previously prepared, and the soup was composed and brought to the table. Easy!

SALAD OF ROMAINE AND FRISSÈ ~ One of my favorite easy salads was invented on a vacation where we had limited supplies of food, kitchen items, and time. I took the inner leaves of a romaine head of lettuce. (You can buy romaine hearts, but use only the smallest leaves.) I piled the whole washed leaves on a large platter and topped them with thinly sliced crimini mushrooms. This time I added the inner leaves of the frissè, which made the salad more interesting. On top of the mushrooms I used a vegetable peeler to add thin slices of parmesan. I drizzled the whole thing with a really good fruity extra virgin olive oil (from your coveted little expensive bottle), and some seasoned rice wine or white wine vinegar, and a generous scritch of black pepper. Toss at the table and arrange on salad plates. Add coarse sea salt to taste.

THE RED PLATE WITH TOMATO, BASIL, AVOCADO, AND MOZZARELLA DI BUFALA ~ Alongside the salad, choices of tomato, basil, avocado, and mozzarella were arranged on The Red Plate. Some of us eat them on the salad; some of us eat them after the salad. Again, each person can develop his or her own relationship with this course.

FETTUCCINE ALFREDO ~ Because we were eating in courses, I dressed the *fettuccine* with a light Alfredo sauce made separately, ahead of time. I added a bit of nutmeg to a basic white sauce. This was tossed with the cooked pasta, to which I added parmesan and chopped parsley. If we'd been having a lighter meal, or were in a hurry for some other event or on a diet, the pasta could have been dressed with a bit of butter, and served underneath the main dish of chicken.

CHICKEN IN A MARSALA SAUCE ~ The chicken breasts were cut into bite-sized slices, not cubed. I seasoned them with salt and pepper, and dusted them with a bit of flour. The chicken was browned with an onion, and then braised slowly in the

“ *La felicità é come il sole: sorride e poi tramonta.*
(Happiness is like the sun: it smiles and then sets.) ”

oven with some Marsala and some chicken broth, until tender. Before serving, I sautéed the thinly sliced mushrooms separately in another pan until they were quite brown. Once they were almost crisp, I deglazed the pan with some more Marsala and added both to the chicken. I covered the entire platter with chopped herbs from my garden (lots of parsley, as a minimum), added some coarse salt, and squeezed lemon over the top.

COLLARD GREENS UNDER TOASTED BREAD CRUMBS ~ Collard greens? We don't live in the south! Well, you know what? They taste pretty good if you prepare them properly. They're very good for you. If you sauté them with a little bit of onion and garlic in some form of pork fat (for flavor), and olive oil, they're delicious. If you want to disguise them even further for your pickier family members, put them in a shallow baking dish, add some of those homemade breadcrumbs you've been itching to use, and add some parmesan or *grana*. Put the dish under the broiler and get some caramelization going, and they will be even better tasting, though a bit more fattening. Eat a little, and make sure you actually get some of the greens with all of those delicious crumbs….

BREWED MOKA COFFEE WITH CHOCOLATES ~ Still sitting around the table? When you have the dishes cleared (which in my house means while I'm clearing the dishes) start a small pot of coffee or plug in the espresso machine. It's hard to refuse an offering of a small bowl of very fine chocolates and a tray filled with steaming espresso cups.

WATER INFUSED WITH MINT ~ Throughout the meal, you can help yourself to a pitcher of filtered water with mint leaves floating on top. A glass at the end of the meal is a nice way to cleanse your palate, especially if someone has to drive.

Start the discussions on world politics, generational differences or religion. Perhaps, after the water, a glass or two of cognac or tea will be necessary. If driving, continue the discussions until you're okay to drive, and chew on those mint leaves.

Braciole di Maiale alla Griglia
GRILLED ROLLED PORK

- ❖ Birra
- ❖ Funghi Stufati
- ❖ Asparagi alla Griglia
- ❖ Ravioli al Carciofo con Burro, Limone, e Parmigiano
- ❖ Braciole di Maiale alla Griglia
- ❖ Mandarini, Fichi Ubriachi, e Semi di Zucca
- ❖ Digestivo a Scelta

Pork loin is one of the leanest, most economical meats you can buy. The entire loin shows up in the markets for an incredible price, or you can buy it as a small roast or individual boneless loin chops for increasingly higher prices. I prefer to be my own butcher and not pay someone for something as simple as slicing a piece of meat. The choice is yours. The pork loin that I'm talking about comes about the size of a human upper leg, without a bone. You can also find the center cut, or pork tenderloin, which resembles the size of your forearm. I like to use the larger whole boneless loin. The larger size is essential for this meal because you will slice and pound each piece into a cutlet. Cutlets made from the tenderloin are just too small for this preparation. If you do opt to experiment with the entire loin, and you're not planning on feeding an army, here's what I recommend:

1. Take it home and immediately cut it into thirds. Each third should just about fit into a large plastic freezer bag.

2. Zip up two of the thirds and put them in the freezer for another meal.

3. Now work with the third you are preparing. This amount of meat will serve four to six people easily.

Appunti/Notes

BEER ~ Beer goes very well with pork and stuffed mushrooms too, now that I think about it.

STUFFED MUSHROOMS ~ My friend Lori gave me some arugula with instructions for making it into a *pesto*, so I did. Follow any basil *pesto* recipe, though I substituted arugula for the basil, macadamia nuts for the pine nuts, and *ricotta salata* for the parmesan. Finish it with some garlic and olive oil, and it will keep for weeks in your refrigerator, in a jar under oil. I pulled the stems out of the largest button mushrooms I could find and mixed the *pesto* with some crab and breadcrumbs. Drizzle a little oil and parmesan over the top so there's something to brown, and pop them in the oven until they're cooked through. You could also start them in a pan and then transfer them to the oven to get the caramelization process happening sooner.

ARTICHOKE RAVIOLI WITH BUTTER, LEMON, AND PARMESAN ~ I didn't make the *ravioli* by hand. In our house, if anyone is making *ravioli*, they'd better have Nana's meat filling—or else. Freshly made store bought *ravioli* are sometimes acceptable as long as they're not cheese ones. If my main dish is really time-consuming, I like bought *ravioli* because I can cook them easily and just put together a simple pan sauce while the meat is resting after being grilled. Brown the

butter a bit, possibly with some finely diced shallot, and then finish the *ravioli* in the sauce. Add the lemon and parmesan upon serving. Parsley? Why not?

GRILLED, STUFFED, ROLLED PORK CUTLETS ~ Slice the pork loin into ½ inch to ¾ inch slices, and pound thin between sheets of waxed paper or inside an opened plastic zipper bag. You should get eight to twelve slices. Ensure that you have at least one cutlet for every person, and two if they're big eaters. Rub both sides with olive oil, and season aggressively with salt and pepper. You will be rolling them up with a stuffing of your choice and securing them with toothpicks or metal pins. I've tried various combinations inside the pork cutlet. Our favorites are zucchini, goat cheese, and sun-dried tomato; and sautéed greens with *mozzarella di bufala*. If you use zucchini, slice very thinly and microwave until they become pliable enough to be rolled up. The sun-dried tomatoes; must be reconstituted so that they're very moist. I've even done these with cheese and prosciutto inside, though they can be a bit dry. Also try wrapping them with *pancetta* or bacon on the outside. Try to keep the stuffing ingredients in the middle of the cutlet, so they don't ooze out during the cooking process. You will notice as you roll them that rolling in one direction usually will be easier to secure than the other. Put the finished packets on skewers and refrigerate until it's time to grill them. Use a meat thermometer and make sure they're fully cooked and food safe on the inside before serving. These little packages can also be browned in a pan and finished in the oven if you don't want to grill them, or if it starts to rain....

SATSUMA TANGERINES, DRUNK FIGS, AND PUMPKIN SEEDS ~ Pull out one of those trays you've been saving for when company comes and use it with your family. A small bowl of tangerines, some pumpkin seeds (a.k.a. *pepitas*) and either fresh or dried figs provides an interesting trinity of choices. On this evening I used dried figs that had been macerating in *grappa*. It never hurts to have one or several dried fruits swimming in its favorite alcohol in a jar on the top shelf of your refrigerator. You can easily throw them into a bowl to serve as is, or cut them up and add into any number of desserts or breakfast choices.

AFTER DINNER DRINKS OF CHOICE ~ So many choices, so little time....

Easy Does It
Pasta Sfoglia con Funghi
Puff Pastry with Mushrooms

- ❖ Aperitivo a Scelta
- ❖ Indivia Belga con Fichi, Prosciutto e Pinoli
- ❖ Zuppa di Pomodoro
- ❖ Pasta Sfoglia con Funghi, Pomodori, e Cipolle
- ❖ Fette di Carne Fredda
- ❖ Uva Rossa

This meal is very easy and can be prepared ahead of time, except for the last step of baking the puff pastry. I recommend it for those nights when you're running in the door moments ahead of your family. The soup can be from an earlier meal or made days ahead when there's more time, and if you take any previously prepared roast (pork loin, prime rib, brisket, lamb) or large steak (tri-tip, top sirloin or London broil), slice it thinly, and serve cold with a relish or chutney, you can satisfy the meat eaters who may not be happy with a meal of soup, salad, and pastry. The pastry can be made entirely vegetarian, although not necessarily vegan due to the butter and cheese. The tomato soup came about completely by accident. We had brought back the sun-dried tomatoes from Sicily years ago. They were the best sun-dried tomatoes I have ever tasted. They came sealed in a plastic bag, in olive oil with herbs. I have spent countless hours on the Internet trying to find a web address for the tiny boutique where we purchased them. I have bought many jars of sun-dried tomatoes since. I have purchased jars and bags of sun-dried tomatoes and put them in my own jars and filled them with herbs. Nothing has ever come close. If you are ever in Scopello, Sicily....

But, back to the soup. Months earlier, I'd bought a bag of very hard sun-dried tomatoes and put them into a jar under one of my best olive oils. When I was ready to try them, I discovered that they were still hard as a rock and I was unable to cut them. In fact, they slid all over my cutting board as if trying to escape from my knife. In disgust I put them back in the jar and left it on the top of my refrigerator, mad at myself for not realizing that I should have re-constituted them with hot water, drained them, and then added them to the jar of oil. Never being one who throws anything away, one day I realized that if I just made them into a soup I could kill two birds with one stone, and get them out of my refrigerator and into my stomach where they had belonged all along. So, I have included the recipe for the tomato soup because it is truly mine. It was inarguably the best tomato soup I had ever made and most likely the best tomato soup I had ever eaten. The oil that they were pseudo-marinating in became a delicious salad dressing after the addition of white wine vinegar, salt, pepper, balsamic vinegar, and *Herbes de Provence*.

Appunti/Notes

YOUR CHOICE OF APERITIF ~ By now, you know I like white wine as an *aperitivo*. Mix your own favorite drink, although this meal is rather light, so something sparkling as opposed to on the rocks would be my recommendation.

BELGIAN ENDIVE WITH PROSCIUTTO, FIGS, AND PINE NUTS ~ The nice thing about Belgian endive is that it's easy to prepare. Just wash and peel apart the leaves and you have perfect little edible plates to fill with whatever rings your bells. Using chopped prosciutto with thinly sliced figs, topped with pine nuts and a drop of honey, is wonderful. You could even puree them together and make a paste. Try toasting the pine nuts and see which flavor you prefer. Get inventive and mix tangerines with goat cheese and walnuts. The list is endless. I have even puréed leftover Chinese food and re-seasoned it to put into endive. As long as it's tasty, most people won't care what it is. No bugs though, please!

TOMATO SOUP ~ The recipe is included below. You could substitute fresh tomatoes, but it wouldn't be the same. The thick cream from the milk bottles could be substituted with heavy cream.

PUFF PASTRY WITH MUSHROOMS, TOMATOES, AND ONION ~ The recipe is in the back. Usually, I will use a slice of white cheese, like a pecorino or a Jack, on the bottom layer closest to the puff pastry, with maybe some feta and *parmigiano* on top. Thinly slice everything you put on it, so they will cook quickly and evenly. Don't overdo it by putting on too many toppings. Simple is better. Sprinkle with fresh herbs, but put them under the cheese, so the cheese can protect them from getting burned. When they come out of the oven, sprinkle with more fresh herbs while still hot, and drizzle with a drop or two of olive oil (the good one), and maybe even some lemon juice or zest, depending on what you chose to put on top. Coarse salt and pepper will wake up the taste buds even more.

SLICED COLD MEAT ~ You can thinly slice red onions, add some chopped olives, add capers and/or make an *aioli* with mayonnaise mixed with any of the above, and herbs, citrus, and garlic. Play. Put the dipping sauce on the side, and if your family doesn't like it, they can pass.

RED GRAPES ~ Wash the grapes ahead of time and discard any robbed stems. Cut into small bunches and encourage the eaters to never pick off single grapes, thereby leaving an ugly, scarred bowl of unattractive half eaten grapes for the next person who comes along. (You may notice that this is one of many food issues I'm passionate about! *Secondo me*, its akin to biting an apple and then putting it back into the bowl.)

Sun-dried Tomato Soup

INGREDIENTS
1 cup sun-dried tomatoes, 2 cups water, ½ leek, ½ cup salsa, cream from top of 2 gallons of milk, salt, pepper, olive oil. The fresh salsa contained tomatoes, onion, jalapeno, cilantro, olive oil, lemon, salt, pepper, and cumin).

PREPARATION
Add the sun-dried tomatoes to the water and bring to a boil. Boil uncovered while adding the sliced leek, salsa, salt and pepper. When sufficiently reduced, puree with immersion blender and add the cream. Serve with a drizzle of olive oil and parmesan toast or *crostini*.

Puff Pastry Antipasto

INGREDIENTS
frozen puff pastry, shredded Italian cheese, thinly sliced red onion, local fresh herb mixture, cilantro, olive oil, salt and pepper.

PREPARATION
Defrost the puff pastry according to manufacturer's directions and cut into ninths, or the desired size. Place on baking sheet. Dock center area of each piece with a fork. Place cheese on each piece, leaving the undocked edge uncovered. Top with red onion, herbs, olive oil, and salt and pepper. Reserve some of the fresh herbs and olive oil to go on after it is baked. Bake at 425 °F until slightly browned on top. Cool on wire rack and serve immediately, or allow cooling and re-heating when ready to serve.

> "*Le ore del mattino han(no) l'oro in bocca.*
> (The morning hours have gold in the mouth.)"

Farewell to Jessica

Pollo alla Cacciatora

Chicken Cacciatore (Hunter's Chicken)

- Vino Bianco
- Insalate Miste Selvatiche
- Pasta o Polenta
- Pollo alla Cacciatora
- Melone o Frutte di Bosco
- Vin Santo
- Biscottini
- Acqua alla Menta

Perhaps I should name this meal *Pollo Frigorifero* (Chicken Refrigerator) because this is where the hunt takes place. Chicken Cacciatore is one of my favorite meals, partly because it's so versatile and partly because it's so delicious. It can be simmered on the stove on very low heat, put into a low oven, blasted on the stove if there is little time, or cooked on high heat in the oven. Whichever way you cook it, it will be delicious. If you look for a recipe for this dish, every one will tell you a different way to make it. That's because it is truly a poverty food, put together with whatever could be found. If your "Hunter" was lucky, it included a chicken, too. The main ingredients are a chicken, a pot, and everything else you can find in your refrigerator. I like this meal in all seasons. It can be comfort food on a cold rainy day, and it can be eaten *al fresco* when it's hot outside. I prefer to cook it slowly at low temperatures. In the summer it will not heat up your kitchen too much if the oven is on low. You can also cook it more quickly, after the house has cooled down, if you prefer to dine later in the evening. It can probably be done on a barbeque if you can get a slow fire and a heavy cast iron pot. I haven't tried it that way yet, but perhaps....

Although you can make this dish with boneless chicken breasts, canned everything, and a microwave, I prefer using the entire chicken (or two), using the broth you produced from the last chicken's bones and the all the herbs and vegetables you purchased that morning or earlier in the week. Perhaps some of them could come out of your garden?

Appunti/Notes

WHITE WINE ~ You'll need some for the chicken, so why not open two bottles?

SALAD OF WILD GREENS ~ So what does this really mean? A good hunter will not pass by a nice dandelion plant, probably can recognize arugula in the woods, and surely knows all the edible greens in his or her local forest. The rest of us, who are worried about pesticides and wild animal urine, will probably get our greens from the local market. Try sticking to the theme and get something slightly resembling wild greens. Romaine and iceberg lettuce would not be thematically correct here. If iceberg is all the lettuce you can find, you are foraging in the wrong forests.

YOUR CHOICE OF PASTA OR POLENTA ~ A hunter would be more likely to have bread or a sack of *polenta* in his pocket next to the bullets—although, if pressed, I bet she would know how to make a colander to strain pasta out of intertwined twigs. I love this dish on top of spaghetti or linguine. Fresh *pappardelle* are excellent, also. You want something that will allow the wonderful sauce to stick to it, which is why *polenta* is also good.

HUNTER'S STYLE CHICKEN ~ If you cut up a whole chicken and make this dish with all the parts (you may cut the breast meat off the carcass, thereby getting boneless breast pieces and the carcass for broth), you will get all the flavors of using meat on the bone and some of the convenience for the boneless meat eaters. No matter how many times I pick out the breast pieces, I find them to be dry and tasteless compared to the coveted thigh and wing pieces. Even the legs, which are not my favorites, taste better than the breast pieces. Dredge each piece in seasoned flour, and brown quickly in hot oil or fat. Remove from pan and hold aside until all the vegetable steps are completed. Sauté chopped onion (or leeks or scallion), carrot and celery. You can add peppers, bells for sweetness and color, *piccante* for a little heat. Now is a good time to finely chop any herb stems (like parsley or cilantro) and add them in to flavor the dish. Season each item with salt and pepper as you add it to the pot. You can add mushrooms at this stage, if you keep them in big pieces and brown them (or sauté them separately and add at the end). Now you are ready for the simmering part. This can be done on the stove or in the oven in a covered pot or open pot, depending on how much time, how much liquid, and how much heat you apply. The desired result is to have the tops of the chicken get a little golden brown, while all of the flavor marry in the broth as it evaporates and thickens into a sauce. So how much do you use? What have you got? For one chicken, a half bottle of wine or less. Definitely add some tomatoes—a soup-sized can with the broth, or fresh, or a combination of the two. I like to always put in some fresh tomato, because I prefer the flavor. Chicken broth is good; use one part broth to one part wine and tomato juice to the point of almost covering the chicken in the pot. Now add herbs, lots of them. I pick parsley, marjoram, oregano, and garlic chive from my garden. Sometimes I'll add a bit of rosemary. I put the entire branch into the pot. It's easy to remove the stems just before serving. Add salt and pepper to taste, and let the whole thing simmer until the chicken is tender. I like to serve it just before the meat starts to fall off the bone (it's easier to get it out of the pot and onto the plate), but it's delicious either way. Place your pasta in a large serving bowl or onto individual plates, place chicken on top and spoon generous amounts of the sauce on top. If the sauce is too runny, take the meat and vegetables out of the pot and boil on high to reduce the liquid until it's thick. Garnish with more chopped mushrooms (if you want), freshly chopped herbs, lemon, and more salt and pepper. Roll up your sleeves and lick the plate when you're finished!

MELON OR BERRIES ~ Cut the melon into wedges, and then cut off most of the rind, leaving it still attached at one end. It looks more attractive when you leave it in its natural state, and the rind makes a useful handle. Or simply wash the berries at the very last minute and bring them to the table in a rustic bowl resting on a tea or paper towel.

BISCOTTINI (SMALL HARD COOKIES) ~ One or two *biscottini* per person, with the fruit, and as you're pouring a small nip of your....

SWEET DESSERT WINE ~ ... favorite dessert wine. Sit under the stars and pretend you are the Hunter or Huntress.

This was our last official meal with Jessica as a caregiver for Kristin. We were sad to see her leave, but knew she would remain a part of our lives. My parting culinary lesson was to show her how wonderful a chicken could be with just the normal ingredients from the refrigerator of a holistic kitchen.

STEWED EGGPLANT AND ZUCCHINI ~ This dish can be made in a skillet or on the barbeque. If grilling, brush each piece of sliced vegetable (including onions) with olive oil and season with salt and pepper. Grill on both sides and arrange whole or sliced on a platter. If using a skillet, slice the vegetables and brown on both sides, then add the tomato and let it simmer until the tomatoes break down. This dish can also be done in an oven. Adding fresh herbs and some lemon juice before serving will help to brighten the flavors.

EMMER ~ I made *farro* (also called emmer), for the first time recently, and everyone loved it. Instead of boiling it alone with salt and pepper, like rice, I added some tomatoes, onion, and peppers in the broth and let them cook together. It was delicious and nutty, with a consistency of brown rice, but tastier. As soon as I find a reliable source for it, we will be seeing it at our house much more often. In the winter, it could become a substitute for *polenta* and pasta under braised meats.

GRILLED STEAK IN THE MANNER OF FLORENCE ~ As with all good grilled meats, taking the time to rub them with olive oil, and at least salt and pepper (and possibly a bit of fresh garlic), will add greatly to the taste. I'm not a big proponent of rubs, because I believe they tend to overpower the flavor of the meat. Rubs are great when you have an old piece of meat or if you're going for barbeque flavors. These bone-in rib-eye steaks were rubbed with crushed garlic and grilled medium rare. I let them rest on the board under a nice pat of butter for five minutes, then sliced them, garnished with chopped parsley and scallion, and served the entire board at the table. Some of us prefer to cut the meat away from the bone and just eat the bones others go for the eye cut. Everyone is happy.

SLICED ORANGES ~ I sliced a couple of oranges and brought them out to the table on a plate. Sometimes one is tossed across the kitchen with the command, "Here, make yourself useful." The citrus does a good job of cutting the fattiness in your mouth. Did someone say chocolate?

Lombata di Maiale al Forno

Roast Stuffed Pork Loin

- Chianti Classico
- Insalata di Michelina con Funghi e Parmigiano
- Zucchine Gialle
- Patate Gratinate
- Lombata di Maiale al Forno
- Fichi
- Acqua Frizzante

Although the weather is hot in the summer, your oven can be used if you can avoid being in your kitchen or house in the afternoon. Prep everything early in the day, or the night before, so that it can be taken out of the refrigerator and added to the hot oven. Try to keep away from your stove, and let only the microwave and oven be the cooking tools today.

Once in Italian class, a dialogue went like this:

"*Che cosa avete mangiato per Pranzo oggi?*" "What did you eat for lunch today?"

I answered, "*Ho mangiato salsiccia, pasta, e un'insalata verde.*" "I ate sausage, pasta, and a green salad."

She replied, "*Va bene, ma ho domandato che cosa hai mangiato per Pranzo, non per Cena.*" "Very good, but I asked you what you ate for lunch, not for dinner."

I answered, "*Sì, per Pranzo. Stasera, per cena cucino Maiale al Forno.*" "Yes, for lunch. Tonight for dinner I'm cooking pork roast."

There are no silly Caesar salads or cottage cheese and fruit lunches occurring in my kitchen. An apple alone will not do for lunch. I take the time to sit down and eat from a nice plate, with a placemat, silverware, and a stemmed water glass. Occasionally, I have a glass of wine. I will frequently finish with a latte and a piece of really dark chocolate, and then another glass of water. After I finish, I'm ready to attack the rest of my day. I don't stop at a drive-through restaurant later for a snack. There are no late afternoon smoothies for me. I'm satiated and content until dinner time rolls around. A left-over piece of the following pork roast, with some of the potatoes and a tomato, is an excellent lunch, but you can't get it if you don't start making roasts and such for dinner. If you cook enough food at night, there's plenty available for packing into lunches, and there's usually some for me, too. The meat can also be sliced and put between slices of very good bread.

Appunti/Notes

CLASSIC CHIANTI ~ The traditional *Chianti in fiasco* (basket flask) is not robust enough for a filled roast. Pick a full-bodied red wine that can hold its own against the richness of the pork, its filling, and the brown gravy that will go with it.

ROMAINE WITH SHAVED MUSHROOMS AND PARMESAN ~ This salad should either be served on a platter or made directly onto individual salad plates. Use the romaine hearts (after you've eaten the rest of the romaine, not from the bag). Use whole leaves, or slice across several at ½ inch intervals. Break apart and place onto platter. If you do slice the lettuce, do not let it sit before eating as the edges will rust. Using a vegetable peeler, shave parmesan slices over the top of the romaine. Add several thinly sliced fresh mushrooms, and season lightly with very good olive oil, seasoned rice vinegar, and coarse salt and pepper. Do not toss before serving. A good variation would be to use *ricotta salata* and thinly sliced red bell pepper. To this I would add a drizzle of balsamic vinegar, because the *ricotta salata* does not have a strong flavor like the parmesan.

YELLOW SQUASH ~ At different times of the summer season you can find all types of yellow squash. This dish can be made with any of them: crookneck, yellow zucchini, small oval-shaped ones, or even green, for that matter. Buy the ones that look like they came out of the ground last. Slice them, add salt and pepper, and drizzle with olive oil. Put them in a pan with some onion and fresh herbs at the last part of the roasting. Cover them first (or microwave) so they steam gently, and then uncover and allow to crisp up a bit.

GRATIN OF POTATOES WITH CHEESES ~ As with the squash, steam or microwave the potatoes so they are partially cooked and easier to slice. Season with salt and pepper and olive oil. Arrange in shallow baking dish and alternate with sliced or grated cheese. Add cream or milk and a dusting of bread crumbs on top. Grate some *parmigiano* on top, and bake in the oven until crispy.

STUFFED BONELESS PORK LOIN ~ When it comes to roast pork, the hard-to-find pork roast with bone in, or crown roast of pork, is the most magnificent, tastiest roast you can prepare. Contrary to popular belief, the roast is not fatty. If you compare it to a prime rib roast (with the bone in), you will find at the end of the evening that there is far more fat in the pan from the beef than from the pork. And as those of us who watch the food channel will attest, "Pork fat rules!" While I will always prefer the pork roast with bone in, the whole loin of pork on sale for $1.99 per pound is just a bargain that is not to be passed up. This cut of meat is so versatile—you have seen it used in other seasons of this book. Depending on the amount of time, you can slice it and stuff individual pieces (if you're in a hurry), or slice it in a spiral direction and stuff the entire roast, which takes longer to cook. Put anything you want into it. Think about color and flavor. In this menu, I stuffed it with the perennial sun-dried tomato, basil (or basil *pesto*), and *mozzarella di bufala*. The trick is to slice around the length of the pork loin, so you're cutting it into a long flat ½ inch sheet that can then be stuffed, rolled and tied. Ask your butcher, if you're afraid. Season the meat as always, and use olive oil. Layer the ingredients, roll, and tie. Brown on all sides, and then place on a rack into a hot oven with some liquid in the bottom of the pan so you will achieve enough pan juices to make the amount of gravy you want. Cook uncovered. Use a meat thermometer to determine doneness, and then let the roast rest for at least ten minutes before slicing. Be imaginative with your fillings. Bread or cracker stuffing could be used. Once, in Vienna, a pork roast was served to me with pickles, bread, and *peperoncini* inside, and a delicious paprika sauce poured over the top.

FIGS ~ We planted our fig tree early last year, and are anticipating a small crop for this, our first harvest. Two years ago, I discovered an abandoned fig tree on the corner of the street that enters into our neighborhood. Sadly, I had been driving past this tree almost every day for the last twenty years. Now, in the summer after a delicious meal, I will surreptitiously take my stainless steel colander basket and say, "I'll be right back." Accompanied by Dylan, I will walk to the corner and hope that none of my friends drive by and see me standing in weeds up to my hips, picking as many figs as are ripe and can be consumed that evening. Perhaps if they drive by they will be on their way to the local health food store to pick up a basket of figs at $12.99 each. Mine are free! Figs can be prepared in many ways, but when they're this fresh I just stand them on a small decorative plate and serve them. Kate will eat hers directly from the colander as I'm still washing them.

SPARKLING WATER ~ Water scooped from a natural spring in your own backyard is desired, and if enough of these books sell, perhaps I will have one behind my casa in Italy someday. For now, it's water scooped from whichever well I can find that is not a stainless steel tank in a factory in Los Angeles.

Pot Roast in the Summer???

Manzo Brasato con Salsa BBQ
Pot Roasted Beef with BBQ Style Gravy

- ❖ Birra
- ❖ Insalata di Cavolo
- ❖ Pane Fresco
- ❖ Manzo Brasato
- ❖ Fagioli al Forno
- ❖ Pannocchia Cotta
- ❖ Sorbetto o Gelato con Uva Congelata
- ❖ Tè di Erbe al Sole, ghiacciato

I tell everyone that I am the Queen of Pot Roast. I can eat pot roast at any season, though in the summer, the thought of slaving over a hot stove is not too appealing. The solution? Start cooking it early enough in the morning so that it's finished by the time the heat of the day rolls around. It can be served hot or cold with pasta, or with fresh bread and microwaved gravy. In the summer months, I will cook it with Thai curries and coconut milk (and an entire bunch of cilantro), or braise it in a barbeque sauce, and serve it as described below. Either way, it will be delicious. As in all braising operations, brown the meat, add some form of liquid, and cook slowly until tender. Thicken the pan juices and have at it. In the colder months, pot roast with pasta, peas, and gravy is my favorite comfort meal.

Appunti/Notes

BEER ~ It can actually get too hot to drink wine. Old Italian-Americans solved this problem by adding ice to red wine. Today, the wine snob police would cart us away. *Vino rosso con ghiaccio? Non è possibile!* A true cellar temperature of 55 to 58°F would yield a cooler wine, and a properly cellared wine would seem cool. But why go there? Drink ice cold beer in the summer. Every one else in America does.

CABBAGE SALAD ~ This is not a true coleslaw. Thinly shave ¼ to a whole cabbage (Napa cabbage will yield a very light slaw). Season it with salt and pepper. Just before serving, add a little bit of olive oil, and white wine or seasoned rice vinegar, and some currants or raisins which have been soaked in *grappa* if they're not soft to start with. You could add a little bit of mayonnaise or yogurt, but treat it more as a topping than smothering the cabbage in it. Drizzle with fresh lemon juice.

FRESH BREAD ~ The meat will be served sliced, with accompanying barbeque sauce from the pan juices. Slice the bread, or serve rolls which allow for the making of a sandwich, if desired.

POT ROAST AND BBQ STYLE GRAVY ~ Season with flour, salt and pepper, and brown the entire pot roast. Add homemade barbeque sauce (or your favorite bottle), an onion or two sliced into rings, and a beer. Partially cover and cook in the oven on low heat until fully cooked, when the meat is just starting to fall off the bone. When ready to serve, or earlier in the day, remove the meat from the bone and slice. Thicken the pan juices by reducing the original liquid amount to half, re-season, and/or add a tiny bit of flour. You're trying to achieve a barbecue sauce, not gravy. Pour some onto the meat, and serve the rest in a gravy bowl or pitcher. Arrange the onions around the meat on the plate.

BAKED BEANS ~ Since the meat is cooking for a large part of the day, why not make some baked beans, too? Do not open a can of baked or barbequed beans! They will be bad. Remember to soak the beans overnight, or boil them for about an hour and a half, until *al dente*. Then put them into a heavy oven-proof pot or casserole dish with onion, barbeque sauce (ketchup? *Marinara?*), chili powder or hot peppers, some of the beer or broth, some mustard, pork or bacon fat (you can always find a recipe for baked beans) and let them cook slowly in the oven with the meat. There is no substitute for real baked beans. Try bringing some to your next pot-luck, and notice the compliments.

Corn on the Cob ~ I am eagerly waiting the day when the Italian cousins come for a visit. After seeing miles of fields of corn being grown there, I asked them why I could find no corn in the *mercato*. Letizia looked at me as if I were crazy and remarked, "We don't eat the corn. It's for the cows!" It's probably also for the *polenta*. I can't help wondering, though, didn't anyone ever think of steaming some and putting butter on it? Good fresh corn can be eaten raw, steamed or grilled in or out of the husk. Steamed is still my favorite because that is how it was served as I was growing up. I get chastised for ruining good corn with butter, but I do admit to using much less than I did as a child. A small amount of salted water, or sugared milk if you're from New Jersey, and you're well on your way. Don't overcook it. Corn was always served after the meal at our house, probably so you could easily melt the butter with the hot corn and roll it around on your plate. Notice who eats across and who eats around the cob. Is their style of eating similar to yours? Do you agree with them politically? Do they squeeze the toothpaste tube the correct way?

Sorbet, Sherbet or Ice Cream ~ This meal is essentially a summer barbeque, although the barbeque itself is not used. Volunteer to be the person who scoops the ice cream or sorbet and stand in front of the freezer a while longer than usual. Pop a few frozen grapes into your mouth. Your hot kitchen or backyard will be instantly more bearable. Kiss your sweetie. Want a grape?

Sun Tea with Herbs ~ When it's really hot, it's a great time to get out the jug or pitcher, put some herbal tea into it, and let it sit out in the sun for a few hours. You will have a delicious tea. Poured over ice, with an added lemon slice or mint leaves, and you're on your way to a cool evening. A mint "*juleppa*" or *limonata* would be okay, too.

> *Chi non vuole quando può, non può quando vuole.*
> (Who doesn't want to when he can,
> can't do it when he wants.)

Pollo alla Griglia con Pesto
GRILLED PESTO CHICKEN

- Campari, Noci e un Fioré
- Grissini e Speck
- Insalata Verde e Condimento Francese
- Il Piatto Rosso con Gorgonzola e un Foglione di Basilico
- Penne con Basilico, Pomodori, e Mozzarella di Bufala
- Pollo alla Griglia con Pesto
- Melanzane alla Griglia
- Fragole Fresche e Cioccolatini con Amarillo

Barbequed chicken is one of my all-time favorite meals. In my attempts to create the Italian version of barbequed chicken, I threw away my jar of barbeque sauce and looked to my "perfectly stocked kitchen" to see what I could work with. My original plan was to make the barbequed chicken for dinner, and serve spaghetti with *pesto* alongside. With the loss of the barbeque sauce, Jim's intense dislike of large amounts of garlic, and my realization that the *marinara* that I was going to use instead of the sauce actually had meat in it I decided to try the *pesto* on the chicken and the sauce on the pasta. I'm probably not the first person who has put *pesto* onto chicken, but I guarantee I will not be the last. Once you've tried it you'll be hooked, too. Now, of course, your homemade *pesto* will be much better than any purchased *pesto*. The purchased *pesto* will have too much garlic and bad oil in it. By making the *pesto* yourself, you can control the ingredients and achieve the consistency needed to stay on the chicken and not slide off of it while it's cooking. If there's too much oil in the *pesto*, you will be constantly fighting the fire. The *parmigiano* will help to keep the *pesto* sticking to the chicken as it marinates and cooks. To achieve the right doneness of the chicken, watch over the grill and use a meat thermometer.

GRILLED EGGPLANT ~ Sliced and rubbed with olive oil and Italian herbs, or grilled whole and then scraped out of the skins; either is delicious, or can be done at the same time as the chicken, if your grill is large enough. If you have a small area for grilling, do the eggplant first and allow it to cool. Grilled vegetables are great served at room temperature. The chicken is best served hot.

STRAWBERRIES AND CHOCOLATE-COVERED BLUEBERRIES ~ I don't really remember who brought the chocolate-covered blueberries, but I filled a medium-sized platter with freshly washed strawberries and added some of the chocolate covered blueberries around the edges. Interestingly enough, the strawberries disappeared first. I think there were too many men at the table that night. The women would never have allowed the chocolates to be left languishing. At least one of the women wouldn't have.

Pesto for Grilled Chicken

INGREDIENTS
2 cups fresh basil leaves, ¾ cup pine nuts, 2 garlic cloves, ½-1 cup olive oil, 1 tsp salt,
½ tsp pepper, and 1 wedge of parmesan cheese (grated).

PREPARATION
Using a food processor, grate the parmesan cheese and set aside. Put basil leaves, pine nuts, and garlic into food processor and blend until chopped coarsely. With food processor on, add oil slowly until a thick paste is formed. Season with salt and pepper. Store in tightly sealed jar until ready to use. When ready to use, add cheese and mix lightly. Use immediately or store in refrigerator adding additional oil to cover all of the *pesto*. As you use the *pesto*, continue to add oil to cover so the basil will not brown during storage. When all the *pesto* is used, use the oil to make a salad dressing.

The Proper Kitchen

CHAPTER 8

Few of us will ever have the perfect kitchen, so let's talk about a proper kitchen. This is a kitchen that may contain some of the features of a dream kitchen. The difference, as I see it, is that a proper kitchen must be functional, and contain the items you need most to be a successful cook. As an added bonus, it could be large, bright, airy, harmonious, and totally outfitted with high-end cabinetry, appliances, and fixtures. Ten or twelve place settings of china in patterns to suit your every whim would be nice, but one simple set of dishes is all that's really necessary.

Some necessities for one chef may be unnecessary for another, depending on the style of foods you like to eat and prepare. I like some Asian foods, and have experimented with sushi making, wok cooking, and deep frying. Some of the implements necessary to be a successful Asian cook have found their way into my kitchen. Mostly, they take up a lot of space because I don't use them that often. This is not an Asian lifestyle book. However, in living the good life, especially in California, I find that a wok is an essential kitchen implement. A rice cooker comes in really handy for parties, and a basic steamer is good for making dumplings and stuffed artichoke hearts.

Here is a list of things I want in my kitchen. Of course, I don't actually have all of them in my kitchen right now; some are on my wish list. None of these items is essential, though they're all quite nice.

A magnetic knife rack. I keep mine in a drawer.

A hanging pot rack. I keep mine in drawers and cabinets all over the kitchen, because I have way too many and keep buying more to play with, while never throwing an old one away.

> *"Your pots and pans can be very bad children, so discipline them with a good scrubbing and polishing now and then."*

Copper range hood. Best with lots of vertical space above the burners. Vertical space is currently a limitation in my kitchen, which makes it really hard to stir when using tall pots. Copper range hoods are just cool.

Triple sink. I do have it, and hope to never live without. One side for dirty, one for disposal, and one side for clean. I love it and highly recommend it to you, if you have the space in your next remodel.

Six burners on the stovetop. I frequently make dinners for ten to twenty people. To cook large quantities, I need a lot of space. I have four, and they're sufficient for all the meals in this book.

Pizza oven. It's been on the list, but I recently discovered that a pizza stone on top of the barbeque grill is an excellent substitute, as long as you're not also grilling the main course at the same time.

Large pot faucet over the stove. I've never actually used one, but they just look really cool, and you don't have to carry really heavy pots of water across your kitchen, especially if you're making pasta for twenty, or soup from a turkey carcass.

Perfectly level stove. Nothing is more annoying than having half the items in your skillet burn because all the oil runs to the downhill side of the pan.

Now, on to the kitchen of *la mia dolce vita*. You don't need any of the items listed above to live the good life. Here's what I think you need. These items are the basics for optimizing your success in the kitchen. You always need the right tools for the right job, whether you're an engineer, mathematician, teacher, plumber, or truck-driver. I hope you are none of these, because these careers could take you away from your kitchen for long periods of time.

Store things functionally, close to the appropriate task station, and in the order of frequency of use. If you use something all the time, it should be out, or in the top drawer. For instance, pot holders should not be something you have to search for. They should be in the top drawer, or hanging near the stove. Strainers should be close to the sink, since you're most likely going to strain something down the drain. Serving platters should be located between the cooking areas and the dining areas, so you can take something out of the oven (or off the stove), plate it, and then bring it to the table.

Cookware

Pots and pans. Buy the best you can afford. I prefer stainless steel and copper, though I feel you should also get a good heavy cast iron pan. The biggest misconception about pots and pans in an American kitchen is that the set of pots and pans must match. This is another example of the genius of American marketing. We think of gleaming pans, all lined up or hanging from an overhead rack. If you believe that there's a correct tool for every job, you may come to realize, as I did, that some recipes will do better in cast iron, or enamel, or copper, or stainless steel. Many restaurants favor aluminum pans because they're economical. My feeling is that you should get the biggest, heaviest conductor of heat that you can lift. I do not have a non-stick pan. You may, of course, purchase whatever you like. My wish for you is that you buy pots and pans that are functional and pleasing to work with. Every time I pull out the copper skillet my husband brought me from Paris, I'm happy to own it. I take care of it (really, I do), and hope my daughter will be sautéing in it some day.

> *"A good burn now and then reminds you to slow down and pay attention to what you're doing."*

I like pots and pans. I visit my favorite copper pans in the local kitchen shop. I tell them my plans for acquiring them some day, and in what order. When a new pan comes home, I introduce it to its new friends. You do not have to be on a first name basis with your cookware, as I am. However, you may find yourself wanting to give some of them names, especially bad names, like when you forget to grab that potholder before lifting the cast iron skillet. Your pots and pans can be very bad children, so discipline them with a good scrubbing and polishing now and then. They will accompany you when you graduate and become a culinary master person.

These are the pots and pans I have in my kitchen. You may not need all of these, though I will try to prioritize them for the style of cooking discussed in this book.

Dutch oven I have two. They are anodized cast aluminum, about 5 quarts and 3 quarts, with a metal handle on each side for lifting. The bigger one is perfect for stews, sauces, large soups, and small roasts or chickens. The smaller one gets used for small soups and small sauces. It would be perfect if you were cooking for one or two persons. Some day I will replace them with enameled cast iron. I've had these pots since I was in my early twenties. They've served me well. The famous chefs on TV will tell you to buy very expensive enameled cast iron pots. Some of them have their own brands. The sponsors clearly pay to get their products placed. They will tell you all about the superior cooking properties.

What they fail to tell you is that really heavy pots and pans have superior clean-up properties. The reason they don't tell you this is because by the time they get to be very famous food personalities, they no longer have to do their own dishes. For the rest of us, cleanup is important. If not done properly, it can make or break your evening, or the morning thereafter. With a really heavy copper, stainless or cast iron pot you can add hot water and dish detergent and put it back on the stove. While you're washing the rest of your dishes, the pot will essentially be cleaning itself. In my opinion, this feature is worth its weight in gold, or at least in copper.

> *Sharp knives don't cut you, dull ones do, because they slip and catch your fingers instead of what you're trying to cut.*

Pots. I still have the original cast aluminum from my youth, the time of my life where I thought all pans were supposed to match. I have 3, 2, 1, and ½ quart sizes. They have long metal handles and metal lids. Yes, I have burned myself many times on them over the years. After all, it is fire, not you, who is the real master in any kitchen. A good burn now and then reminds you to slow down and pay attention to what you're doing. What you're doing is cooking with some form of fire. My copper sauce pan, from another trip to Paris, is probably my most used one. It takes two hands to pick up even when

CHAPTER 8 • THE PROPER KITCHEN   213

empty. It's a beauty, and I strive to never prepare anything mediocre in it. When you cook with the finest implements, the food that comes out of them must be good. Really, really good; otherwise it's just a joke, like a guy in clean leathers, who rides up on a brand new Harley Davidson and then drops it as he's getting off. Everyone will know he's faking it.

The 3 quart sauce pan is always used for tomato sauce. It's pleasing to me to see it simmering on the stove, hear it sputtering, and to smell the rich aromas coming from it. When my family comes home and sees it on the stove, it's usually the first place they go, to see what's cooking for dinner. Even if I tell them it's spaghetti sauce for tonight, "Don't open it," they will immediately open it and judge for themselves whether I've reached perfection in sauce. They will taste it and then let me know if, in their opinion, it needs something else. Kate will not tell me what she thinks it needs. She'll reach over and add it herself.

Frying pans and skillets. So, if I have this straight, frying pans have sloping edges and are usually shallower than skillets, which have higher straight sides and come with a lid. I think everyone should have at least two small frying pans, 9 inch or 10 inch. You need one for the eggs and one for the bacon, or one for the potatoes and one for the eggs, or one for the bacon and one for the potatoes. Oh, heck, just get three, or get two small and one larger one. Once you start focusing on your food and cooking, you're bound to have guests. I have two small cast aluminum, one small copper, and three of the graduated stainless steel variety with the black handle and copper bottom. Some have lids, some borrow lids, and some go in the dishwasher. I'm waiting for those black handles to break off in the dishwasher so I can replace them with something nicer, but I must say they've been hanging in there for over twenty years.

Braising pans. I like braising pans. This method of cooking starts out on the stove top and finishes in the oven. I cook this way a lot, and the small handles on either side of a braising pan make it easier for the pan to fit into the oven. Otherwise, a covered skillet is just as useful. A big one that can hold a roast, or a whole cut up chicken swimming in the sauce of the day, is essential in my house. If you're cooking for one or two, the smaller size will work just fine.

Sauce pans. Any of the covered pots can be used for making a sauce or gravy, though I prefer a small one with a rounded side so whisking is easier. If your pot has a square edge, the whisk cannot get into the corners very well, and your *béchamelle* can burn. It's worth finding one as a later addition to your kitchen when you begin reducing sauces and pan juices for dressing the entrees before serving.

Knives

Knives. I love knives. They are, after all, one of the most important kitchen tools. You must make the investment and get at least one really, really, well-made knife. I started out with an 8-inch chef's knife, the best I could afford in my twenties. I acquired others as the years rolled on, most slightly better in

quality as I learned new skills and became a kitchen fanatic. Even though I now have enough knives to fill a large kitchen block, this original knife was the most used, and yes, the sharpest knife in the drawer. About a year ago, I bought a small, well-made Santoku knife, and I find it has become the most sought-after knife. However, when more than one person is cutting in the kitchen, they both get used and are frequently traded back and forth.

Keep your knives sharp. I have tried many different sharpeners, including a whetstone. I prefer to take my knives to a professional sharpener. Someone who spends his or her entire life sharpening things will know how to get a good edge. Don't bother with the local kitchen store when they have a free sharpening special! This is a marketing ploy to get you into the store (usually twice) and the person who sharpens your knife is probably a salesperson. A good honing steel is essential to keep the edge sharp on the expensive knives you will eventually acquire. Whether you sharpen your knives yourself or have them professionally sharpened, keeping them sharp is important. Sharp knives don't cut you, dull ones do, because they slip and catch your fingers instead of what you're trying to cut. I always travel with my knives if I'm going to be staying at a place with a kitchen. It's annoying, and potentially dangerous, to cut foods in someone else's kitchen using inadequate tools to do the job.

Now, about knife sizes: I have a small hand, so I like the 8-inch chef's knife and 5-inch Santoko. I've noticed that the men who cook in my kitchen tend to reach for the 10-inch chef's knife that came to me from my husband's knife collection when we were married. Most important, buy knives from shops that let you feel the knife in your hand. You'd be surprised to know that they have different weights and the blades are all slightly different. The day I proudly took my birthday money to the store to buy the boning knife I had been coveting for over a year was a surprise. I closed my eyes and took turns feeling which one felt better in my hand, and the one I had intended to buy was the not the one that won the blind test. Again, if you have the best tools for the job, you increase your odds of success and enjoyment.

The secondary knives that I believe you may want to acquire someday are a serrated knife for cutting bread, a thinner rounded knife for boning poultry, a long thin knife with cullens for slicing cooked meats, and a carving knife or cleaver for cutting raw meat. A carving knife has a rounded blade edge and resembles a pirate's cutlass. (Yes, Hunter, you really should play with one some day!) Steak knives and paring knives are also useful, depending on your style of cutting and eating.

If you're cutting, you will need cutting boards. After a lively discussion with Jessica about cutting board sanitation, I spent several hours researching various websites for a definitive answer on cutting board choices. There is none. The important thing is that no matter what type you use, you have to keep it sanitary. Glass and stone may look great, but they will dull your knives. It's your choice to use plastic cutting boards. I hate them. If you prefer to use different color-coded plastic cutting boards, suit yourself. You will still need to keep them clean. If you have too many boards, you may lose track of what you used one for and whether you sanitized it or not. I use wood. Wood was good enough for my grandfather, who was a butcher, so it's good enough for me. I have three wooden ones, and they get washed and sanitized frequently.

STORED ITEMS

Graters. I still get angry about when I listened to a friend's advice that graters can go into the dishwasher. The plastic handle immediately cracked and broke off, so now the metal handle is a little harder to hold. I have three—one flat, for larger jobs, and two smaller ones for bringing to the table for parmesan or chocolate. They don't seem to rust if you wash them by hand. The micro-plane grater is one of the next big kitchen implements I hope to acquire. It will not have a plastic handle or go in the dishwasher.

Strainers. Strainers become very useful if you're doing your shopping at farmers' markets. Farmers' market produce tends to have a lot more dirt than at the grocery store. Also, strainers are great baskets to use when you pick the produce out of your own garden. Buy several, and use them to wash your produce when you bring it home from the market or store—or from your garden. When everything is washed as you acquire it (except berries), you will tend to eat more of it and use more of it. This goes for herbs, which are always too much trouble to grab at the last minute if they're caked with dirt, but very easy to grab if washed. My counter is usually covered with strainers of various sizes, filled with the freshest produce on hand. We eat out of them and they are my kitchen art. In my house, once I put it into the refrigerator it's usually lost and not discovered for weeks afterwards. Keep your produce where you can see it and use it while it's fresh. (Strainers are not for pasta, see below.)

Ladles. A big flat ladle is most useful. I also have a smaller, deeper ladle for use with smaller pots and bowls. It's good to have a nice ladle for serving soups and stews at the table. A flat stainless steel ladle or screen is essential if you're going to make stocks. You'll need it for skimming off the scum and for lifting bones and veggies out of the stockpot.

> " *Another way to remove the fat is to refrigerate the whole strained stock overnight and then pick the hardened fat off the top before using.* "

Spatula. Purchase a spatula that will survive you. Get a good sturdy blade and heavy handle. A cheaply made spatula will just break, especially when you get lazy and put it in the dishwasher. Pick one large, one small, and one very flexible, or slotted for turning delicate items like fish. These items are extensions of your hands, so treat them well.

Spoons. At a minimum, you should get a wooden spoon with long handle for soups, and stainless (one standard, one slotted) for just about everything else. Serving utensils sized to fit the types of foods you serve and the size of dishes helps make things more pleasant at the table.

Measuring cups. Best to have both dry measure and liquid. I like the metal ones that fit into each other. So far, they've been fairly indestructible. I added a 2-cup measure, which gets used every time I make rice. I use them to store the prep items prior to going into the pot. They can go into the dishwasher. I still prefer old-fashioned glass measuring cups. When something works, stick with it. I inherited one a while back, and was surprised to see that those acquired in my youth had the innovation of being stackable, while the earlier model was not. I kept them both. They haven't broken, and are used frequently. You may have noticed by now that I do not like a lot of plastic in my kitchen. There are some things that have to be in plastic. I do, however, find that the glass is more esthetically pleasing to me and, because it's glass, I tend to treat it a little more carefully.

Pasta colander. When I married my Italian husband, I inherited a yellow plastic colander with a long handle on it. It was one of the most hated items in my kitchen, particularly because it was yellow, and my kitchen is red. Like a good dutiful wife, instead of immediately throwing it out and buying a new one, I humored him and used it. I used it, and used it, and used it. I banged it on the sink very hard every time I made pasta, to get all of the water out. Finally, after about 17 years of marriage the handle got a small crack in it. Two days later, I was at my

favorite kitchen store, buying a new stainless steel pasta colander. I was truly a happy camper. Yesterday, I banged the steel colander on the sink bottom to drain the pasta water—and the handle broke off! I think the yellow colander was getting its revenge. Luckily, the metal colander had two handles. I'll probably never throw it away. Don't put a metal colander in the dishwasher after using it on pasta, unless you like to spend your time scraping off the hard pasta that will cook itself into every hole in the colander during the dishwashing process.

Potholders. Believe it or not, thickness is more important than color. I use mitts and small square ones. I haven't tried the silicone mitts yet; they just don't look right in my old-fashioned kitchen. I've used the cloth and silicone mitts on my pot handles out of desperation, and as a life-saving gesture to the guest cooks who invariably grab the metal handles of my pots at least once every time they are over.

Locking tongs. I never really will understand how I lived more than 45 years of my life before ever trying a set of industrial locking tongs. They have since become the most important tool in my kitchen, next to the Santoku knife. They're always out, and I must wash them thirty times a day when I'm really cooking. I eventually bought a longer pair for using with the barbeque, but only after singeing my hands several times. Some things you learn the easy way, and some things you learn the hard way.

Pasta fork. A beautiful stainless steel work of art, it is one of the most expensive tools in my kitchen, and was an early acquisition after having the stupid bamboo tines fall out into a hot colander full of pasta one too many times. Since I use it almost every night, why not have the best one that my money can buy?

Kitchen scissors. Kitchen scissors are for the kitchen; otherwise they would just be called scissors. Scissors

are for everything else your family wants to cut. Keep them out of the kitchen. Good kitchen scissors are for cutting meats, veggies if you prefer, and twine for the wrapping of roasts, etc. Yes, they can also cut flowers. The next person who uses my kitchen scissors for cutting duct tape will be summarily shot. Wash them frequently, and if you see someone taking them out of the kitchen, they had better return with an armful of flowers or herbs....

Specialty Items

Items for meat preparation. Roasting rack, roasting pan, meat fork, kitchen twine, steel skewers and/or toothpicks, meat thermometer. You will need these items to make many of the meat dishes in this book. The meat thermometer is essential, as cooking times are not identified. You must learn to measure doneness if you want to be a good cook. A recipe cannot accurately determine what the dynamics of your stove, barbeque, and oven are in conjunction with the size of the meat. You will need to think. It's disappointing to cut into an expensive roast only to find it's too rare to eat. Now that you've let all of the juices pour out onto the platter, it can still be re-cooked in the oven, but it will not be as good. It is also disappointing to cut into a piece of meat that's overcooked. Besides using the meat thermometer to determine doneness, look at it, feel it, smell it, and become accustomed to knowing what the dynamics of a properly prepared piece of meat are. Whenever you are roasting, the kitchen will start to smell good when the meat is nearly cooked. Listen to the sizzle in the pan. If you smell something burning, something probably is.

Items for the preparation of stocks, soups, and sauces. Stockpot, sieves, containers for stocks, food processor, stand mixer, hand mixer (a.k.a. boat motor), gravy separator, whisk, hand-held juice reamer, stand juicer.

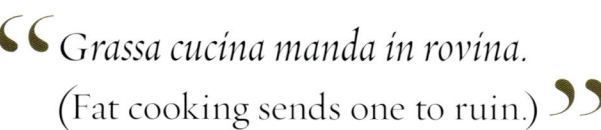

> *Grassa cucina manda in rovina.*
> (Fat cooking sends one to ruin.)

Making soup is difficult only if you aren't willing to try it. If you have the correct implements, the stocks will essentially make themselves. Use your biggest pot—the one you boil spaghetti in if you haven't yet acquired a stock pot, and put bones in it. You can use a whole chicken or roast, but why not eat the meat and use the leftover bits, including the skin and fat, for the soup? Now go around your kitchen and get an onion or part thereof, some celery, and a carrot or two. Wash them and add to the pot. Cover with cold water and bring to a simmer uncovered, so the water can boil off and the flavors become concentrated. Many books will tell you to simmer all day, or only for an hour. I do both, depending on what I'm doing the rest of the day or evening. I like to start stocks in the morning or at the end of the meal. Cook for several hours until you're ready to deal with it again. During the evening, while you're watching TV, is also a good time. Add in any other leftover vegetables and take the bottoms of your bunches of parsley, asparagus tips, mushroom stems or wilted vegetables you haven't used yet, etc. I add in whole herbs, stems and all if I already know where the stock is destined to go, and the herbs are appropriate to the finished soup. When it's done (and this means it's simmered enough for the bones to give up their flavor), turn off the heat and let it sit for a while to cool enough so you can handle it. At no time let it get below temperature for maintaining food-safe conditions. Pull out the bones with either tongs or a slotted spoon. Now comes the fun part. Pour the stock through a sieve (finely meshed screen) into a large measuring cup or bowl big enough to handle the amount of liquid you put into the pot originally. This is also a good time to put it through a gravy separator. This step is essential to remove the fat. Another way to remove the fat is to refrigerate the whole strained stock overnight and then pick the hardened fat off the top before using. Now you are ready to make a soup. Start with the essential *mirepoix*, which in French is usually onion, carrot, and celery, or, in Italian, *soffritto*, which can include onion, carrot, and celery, but may also contain parsley, fennel or tomato. Add your desired soup ingredients to the stock and simmer again, uncovered. Season it as you add each ingredient, and add plenty of fresh herbs at the end. The mixers and food processor can be used to puree the soup. You can serve a soup one way the first night, and puree it the second night. Add a bit of cream, and serve the same soup re-presented the second night. The gravy separator and whisk are essential tools for making sauces and gravies from the pan juices, after you've roasted meats and/or vegetables.

Items for salad preparation. Large bowl for tossing salads, salad spinner, tongs or two large spoons. The salad spinner is another item I've wondered how I did without for so many years. Use it to wash, spin, and dry whole or partially torn lettuce leaves and herbs. Keep re-filling the spinner with fresh water until you no longer see sand or grit in the spun rinse water. If you don't tear the lettuce, it can be kept in the spinner in the refrigerator for several days. Once again, if it's easy to grab a washed lettuce leaf, you'll find that making a sandwich is easier. Using a leaf as part of the food presentation process is faster, and adding some shredded lettuce on or under an appetizer is more easily facilitated.

Items for pizza, breads, and baked goods. Pizza pan/cookie sheets, pizza stone, dough paddle, baking dishes, mixing/storage bowls of various sizes, drying/cooling racks, pastry/marinade brush. The most important items needed for good pizza, besides the flavored ingredients themselves, are a pizza stone (to ensure a properly cooked crust) and a hot oven. Bowls for rising dough, and a paddle to keep the dough from sticking to the board are also needed.

Baking dishes and gratins. Buy the ugly glass ones for baking things that aren't going to be served in them. Buy the nicer white or decorated ones for dishes that go to the table. Yesterday's leftover vegetables with some breadcrumbs, parmesan, and cream, placed under a broiler, can become a whole new dish today.

Ramekins. I use them for holding the bacon fat, small amounts of leftovers, making individual custards, saving an egg white, individual dipping sauce holders, and storing chopped herbs that didn't get used for dinner but may find their way into a future omelet.

Food-processor/blender/mixer. Although many tasks are equally accomplished with a good knife and a little time, a food processor becomes essential in making breadcrumbs (from stale loaves of bread), *pesto*, and creamed soups. Do not try to mash potatoes in a food processor, because the starches will combine to form an inedible glue-like substance. For potato mashing you'll need a potato masher and/or a potato ricer. A standing, or hand-held mixer is not necessary for baked goods. Strong arms and a whisk can be an effective substitute, especially if they're someone else's arms.

Toaster oven. Not actually necessary if you have a real oven, but they're faster and provide another space for cooking and warming foods. They do take up valuable counter space, but could be mounted under the cabinet. Either way, they contribute to the visual clutter in your kitchen. You decide whether or not they work for you. I don't actually own a toaster anymore. Toaster ovens are more versatile. I have a cheap one, and it gets replaced frequently.

Items for serving. These include consumption, and storage of food and beverages. Dishes and eating utensils, serving dishes and platters, vases and jars for flowers and herbs, pitchers for cream, syrups, sauces, and drinks, leftover dishes, plastic bags, lots of wine glasses, wine

CHAPTER 8 — THE PROPER KITCHEN   221

opener, and vacuum bottle corker. If you don't consume an entire bottle of wine at dinner, you can reseal it with a vacuum bottle corker, and then the wine is available during the cooking process the next day.

Dishtowels. I never cook without one tucked into a waistband, belt loop or pants pocket. They're important for grabbing hot pots (where *did* you hide that potholder?), wiping a rinsed knife when something needs to be chopped and added to the sauce in a hurry, and for quickly drying hands when the phone rings. Spreading clean dishtowels on your counter for the dishes to dry on makes an excellent substitute for an unsightly dishrack. When the dishes are dry, you can remove the towels. Your counter is then empty, thereby freeing up counter space for visual relaxation and other items, like kitchen art or bowls of ripe fruit. Buy at least a dozen dishtowels.

Placemats. (They dampen the noise of scraping plates, look attractive and catch many inconvenient spills) and cloth napkins. Get mats that can go in the washing machine, and wash them often. The laundry gets washed regularly anyway, so why not add a few more items to the many small loads you're already doing? You can save some room in the landfill for everyone else's paper napkins and excess non-recyclable food packaging. I was once a guest in a proper Bostonian home, and each person was given a different color napkin to use during their stay. I'm not sure whether it was implied that when the napkin was no longer clean, perhaps you had over-stayed as a guest.

On the Counter

Salt boxes. Keep them next to the stove with the oil and vinegars, so you can reach them. If they're across the kitchen from the foods you're preparing, you won't take the time to put them in your foods.

Bench flour. The small measuring cup of unused flour will sit on my counter for days before I suddenly need a bit of flour and am grateful that I didn't put it away when I last used it. Eventually, I'll find the perfect crock, and it'll become a permanent feature next to the salts, pepper grinders, oil cruets, and whatever else I'm currently playing with.

Moveable paper towels. They can go to where the spill is, though sometimes they don't return to the kitchen after the spill is cleaned up.

A fruit bowl. It's a beautiful and necessary piece of kitchen art. It must be filled with fresh fruit, washed and available to eat. It must be functional and allow the produce to breathe, or your foods will spoil too fast. Use the fruit. You won't use it in a timely manner if it's hidden away in your fridge. Mine is always filled with bananas and mangos, which go into

> *" Lontano dagli occhi, lontano dal cuore.*
> [Far from the eyes, far from the heart (and stomach).] "

Kristin's daily smoothie. They're always welcome as a dessert, or an after dessert item, and can frequently be put into a salad, sauce, salsa or marinade. Other fruits are added in season, and sometimes when entertaining I fill the fruit bowl instead of a vase.

The tray. Coffee and tea are always nicer when served from a pot that's placed on a tray, with the accoutrements (strainer, sugar bowl, lemon, cream or milk) along with it. We all like to lounge on vacation and be served at breakfast. Some of us even receive coffee or tea in bed. It's one of the *Dolce Vita* aspects of life that is so easy to do and makes the rest of your day seem more worthwhile.

Fresh bread, bell peppers, tomatoes, zucchini, fresh fruit to be consumed immediately, and recently picked or drying herbs. The meal plan should be handy, and a snack to keep the hungry ones from stealing all your prepped items out from under your meal. Most important, pour a glass of wine, because this is when the best part happens. Most of the wine in my glass gets into the food before I drink it. That's why the rest of the bottle is also on the counter or in the refrigerator.

Items to prep for the night's dinner. If they're out, and you have five minutes, do some preparation. Chop the onion, defrost the shrimp, and take out some carrots so you won't forget to grate them later, or grate them slightly ahead of time. Obviously, you must keep food safety and kitchen cleanliness in mind at all times and practice smart kitchen habits.

The meal plan or pencil and pad. For me it's a blank piece of paper. I start with the date, sometimes a proverb, or the day's theme. Themes can be *"Da Vinci e Da Verde,"* from the night of the movie premiere, and a lot of green foods that had inspired me one day, or "Jessica's last day," or "Grandma's 85th birthday." Sometimes the meal plan starts on the day the event is conceived. It can have little notes about what to buy, or what the featured foods will be. Sometimes I lay out an entire meal, but by the time it's cooked it turns out to be something entirely different. Sometimes I write it down just so I remember what I planned (the ability to remember being what it is later in life), and every time I have a spare moment, I look at each item and think to myself "What do I have to do next to move this course to its next stage? Which ones should I do next, what can wait until the last minute?" Just before I sit down to dinner, I look to see, "Did I get everything I wanted? Is something still in the oven or refrigerator? What's for dessert, and should it sit out while we're eating?"

Now that you've read through the menus in this book, take a good look at your kitchen. Is it organized to support you in cooking the meals you wish to prepare? Do you have the tools necessary to do the job? Are they easily accessible when you need to reach for them? Start by spending a day re-organizing your kitchen with the help of your ever-hungry family. Get rid of the things that are taking up space and are not functional. Perhaps you can reward yourself and take a shopping trip to the local kitchen supply store.

The Proper Pantry

CHAPTER 9

Before I discuss the things you should keep inside your kitchen, I'll discuss what can be useful to have outside of it. I'm not a gardener. I frequently tell people that the extent of my gardening is to occasionally buy an edible plant that I would like to cook with, and less frequently put it in the ground. Beyond that, my gardening consists of going outside with a pair of scissors and cutting something to go into a container—either a pot or a vase. I've never minded getting my hands into the cavity of any obsure poultry carcass, but dirt under the fingernails, never!

> *" Tanto va la gatta al lardo che ci lascia lo zampino.*
> (The cat keeps going to the larder; sooner or later she leaves footprints.) "

These are the things I have been successful at growing, probably because they grow by themselves.

Tomatoes. Lots of them, in a sunny place. Some years I have tomatoes growing all over, with very little effort on my part. Other years, only one or two plants will survive. This year, I lost four plants completely. Rumor has it that my dog may have contributed to their early demise.

On my very first trip to the nursery to get tomato plants, two senior women were discussing which varieties were their favorites. One of them said, "I always plant Early Girls and Better Boys."

If they're good enough for them, they're good enough for me. I look for them every year, and yes, they do seem to grow quite well. The most prolific ones I've had success with are the yellow pear and the small orange grape-like varieties. Both of these seem to be welcomed by my family members and most friends. I've managed to slip them into almost every meal during the summer, and even put bags of whole tomatoes in the freezer for later in the year, when the tomato onslaught diminishes. The frozen tomatoes defrost and get a bit soggy, but they make a perfect fresh-tasting sauce in the middle of winter.

Herbs. These include oregano, marjoram, sage, rosemary, parsley, mint, garlic chives, and lavender. Mine are finally on a drip system, and seem to be doing quite well in a sunny, south-facing bed. Occasionally, the gardener or my husband will cut them down to the ground. They seem to come back every spring. The mint likes to invade all the other zones, so be careful. If you don't use a lot of mint, you may not want to plant it. Then again, we recently learned how to make *mojitos*, so now too much mint is not such a bad thing.

Vegetables—none, except *cardone*, which is a weed that should only be utilized by starving Italian women. Occasionally, I get a gift from God through

my compost pile. Several tomatoes and an occasional squash have sprung up either at the base of the compost pile, or in various places in the yard where the compost has been used to start some other planting. This is always a welcome benefit for us non-gardening types.

Citrus. I'd like to say that I'm successful at growing citrus, but I found out the hard way if you submerge a lemon tree under water for too long a period of time, it will die. However, my darling husband Jim eventually planted another lemon tree. It rarely has any fruit on it, because I'm always pulling them off, even before they ripen. Lemon juice never, never, never comes in a lemon-shaped plastic bottle, or in any bottle (unless, perhaps you live in the Arctic). I suppose it can come in little ice cubes, but only if you squeezed the juice yourself.).

Macadamia nuts. No, I'm not recommending that you grow them, but if one happens to be in your front yard, or hangs over your front yard, for god

> *Per un grano di sale, si perde la minestra.*
> (For a grain of salt, one loses the soup.)

sakes, pick up the nuts, husk them, dry them, crack, and roast them, after, of course, eating many of them raw. You'll understand why they're so expensive when you have to process them yourself. Plus, as an added bonus, see number 15 following for making a marriage of two very fine ingredients.

I admire all those people who can actually grow things. I, myself, could never take the time away from the kitchen to actually garden.

We have recently planted fruit trees. The menus of the next few years will change, to incorporate more fruit, and will show up in a subsequent book or culinary rant. Some day, when Jim retires, he'll tend the tomatoes. It's every Italian grandfather's destiny. And the cardoons, of course.

Here's what I think you need to keep stocked in your kitchen at all times.

1

Salt, several kinds and grinds, and a grinder too, if you want one. Get salt boxes, or easily accessible jars or bowls. Play with them. A coarsely ground salt sprinkled over the top of any dish just before it's brought to the table adds a whole new textural component to the dish.

2

Pepper, whole black, as a minimum, with the best grinder you can get. I prefer metal gears in that grinder, though ceramic is supposedly okay. Plastic will break, some day. Play with green, white, red, and mixed pepper. White is essential for any white sauces or cheese sauces. It can also substitute for missing jalapenos when making salsa. Green pepper is milder. I tend to use it for fish.

3

Sugar, pick any kind, except for corn syrup. Try experimenting with the subtle differences between brown, turbinado, and raw sugar. Try honey (local of course, bought from someone who actually has a relationship with bees).

4

Flour, I don't bake much, so a good multi-purpose, a whole wheat, a granular flour for gravies, and a little bit of rye, go a long way for me. I've played with the double zero and specialty pizza flours, but in my experience, it's the oven, not the flour, that makes the biggest difference in pizza.

5

Olive oil, butter, and other oils, like canola and peanut, or as Mario Batali calls them, the lipids of choice. Olive oil is the best. You need one to cook with and one to anoint with. I use canola and peanut if I'm making non-Italian foods or pancakes, or anything which doesn't need the olive flavor. In our house, even the pancakes will get olive oil, sometimes. As you begin to experiment more, bring in specialty flavors like oils infused with citrus or truffles, although a lemon or an orange, or better yet, a whole truffle, can be much more fun to experiment with. Sesame and toasted sesame are great for adding an Asian touch. I keep large pieces of fat cut from meats in the freezer for occasional rendering. Bacon grease is always saved for adding bits of flavor. Yes, pork fat rules, and duck or goose fat is prized, though not used too often.

6

Vinegar, as we make every salad dressing from scratch, every night. When the right ingredients are available, it's easy and tastes a whole lot better. (If you ever read the back of a salad dressing bottle, you'll find lots of strange-sounding ingredients that go way beyond oil, vinegar, and herbs. Why pay extra to put that junk into your body?) Again, specialty vinegars like *aceto balsamico* (only the real stuff), champagne, and sherry can spark up many salads and sauces. Definitely have red and white wine vinegar on hand at all times. My favorite is seasoned rice vinegar. It's all you need for a salad dressing, besides extra virgin olive oil, black pepper, and a handful of chopped herbs.

7

Italian herb and *Herbes de Provence* are essential blends, and can be used in almost everything you cook. (Chinese five spice and curry blends can also take any stew and give it a completely new twist.) Fresh herbs are always better, but sometimes it does rain…. Bay leaves and cayenne (and/or chili flakes so you can add heat if you need it), and other spices, depending on the flavors you prefer.

8

Beans, rice, and grains like barley for soups and emergency natural disasters. Assume in any disaster that you can hydrate them and cook them over an open fire, if necessary, or smash them and eat them dry if your survival depends on it. Anyway, all those great soups you'll be preparing

once you start making your own stocks and broths will need something in them. Old fashioned dry ingredients in glass jars make your pantry more interesting and hopefully more inspirational. I'm a particular fan of *polenta*, which lends itself to many of the braised foods I like to cook and eat. *Polenta* takes a bit of time. Couscous is the best instant starch I've come across. Arborio rice for *risotto*, sushi rice if you prepare Asian foods, and long grain rice, are basic staples. I like short grain brown rice and wild rice on occasion. They're not the most popular in my household, though they may be in yours.

9

Potatoes and onions. The three basics, Idaho potatoes, yellow and red onions. Any of the others, as you wish, remembering that the price goes up with the rarity and perceived trendiness. Leeks and scallions are especially nice fresh varieties in the onion category.

10

Garlic, fresh. There are no substitutes. None. In the spring, you may be able to find fresh garlic with the tops still attached. They have a milder flavor, are delicious, and you can use the tops as well.

11

Canned tomatoes, whole, crushed, chopped, paste or sauce. It doesn't need basil, onion or garlic already added. Add them yourself, lazybones. A tube of super-concentrated tomato paste is an excellent way to add flavor and acid

to any sauce. It, along with a tube of anchovy paste, is allowed, though I've had excellent results when experimenting with the salted whole anchovies. Coconut milk, green and red enchilada sauce (for those non-Italian main dishes) are the only other canned items that should be allowed.

12

Bread crumbs, made from all the stale loaves of fresh bread you will now be buying every few days. Keep the loaves in the paper on the counter. They will go stale, and if you live in a dry environment, they should not get moldy. When they're really dried out, or when your housekeeper/spouse/significant other kitchen cleaning person is going to clean the kitchen and threatens to throw them away (remember, in a perfect world the cook should never have to do the dishes), put them in a food processor, or put them in a plastic bag and smash the hell out of them. Save them in an airtight container, preferably glass, so you'll remember you have them and use them. Stale bread can also be added to soups, made into bread puddings (Kate?), or, if sliced before they become completely hard, seasoned, toasted, and oiled as *crostini* or croutons. (I once heard that the reason the French despised the Americans was because we bought our croutons. Since then I don't.)

13

Coffee, whole bean, caffeinated, and decaffeinated. A grinder is one of the essential kitchen tools, especially because you can use it for spices, nuts, and seeds. It's not essential that it be electric. It's your call on whether you prefer noise or convenience. I abhor noise, but I do like some

conveniences. Oh, yes, and get rid of your drip coffee maker. It uses coarse grinds, thereby requiring you to spend more money on coffee than you really need to. Since visiting Italy, we prefer the taste of espresso and will use an espresso machine, *moka*, or stovetop espresso pot. Because you use a finer grind of coffee for these types of makers, you use less coffee on a monthly basis and actually save money in the long run. Buy good coffee; don't get it pre-ground in a can. Know your coffee roaster. French presses also make excellent coffee and allow you to control the strength, though they require a slightly coarser grind.

14

Tea, lots of varieties for every guest and every whim. Take time out to make it a pot at a time. It's part of the ritual, and the time it takes to brew is a good time to spend talking with the friend, relative, or guest who is visiting you.

15

Nuts, because you never know when you have to make something in an emergency, and as toppings or ingredients for a basil *pesto*, they're unbeatable. Use them regularly, or they may become rancid.

16

There are a lot of other things that go into the average pantry, including popcorn. The actual kernels are the cheapest, and that's what pots are for anyway. Popping popcorn in a good olive oil is not really that difficult, and think of all the partially hydrogenated god-knows-what you'll not be ingesting. Oatmeal, whole grain cereals, and granola are all cheaper and better for you than most store-bought cereals. No, I don't make my own granola, but I've thought about it.

17

Chocolate! It must be in your pantry at all times. Not candy bars—solid pieces of high quality dark chocolate are the healthiest. Anything less just has milk, sugar and/or cream added, or worse. You should keep bars for having a *dolce* at the end of a meal, or with the after-dinner wine or tea. It can be made into any other dessert you want, or grated on top of ice cream, cappuccino or fruit. Powdered cocoa is okay if you bake, and I hear cocoa nibs are a sin unto themselves. They're definitely on my "To Play With" list. Now remember, don't eat all the chocolate in one sitting. When you have the very best, you only need a little bit.

18

Raisins, currants and/or cranberries, or other dried fruits. You can put them into a salad, eat them plain, or use them to whip up a quick breakfast bread when you hear, "Hey, mom, I need to bring something to school for the such-and-such pot luck or fundraiser…." They can also be added to poultry stuffing or braised meats.

19

Cornmeal, aka *polenta*. In our house cornmeal is an essential ingredient to pancakes. Yes we do use a mix for pancakes, only because my family insists. Since I only eat the pancakes and don't have to cook them, I try not to argue about it. Just once, I wish they'd make wheat germ or blueberry pancakes, but no! It's not my area. *Polenta*, on the other hand, is my area. I love it. I love making it. Yes, it takes a long time. My experience is that on a cold winter night, the hungry people are willing to gather in the kitchen to watch and talk with the *polenta* stirrer, me. It's a good thing when there are people in your kitchen. The Italian cousins sent me a *polenta* pot one year, so now there's even more of a ritual for the preparation of this dish. The pot is proudly displayed in the kitchen, and people know that when this pot shows up on the stove, some delicious stew is bound to be served shortly.

Fill your pantry. Determine which things you want to store or use on a regular basis, and always keep them on hand. Watch for them in the stores where you shop. When they go on sale, buy a bunch. Buy as much as you can afford to store and are willing to use. Use them in a timely manner, because even dried, canned, and bulk items will go bad eventually.

"*Gallina vecchia fa buon brodo.* (An old hen makes a good soup.)"

Your Refrigerator

CHAPTER 10

Before I discuss the things you should keep inside your refrigerator, I'll discuss what can be useful to have outside of it. The things you should keep outside your refrigerator are probably most of the things you're currently keeping inside of your refrigerator. The fresh produce you bring home from the farmer's markets should be used as your kitchen art and meal inspiration. Since these are the foods you are purchasing every couple of days and are consuming quickly, perhaps there is no need to refrigerate them at all.

You know the old adage, "Out of sight, out of mind?" It applies to your groceries, too. If you leave something in the dark corners of your refrigerator, bad things can happen. Keep them in sight on your counter and use them. Use them fast, or bad things can develop there, too. Currently, I have tomatoes on my counter, among other things. You should never put them in the fridge. Most fresh produce will welcome a chance to ripen to its peak of freshness. When it's in full view, you can see the changes and will know when something is ready to be used. Then use it. Plan your meals around what you have on hand that's at its peak. You'll begin to notice how much better foods taste when used properly. A tomato from the refrigerator that never had a chance to ripen will not taste good. Try a comparison and see for yourself.

The other things on my counter today are peaches, plums, bananas, mangos, limes, and fresh sage. All these will need to be eaten in the next two days. Isn't that what you want your family to be doing with your fresh produce items? Sometimes, I'll come home and the fruit will be gone before I can get it to the table or into the lunches. So, I buy more. This goes for vegetables, too. Kate once ate an entire bunch of asparagus, raw, before I could add them to that night's dinner. She got her vitamins that day.

Use your refrigerator for items needing longer-term storage.

Eggs and cheese. I always keep one to two dozen eggs, bought fresh each Friday at my local farmers' market. Taking the time on a weekend morning to make eggs together as a family tends to make the weekend breakfasts into a brunch. Once you actually sit down to eat a morning meal (in our family, it's the mid-morning or second breakfast) you can take your time eating and conversing. Sure, the extra dishes are a pain, but they're well worth the trouble for spending quality time at the table with family. And of course, if you're lucky to have friends or relatives sharing your morning meal, it's even more special. Aside from the Friday evening meal, I think the Saturday or Sunday morning impromptu brunch is the next best time of the week for me. Even without guests, I'm frequently still in my pajamas at 11:00 AM on the weekends.

But, back to eggs and cheese. These two items go so well together that I'll talk about them in one paragraph. I like to make frittatas or *fritate*. We all like eggs over easy, and omelettes find their way into our kitchen frequently. Even the lowly scrambled egg can be encouraged to greatness when properly cooked and dressed with a little crumbled cheese on top or within. Cheese and eggs can be utilized for many an impromptu meal or snack by being served on toast, as French toast, as grilled cheese, instant *pizzette* with a little extra sauce, as *crostini*, egg salad, cheese sauce on top of leftovers, cheese and crackers, and of course cheese and bread with some salami or other small *antipasto* item. Eggs can be dropped into a clear broth for egg drop soup, and used to add protein to a shake or smoothie. We forget, but hardboiled eggs used to be a frequent lunch bag item. Although I usually don't, cheese and eggs can be crumbled onto a salad, and even on top of leftover pasta or potatoes. Cheese and eggs are fattening, you say? Well, don't eat the whole dozen or the whole block at one time. You are buying your cheese in blocks, aren't you? If you are unable to crumble or slice or shred your own cheese, you probably should stay out of the kitchen altogether. The more you allow others to process and handle your food for you, the more money you waste doing things that are pretty easy and fast to do anyway, and the more you risk introducing bacteria into your food. There are worse places to be than spending time in your kitchen, like sitting in traffic to go to the fast food places so that you can bring cold, unhealthy food into your kitchen to feed your family. Okay, yes, I'm ranting, so let's move on to pork products….

Prosciutto, pork products, and bacon drippings. Prosciutto is one of the finest pork products you can keep on hand. It doesn't keep forever, and yet in a way it does. Freshly sliced prosciutto, either alone or with a slice of melon or some figs, can be an orgasmic eating experience all to itself. Never cut off the fatty part—it's where much of the flavor is. Again, a little bit is not going to kill you. After a few days of being in the fridge, it starts to absorb moisture and is no longer in its prime. So, if you don't serve it immediately, don't throw it away. Use it to infuse flavor into other foods. Chop or shred the slices of prosciutto, and use them as starts for egg dishes, with vegetables, and in hot salad dressings, pasta sauces, or in soups. A little bit goes a long way, so don't try to overpower your other flavors. Use the pork products to enhance the flavor. I never throw away bacon drippings, and have been known to render fats trimmed from meats into a small container, kept in the fridge, for starting the onions sautéing. Yes, olive oil is lower in unsaturated fats, etc., and I am not recommending getting rid of it for cooking in lard, but every now and then you'll eat somewhere where the flavor is unmistakably delicious. It could be that some of old Bessie or Arnold Ziffle found her/his way into the pot. Any of the many *salumi*, ham, and *pancetta* products available are equally useful and delicious. Try them all and notice the subtle differences in your standard meal items.

Lettuce, more than one variety, in head form whenever possible. It's very easy to buy pre-prepared lettuce mixes, pre-washed, dried and put into a bag for you. Frequently there is a preservative added to enhance freshness. Enhanced freshness is an oxymoron. It's either fresh, or it isn't. If you buy your lettuce from the farmer, ask him when it came out of the ground.

How long do you think it takes for the lettuce in your bag to be driven to the washing, bagging and preserving place before it's shipped to the market, and eventually placed in the refrigerated bin? Ever notice the farmer's truck? It's usually not refrigerated. Buy what you'll need for the next couple of days, and then buy it again. Lettuce, when wilted, can only be used in stock or compost.

Here's an Italian lettuce story. Several years ago, while vacationing in Sicily, I went to the *frutti-vendolo* and purchased two heads of lettuce, one for that night's dinner and one for the next night's dinner. The first night's salad was delicious; we thought to ourselves, "Even the lettuce tastes better in Italy!"

When I took the second head of lettuce out of the refrigerator the second evening, it was completely wilted, mushy, and slimy. I couldn't believe it! How could a perfectly beautiful head of lettuce go so bad, so fast while in a refrigerator? It took me several days to find out. Yes, the lettuce for the first night was as fresh as it could be. I had seen the trucks carrying the produce to market on the roads every day. So what was the story? Well, the story was exactly that. I had seen the trucks carrying the produce to market every day. Every day, an open air pickup truck, no camper shell, no refrigeration, not even a cardboard box top to protect the freshly picked produce from the glaring Italian sun! Their produce was picked at its peak of freshness and meant to be eaten that day. It was not meant to be held at all. This is an almost foreign concept to the American cook. With all our modern conveniences, we're missing the original concept, which is to eat as close to the field or butcher as possible. The farther we get from the source, the more we sacrifice in quality, the more we pay for transportation, the more we pay for non-essential additives and packaging, and the more energy we consume holding these foods in refrigeration. Is your supermarket iceberg lettuce wrapped in plastic really cheaper than your organic, freshly picked head of lettuce that you take home in your canvas bag, wash in your own sink and eat that night?

Milk, cream, butter. Last time I looked, we are not related to cows, sheep, goats, and water buffaloes. Most of us are no longer nursing, so our consumption of milk does not need to be in large quantities. Yes, all these foods contain fat. I prefer to use whole milk, real cream, and unsalted butter. Use in moderation, and/or as the finishing touches to your pan sauces and soups. A little goes a long way. If I die as a result of a massive coronary some day, you can say, "I told her so. I knew she should have been using non-fat milk…." Until my doctor tells me my life is in serious danger, I'll keep using real, unadulterated fats.

Yogurt. I keep plain whole milk yogurt in my fridge at all times. It's very versatile, and can be used to enhance fresh fruit, salad dressings, potatoes, and sauces. Most of our yogurt gets put into a daily smoothie. I also like it on top of granola, in pancake batter, and with horseradish alongside rich steaks or beef. It can be used in place of sour cream, and, if strained, can be used as a base for dips. I make my own. Thank you, Mirielle.

Pure maple syrup. Grade B dark amber is considered to be the best variety of maple syrup I've come across. If it doesn't say pure maple syrup, you're probably buying corn syrup with brown coloring and imitation maple flavoring. Why save a few cents to put additives into your body? Again, eat closest to the tree, the maple tree, that is!

Sauce. Usually red, sometimes *béchamel*, frequently gravy. Never throw away more than a tablespoon. Sometimes your sauce from one night is perfectly completed with the leftover soup or sauce from an earlier meal.

Carrots and celery. Always better fresh, but they'll keep a long time in the fridge. For me, I want them always on hand to be added to the stockpot, or for a last minute *marinara* sauce. Both, coupled with an onion and a small piece of meat or fish can make an instant stir-fry or be simmered longer for a stew. Also, either can be cleaned and sliced for a healthy snack or *crudité*. If I take the trouble to peel and pre-slice, and put into a bowl of water in the fridge, they're the first thing that gets eaten by my hungry fridge foraging family. I have seen Kate with a carrot in her mouth and an armload of eggs, cheese, and bacon walking toward the stove to prepare her post-volleyball practice, pre-dinner snack.

Stocks and soups. They don't come out of cans, ever. They come from the bones and carcasses that are the natural by-products of a holistic kitchen. It's hard to understand the true miracle of soups without procuring the right sorts of ingredients, as discussed throughout this book. Soups occur naturally when you're taking stock (pun intended) of your items on hand in preparation for the next shopping experience. Soups begin to happen when you look in your fridge and say, "Uh-oh, what am I going to do with that pot of chicken broth I made out of last night's roast chicken bones? Oh, look, those zucchini had better get eaten soon. Thank god, I still have some onion, carrots, and celery left. I'll just use these up and buy fresh ones at tomorrow's farmers' market. Oh, here's some cream from an earlier fettuccine alfredo. I might as well throw it into the pot, too."

Citrus. Unless you have a tree, citrus keeps a long time in the fridge. Take out one or two on a daily basis and either juice them, eat them, or cook with them. You'll be healthier if you get your sugars from natural products inside of refined processed products. An orange and a small piece of chocolate after lunch will go a long way towards satisfying your hunger and curbing your appetite, thereby preventing binge eating later that day before dinner.

Sandwich meats. The exception to leftover meats, or for making lunches that can't be microwaved the next day. By sandwich meats, I mean really good roast beef, ham, turkey, or chicken that was cut from a larger piece of meat by a butcher or deli person recently. If it's processed to last more than a day or two, leave it at the store. Remember when you bought meat at a deli and the butcher actually sliced it in front of you and put pieces of waxed paper between each slice? This will usually happen when you order prosciutto or other specialty meats. It will always be better than getting it grabbed from a bin....

The Functional Freezer

CHAPTER II

The freezer is not designed to hold all the unhealthy pre-prepared foods you bought from the freezer section of your local grocery store, the foods that you thought you couldn't make yourself, or the last minute microwavable items you plan to feed yourself or your family while you're off paying someone to tell you how to live your life. If you want to live the good life, you have to recognize that living *La Dolce Vita* centers on a lifestyle that includes simply prepared, exquisite foods you're capable of making yourself, if you give yourself the time and set up your habits and kitchen to achieve success.

The Italian food culture and the food culture of many other parts of the world have their roots in poverty cooking. They made the best meals they could with the ingredients that were available. When meat was available, it didn't come all nicely wrapped in a Styrofoam package. Chicken breasts certainly did not come in fives, and certainly started out having bones in them, usually with the rest of the chicken still attached. We in the U.S have forgotten our food roots. We live in the land of plenty, or so we think. A common response to people who hear about my style of cooking is, "Who has the time to cook?" However, when asked, "What's the one thing people want most in their lives?" the answer is frequently, "More leisure time, and more time to spend with my family."

Before the American mass exodus from the kitchen, these things just happened. People spent more time in their kitchens and at home, because after all, that's where the hearth is.

"What's a hearth?" you ask. The hearth is 1. The brick, stone, or tiled floor of a fireplace, often extending into the room, and, 2. (a) The fireside as the center of family life; (b) the home; the family circle.

Over the years, fireplaces disappeared from kitchens. Luckily, with family rooms and wood-burning pizza ovens, the physical hearth is returning. Now we just have to bring the family circle back into the kitchen.

Getting back to the question of, "Why should I cook like this? I have plenty of money to pay my butcher

to trim the bones off my chicken, and for god's sake don't show me any chicken feet!" You should do it because there needs to be recognition of where our food comes from and at what cost. Vegans will tell you that someone has to kill something in order for you to eat it. I say if you are going to kill something, recognize that it gave its life for you so you could eat it, and eat all the parts. Perhaps fewer beings will have to die to satisfy our hunger.

I haven't yet bought an entire side of beef and learned to use all of the parts, but I'd like to. A cow is not made up of only filet mignon. I believe that part of our American obesity problem is that we tend to forget about eating the leaner, less popular parts of our animals. If we ate more meals from a whole side of beef, we would get a larger variety of foods, some succulent and prized, others leaner, making a balance that could only be beneficial, especially to the animals involved. So, what does this have to do with the functional freezer?

Everything.

Because, as we reintroduce bigger pieces of meats, poultry, and fish to our diets, there will be a need to preserve them, and perhaps a need to hold the remaining parts until we're ready to consume them. Remember hearing of root cellars? I'll bet they held more things than roots!

These are the types of things I keep in my freezer. And yes, there are a few instant things for surprise guests, or surprise illnesses.

Bones. Lots of them! All soups start from bones, even if they're from vegetables. Yes, you can buy bones from your butcher, and yes, you can buy broth from your local supermarket. The former requires you to pay someone to get what you already paid them to take away from the food you bought the first time. Plus, it now has to be packaged which produces waste. The cans, or thank god, recyclable boxes of broth, are nifty, but are you going to trust a great big food processing facility to make sure only the bones and no food-borne illnesses are going into your soup? Not me. I will personally say that I knew every item that went into the soup and even the person who last chewed on the bone. Disgusting? Compared to food processing plants, I don't think so. Soup bones are boiled, so why not take them off the plate? Not off the floor, but certainly off the plate. My standard response to criticism on soup bones is that in life, like in the Donner party, there are eaters and eat-ees. If you die first, and I've got water and a match, I will eat you. After, of course, we've exhausted every other possible thing to eat in my freezer and root cellar. You can be doing something else for hours while a stock simmers. It will only take you minutes to strain and discard the vegetables and bones. With the right pot and a few kitchen tools, you can be creating the foundation for many delicious meals.

Carcasses. When I cook a chicken, it's either roasted whole or trimmed into parts. I like to use the wings, thighs, and legs with the bones in them and slice the breasts off the carcass. People do like boneless breasts, and this method leaves the carcass intact to be easily frozen for a future soup. A large chicken carcass or two small ones can fill one zipper bag. These bagged carcasses become instant starter packages on a cloudy or rainy day when soup-making is in the air. Yes, I'm one of those people who will take home a turkey carcass on Thanksgiving. One year my family gave me infinite grief for taking my aunt's turkey carcass back home to my brother's house. We were staying at his centrally-located and available condo while he was on vacation. They all thought I was crazy—but two hours later, after simmering that carcass with an old onion and, luckily, some carrots and celery that were abandoned in his vegetable drawer, a soup emerged. After two hours of smelling this simmering soup, everyone suddenly wanted a bowl, though they'd stuffed themselves on the real meal earlier that evening. And yes, we spent quality time together and didn't have the need for a late-night pizza order. Everyone remembers that evening. They would never have remembered takeout pizza.

Large pieces of meat. I usually buy two to four nights worth of meat at one shopping. Many times it's one for tonight, one for tomorrow and two for the freezer to be taken out on nights three and four. We prefer to not eat meat that's been sitting around at home, refrigerated. Frequently, meats three and four get used at another time, because chances are I'll be at the market again buying something fresh. These large pieces of meat get defrosted and used on those days where I don't spend all day in the kitchen. Slow roasting or braising a big piece of meat takes very little preparation time and can be very nicely presented for guests. These items in my freezer would be a whole prime rib, preferably three to four ribs, several whole chickens, and pork tenderloins (cut into three sections and then frozen), or a whole top sirloin (also cut into steaks for meals of four to six persons). I also keep racks of ribs—not pre-marinated, and packages of short ribs, both of which can be easily and tastily prepared in less time than you can say "take-out." Recognize that the time you take to prepare a food item, and the time it takes to cook, are not the same. What matters is the time you spend on it, not the time it spends slow cooking itself in your oven.

Frozen turkeys. Most markets give out frozen turkeys at Thanksgiving. They are usually not the ones I cook for Thanksgiving dinner. I prefer a large, free range, fresh variety, though yes sometimes you can't taste the difference. Just because you can't taste it doesn't mean they're not filled with additives that you don't want to ingest. Fresh turkeys are more expensive, an expense I'll gladly pay to support the organic turkey farming community. And yes, I'll also take the free turkey, because, after all, it's free. The second turkey gets cooked and eaten; although with a little bit of added guilt. Oh yes, before I forget, leftover turkey makes excellent enchiladas, if you use green enchilada sauce or *tomatillos*. If you don't believe me, ask anyone who has ever been on a skiing trip with me. They didn't believe it until I dragged a frozen turkey along on a trip. The turkey cooked itself while we were skiing, provided sandwiches for the next days' lunches, provided enchiladas for a later dinner, and eventually wound up in a soup.

Vegetable parts. (Waiting to be married with the above, in the stockpot of marital bliss.) At this moment I know that there are asparagus bottoms and portobello mushroom stems because I just put them in the freezer. These items get thrown away by most home cooks, but they all participate in the miracle of a good stock or broth. How could I possibly fit all those boxes of frozen pizza in my freezer, when there are so many components clamoring for shelf space?

Fast hors d'oeuvres. Pot stickers, tacquitos, bags of shrimp, seafood mixes for an instant *cioppino*, given that the other ingredients are floating around.

Italian sausage. I keep it by the box because it's easy to store, and coupled with a plate of spaghetti, some sauce, and a salad, it becomes its own instant feast.

Bacon, bits of leftover ham, *pancetta*. They all freeze well and can be added as flavorings to many things. On top of pasta with the local fresh vegetable of the day, they can become a main dish. Also perfect for instant breakfasts, either alongside or inside eggs or a *frittata*.

Frozen *ravioli*. It has to be a good one, usually chicken or mushroom. I find them to be most versatile. If you take the time to make them yourself, always put some in the freezer. Your family will eat as many as you make, so if they eat a half batch without knowing the other half has already been squirreled away, they're none the wiser. *Ravioli* are easily defrosted and sauced, and make an excellent *contorno*, or side dish.

Frozen fruit. Leftover from your orchard, or from the half flat or triple box of strawberries you bought at the farmer's market and didn't finish. Freeze berries whole and put them in a plastic bag, or buy a frozen bag of mixed berries so you can top ice cream or a cake, or make a fruit sauce. I freeze whole, skinned bananas when they get overripe, for future banana bread and smoothies.

Plain cheesecake or pound cake. Get small ones; they make a great instant dessert under fruit or ice cream. Top with those nuts or chocolate you'll always have on hand. It's great to drizzle them with a liqueur.

Ice cream. I buy Ben and Jerry's, (my family's favorite single-serve size) by the dozens when they're on sale. Most people will not refuse a small spoon of ice cream with some fresh berries after a meal. It's good to keep a large container of a really good vanilla ice cream. Kate made her own ice cream cake one day, with ice cream, small pieces of leftover chocolate cake, strawberries, and some chocolate *ganache* that I'd frozen after an earlier party. Everyone thought it was delicious, and again, it was leftovers!

Limeade. At least one, for that evening when the sun is setting, it's warm on the patio, and it's margarita time. Add a little lime juice, some *Triple Sec* and tequila, and put on a Carlos Santana CD....

The freezer message here is simple. Don't fill it with pre-prepared store-bought meals. Fill it with the ingredients you need to make your own delicious meals. You won't need to go to the gym after you start lugging those frozen turkeys around.

Closing

CHAPTER 12

It will be interesting to see if your life changes after reading this book. Perhaps your next shopping trip will involve purchasing larger pieces of meat with bones in them, or a new organic item that wasn't organic the last time you procured it. Maybe you're thinking about starting a soup? I welcome your thoughts. I hope you begin to live your life as if every day is a part of *La Tua Dolce Vita*, and that you begin to express time in food bytes.

Every thought and action I have experienced has led up to the writing of this book. Before the day I was driving in my car and the flash of inspiration hit me (that I could write about what I knew best in my own life and its transformations from a culinary standpoint, and that I could share it on paper), I would not have believed it possible. It has been an adventure ever since.

So what's next for me? Many more *Venerdì*, I hope. I'm sure I will have lots to say. I am rarely at a loss for words. Perhaps you would like to hear about some of our Saturday evening dinners?

The files are already building for *Saturday Evening*. For inspiration, I will continue to live *La Dolce Vita* in my own humble way, one meal at a time.

And, if by chance, I realize my dream to kiss Brad Pitt, Johnny Depp, or Bono while holding a glass of good wine in my hand, somewhere along the European or American Riviera, (or in the Caribbean, Johnny), that would be nice...

(Don't worry, Jim, you will always be at my side sharing *Ma Dolce Vita*).

Oh yes, and chocolate, for I am my mother's daughter, after all.

Acknowledgments

There are certain people in my life who have altered it and showed me the trailheads to new paths.

First and foremost, I must credit Kristin Nicole Carbone. If she had not incurred her serious brain injury, thereby ripping me from the very routine life I had envisioned for myself, I would not have started to question my existence and certainly wouldn't have had any time to think about *La Dolce Vita*, let alone actually try to live it. Her constant care requirements forced me to rethink my cooking style; and the ten years we spent exploring culinary avenues in our kitchen provide the groundwork for much of the content of this book.

I must also thank Jim Carbone, Kate Carbone, Anthony Carbone, and Rudy Medrano. You were there every Friday evening expecting some new culinary wonder, critiquing the least imperfection in my latest experiment, and hungrily eating it anyway. I would never have had the impetus to pull together this book without our own Friday evenings.

I would like to thank my mother, who provided me with my early education in cooking, and my father, who always came home for dinner. If they hadn't been hardworking parents who sacrificed for my private education, I would never have had to start preparing dinner while they were at work. I would like to thank Rick who was the first one to say "Let's add something to this to see if we can make it taste better." I would like to thank Jeff and Rick for rolling up my first box-prepared brownies and bouncing them across the table at me. If it hadn't been for this incident and the resurrection of the botched angel food cake from the trash can, I might never have switched from baking to the more forgiving cooking of main dishes in large pots.

Photographs by Mike Verbois, Michele Carbone, John Houchin (pages 50, 85, 128, 169, 170, 226, 232, 233, 242, 247, 248), and Joe Standart (page 17)

I would like to thank Susan Owens, Nicholas Sluchevsky, and Vern Binion for their early introductions into the kitchen as a social scene. Susan taught me that fresh vegetables and fish were excellent things to eat and that dishes needed to be washed. Nick taught me that no matter what your fortunes were, you still need to eat the very best foods, from the very best dishes, with the very best company, and with the very best wine (all within the realm of your financial situation). Vern taught me that no matter what time you arrived to a dinner party, you may still be required to cook. Some hosts enjoy the preparation time in the kitchen. These times can be even more fun than enjoying the meal itself.

I would like to thank my *Cugine italiane*, Letizia, Martha, Francesca, and Manuela who invited me into their kitchens and showed me how to prepare their traditional specialties.

I would like to thank Laura Salvi Morrison and *Le Italianucce* for helping me to realize that I was already living *La Dolce Vita* and that a great dish of pasta or a pizza just out of the oven was the perfect thing for a Wednesday lunch.

I would like to thank Merrily Peebles, who had the vision to see a book among my menu outlines and the stamina to help me create it.

I would like to thank my grandfather, Joseph Bressler, for passing down his butcher's genes to me. If it's a piece of meat, I can and will cook it.

I would like to thank the numerous suppliers of excellent produce, including Kanaloa Seafood Market, Montecito Village Grocery, Shalhoob Meat Company, Lazy Acres Market, the Cronshaw family, and Margerum Wine Company. *Il Piatto Rosso* and many of the Italian ceramics can be found at the Italian Pottery Outlet, www.italianpottery.com. Image courtesy of Viking Range Corporation; Joe Standart, photographer. Cover photo location courtesy of the Franz family.

I would like to thank Walter L. Kleine, Harry Sims, and Media 27, who understood my vision of *La Dolce Vita* and made it into the beautiful reality that I now can share with others.

Grazie in existere...

Word and Phrase Glossary

alle otto in punto ~ At eight on the nose 108

Anaheim chiles ~ Long pointed light green pepper frequently used in Mexican cuisine 70, 95

Aperitivo, Aperitivi ~ Aperitif before dinner cocktail, cocktails 39, 40, 41, 51, 131, 133, 137, 166, 187, 188

Appunti ~ Notes 54, 57, 58, 61, 63, 69, 73, 77, 80, 82, 89, 95, 99, 102, 106, 109, 112, 116, 119, 123, 131, 137, 140, 143, 147, 150, 156, 159, 163, 166, 173, 176, 181, 185, 188, 192, 195, 199, 202, 206

Assaggino, Assaggini ~ Small taste or first course of small tastings 41, 42

Béchamelle ~ Béchamel; white sauce consisting of flour, butter salt and milk 138, 214

Birra ~ Beer 88, 146, 184, 194, 202

Caffè ~ Coffee 46, 97, 101

Campari ~ A bitter Italian liqueur 40, 52, 56, 57, 72, 73, 205, 206

Campari Negronita ~ A variation of the Negroni, which is mixed with gin, Campari and sweet vermouth, the Negronita contains Campari with soda, vodka and triple sec served over ice. 72, 73

Cardone, Cardoons ~ Cardoon (Cynara cardunculus), is a member of the thistle family and is also known as artichoke thistle, cardoni or cardi 92, 134–138, 227, 228

Carrota Bruta ~ Ugly carrot 53

Contorno ~ Vegetable or side dish 35, 39, 41, 43, 45, 151, 246

Crostini ~ Small crusts or croutons 48, 53, 56, 60, 75, 97, 108, 109, 111, 112, 115, 146, 159, 168, 176, 190, 232, 237

Crudité ~ An appetizer usually cut into bite-sized pieces of vegetable(s) and served with a dipping sauce 240

Cucina ~ Kitchen, cooking or cuisine 8, 150, 220

Digestivo ~ An alcoholic drink usually served after a meal 39, 46, 122, 184

Dolce, dolci ~ Sweet, sweets 14, 39, 45, 58, 60, 68, 93, 110, 139

Dov'è la strada per andare alla piazza del Duomo? ~ Where is the street for going to the cathedral square? 24

Espresso ~ Strong coffee that is brewed or expressed while under pressure 22, 46, 93, 121, 183, 233

Farro ~ A barley like grain, emmer 194, 197

Fava ~ A broad bean similar to a lima bean but darker green or brown in color 146–149

Fettuccine Alfredo ~ A pasta dish usually made with fettuccine pasta with a cream or egg sauce 179, 182, 240

I Film: Il Padrino, Il Notte Grande o un film Italiano classico come La Strada, Cinema Paradiso, Mediterraneo, La Dolce Vita, o La Meglio Gioventù ~ Films: *The Godfather, Big Night* or a classic Italian film such as *La Strada, Cinema Paradiso* or *Mediterraneo, La Dolce Vita,* or *The Best of Youth* 104

Foodie friends ~ Friends who are also into the pursuit of happiness through food 16

Formaggio, formaggi ~ Cheese, cheeses 36, 45, 56, 63, 68, 72, 76, 93, 105, 120, 130, 142, 166, 179

Frittata or frittate ~ A form of omelet 156, 237, 246

Frutta ~ Fruit 45, 105, 106, 120, 153, 175

Frutti-vendolo ~ A merchant who sells fruit and vegetables 238

Galette ~ A type of cake or pie frequently filled with fruit, and usually without a top crust. 104

Gorgonzola ~ A blue cheese from Italy 57, 68, 69, 72, 73, 97, 99, 108, 109, 116, 145, 164, 167, 181, 205, 206

Herbes de Provence ~ A herbal mix from Provence, France usually consisting of lavender, thyme, basil and other herbs 188, 230

Il Piatto Rosso ~ The Red Plate, used for presenting accompaniments to a green salad 43, 53, 60, 61, 72, 75, 76, 79, 93, 108, 115, 139, 166, 175, 179, 194, 205, 251

Insalata Verde ~ A green salad 53, 58, 60, 72, 79, 102, 105, 134, 166, 194, 198, 205

Insalatina Verde ~ A small green salad 42

L'autunno ~ Autumn 49–51

L'estate ~ Summer 169

L'inverno ~ Winter 85

La Dolce Vita ~ The sweet life 1, 3, 4, 8–10, 13, 17, 24, 25, 30, 32, 33, 93, 96, 104, 172, 242, 249–251

La Primavera ~ Spring 127

Liquore Italiano ~ Italian liqueur 104

Maiale ~ Pork 72, 146, 161, 184, 198

Manzo ~ Beef 58, 88, 202

Marsala ~ An Italian sweet wine made near Marsala, Sicily 179, 182, 183

Moka ~ An Italian stove top espresso pot conprised of a lower chamber which is filled with water, a filter basket and an upper chamber and filter that screws onto the lower chamber which then receives the espresso 22, 96, 183, 233

Mozzarella di bufala ~ Mozzarella cheese made from the milk of an Italian water buffalo 61, 67, 93, 182, 186, 201, 206

Nel pacco con un cucchiaio ~ In the container with a spoon 45

Non importa ~ It's not important 51, 139

Omelettes ~ Omelets 237

Parmigiano ~ Parmesan cheese 55, 71, 88, 108, 137, 138, 143, 149, 159, 184, 189, 200, 205

Piccola Pasqua ~ Little Easter 134, 136

Pinot Grigio ~ An Italian white wine 15, 134, 137

Pizzette alla Griglia ~ Grilled pizza 161

Pomodoro, Pomodori ~ Tomato, tomatoes 31, 54, 56, 60, 72, 76, 108, 115, 120, 139, 150, 153, 166, 179, 187, 194, 205

Prego ~ Thank you, you're welcome 194

Pranziamo ~ eat lunch together 194

Prosciutto ~ A cured ham originally made in Italy 43, 53, 54, 58, 68, 70, 76, 78, 97, 99, 131, 140, 160, 173, 174, 186–188, 206, 238, 240

Secondo ~ Second course 39, 43

Secondo me ~ According to me 189

Speck ~ Smoked Prosciutto 205, 206

Soffritto ~ Aromatic vegetables, usually chopped and sauteèd at the beginning of a preparation 51, 101, 112, 220

SPA is Stazione termale, or semplicemente: Terme ~ spa 150

Spuntino ~ A small snack 41

Tuaca ~ An Italian liqueur 46, 102, 104

Venerdi sera ~ Friday evening 1, 3, 4, 17, 31, 51, 87, 91, 108, 172

Verdura, verdure ~ Vegetable, vegetables 60, 76, 82, 88, 108, 111, 115, 142, 175, 179

Menu Index

Polpettine e Spaghetti con una Carota Bruta ~ Meatballs and Spaghetti (with ugly carrot) 53

Bistecca alla Griglia ~ Grilled Steak 56

Scalloppine di Manzo al Forno ~ Top Sirloin 58

Claire's 85th ~ Bistecca Tripunta alla Griglia ~ Tri-tip 60

Stinco di Agnello — Kate wants Indian food ~ Lamb Shanks 63, **64**

Pollo al Forno ~ Baked Chicken 68

Costole di Maiale con troppo Cavolfiore ~ Pork Ribs with too much Cauliflower 72

Gamberoni con Pesto e Prosciutto ~ Shrimp with Pesto and Prosciutto 76

Zuppa di Pesce ~ Sea Bass and Watercress 79, 179

Agnello alla Griglia ~ Grilled Lamb 82, 108, 134

Cotolette di Manzo ~ Short Ribs on Polenta 88

La Prima Sera di Bill Maher @ Teatro Arlington — Cotollette di Agnello alla Griglia ~ Grilled Lamb Chops 108

La Cena per Federico, Tami e Verni — Rollini di Vitello Brasati ~ Rolled Braised Veal (almost) 93

Cioppino ~ Fisherman's Soup 97, **100**

Tornados di Bistecca "Filet Mignon" ~ Individual Beef Wellington 102

Una Celebrazione di Frutta di Canale — Stufato di Melanzane ~ AKA Eggplant Ratatouille 105

TGIF/GDEV* — Galline Farcite ~ Stuffed Cornish Game Hens 115

Minestrone ~ Minestrone 118

"Osso Buco" di Vitello ~ Veal Osso Buco 111

La Festa di San Martino e Il Compleanno di Nicholas Sluchevsky — Oca al Forno con Ripieno di Frutta Secca ~ Roast Goose with Dried Fruit Stuffing 120, **124**

Burnt Offerings — Anatra alla Griglia ~ Barbequed Duck 130

Una Piccola Pasqua — Salsicce e Agnello alla Griglia ~ Grilled Lamb & Sausages 134

Alice doesn't live here anymore — Capesante su Fettuccine ~ Scallops on Fettuccine 139

Little Green Things — Spaghetti con Verdure Verdi in Padella ~ Spaghetti with Sauteèd Greens 142, **144**

Experimenting with more Little Green Things — Costole di Maiale alla Griglia e Orecchiette con Fave ~ Grilled Ribs and Pasta with Fava Beans 146

Cucina di Stazione Termale — Medaglioni di Pescecane ~ Medallions of Shark 150

When Life Hands You Eggs — La Colazione di Sera ~ An Evening Breakfast 153

Non Fa Bel Tempo Oggi—*Minestra di Piselli* ~ Pea Soup 158

If you grill a big pizza—*Pizzetti alla Griglia* ~ Small Grilled Pizzas 161

Salmone alla Griglia ~ Grilled Salmon 166

Devo Andare Via (I've Gotta Go)— *Insalata di Gamberetti* ~ Shrimp Salad 173

Dinner with the Neigabors—*Pesce al Forno* ~ Whole Baked Snapper 175

Pollo al Marsala ~ Chicken Marsala 179

Braciole di Maiale alla Griglia ~ Grilled Rolled Pork 184

Easy Does It—*Pasta Sfoglia con Funghi* ~ Puff Pastry with Mushrooms 187

Farewell to Jessica—*Pollo alla Cacciatora* ~ Chicken Cacciatore (Hunter's Chicken) 191

Bistecca alla Griglia di Firenze ~ Grilled Steak Florentine Style 194

Lombata di Maiale al Forno ~ Rolled Stuffed Pork Loin 198

Pot Roast in the Summer???—*Manzo Brasato con Salsa BBQ* ~ Pot Roasted Beef with BBQ Style Gravy 202

Pollo alla Griglia con Pesto ~ Grilled Pesto Chicken 205

COURSE INDEX

SPUNTINO E PANE

Crostini al Prosciutto ~ Prosciutto on Toast 53

Crostini con Mozzarella, Pomodori e Basilico ~ Tomato, Basil and Mozzarella on Toast 60

Crostini con Pomodori, Basilico e Mozzarella di Bufala ~ Tomato, Basil, and Mozzarella on Toast 56

Crostini con Prosciutto Crudo e Asparagi ~ Toasts with Ham and Asparagus 97

Crostini con Purè di Fave ~ Puréed Fava Beans on Toast 146

Formaggio e Pane, Salsa e Olio ~ Bread and Cheese, Salsa and Oil 105

Formaggio Pecorino e Croccantini ~ Pecorino on Crackers 63

Grissini con Prosciutto ~ Bread Sticks with Prosciutto 173

Grissini e Speck ~ Breadsticks and Smoked Prosciutto, aka Speck 205

Formaggi e Noci ~ Cheese and Nuts 179

Pane Fresco ~ Fresh Bread 68, 79, 82, 158, 202

Pane o Toast ~ Bread or Toast 153

Pane Rustico Croccante ~ Crusty Rustic Bread 58

Trota Affumicata con Crostini, Asiago e Basilico ~ Smoked Trout with Crackers, Asiago Cheese and Basil 111

Vongole Affumicate su Crostini ~ Smoked Clams on Crackers 108

ANTIPASTO

Antipasti del Giorno ~ Today's Antipasto 175

Antipasto di Salame e Formaggio ~ Cheese and Salami 93

Assortimento di Pane con Pâté di Anatra, Salumi, Olive, e Melanzane ~ Assortment of Breads with Pâté, Salami, Olives, and Eggplant 97

Assortimento di Salumi, Formaggi e Pane ~ Deli Meats, Cheese, and Breads 130

Cocktail di Scampi con Salsa Fresca ~ Chilled Shrimp with Dipping Sauce on toast 68

Formaggio Cheddar sopra al Pane di Segale con Condimento di Granturco ~ Cheddar cheese on Rye Toast with Corn Relish 72

Granchio sul Cetriolo ~ Crab on cucumber 60

Indivia Belga con Fichi, Prosciutto e Pinoli ~ Belgian Endive with Prosciutto, Figs, and Pine Nuts 187

Indivia con Purè di Qualcosa ~ Endive with something Puréed 158

Patate, Formaggio, Salsa, e Olive Nere ~ Potatoes with cheese, salsa, and black olives 76

Un Piattino di Avocado e Insalata di Granchio ~ A Small Plate of Crab Salad with Avocado 102

APERITIVO, VINO E BIRRA

La Dama Bianca ~ White Lady 130

Aperitivo a Scelta ~ Your choice of Aperitif 187

Assaggi di vari Vini Rossi ~ A Tasting of a Variety of Local Red Wines 111

Birra ~ Beer 184, 194, 202

Birra Italiana o Microbrew o Vino della Casa ~ Italian Beer or Microbrew or House Red Wine 146

Birra o Vino Rosso ~ Beer or Red Wine 88

Campari e Acqua di Seltz con Ghiaccio ~ Campari and Soda 56

Campari Negronita di Michelina ~ Campari Negronita 72

Campari, Noci e un Fiore ~ Campari, Nuts and a Flower 205

Chianti Classico ~ Classic Chianti 198

Pinot Grigio ~ or Your Favorite White Wine for Aperitivo 134

Prosecco ~ Sparkling Wine 60, 153, 166

Tempranillo 2001 ~ or House Red Wine 82

Vino Bianco della Casa ~ House White Wine 63, 68, 150, 179

Vino Bianco della Casa o Cocktails "Bellinis" ~ White Wine of The House or Bellinis 76

Vino Bianco di Casa Nostra ~ White Wine of the House 58

Vino Rosso della Casa ~ Red Wine of The House 53, 108

INSALATA

Condimento di Crescione, Barbabietola e Sugo di Arancia ~ Salad Dressing of Puréed Watercress, Beets, and Orange Juice 97

Insalata "Cesare" ~ Caesar Salad 115

Insalata Capricciosa ~ Chopped Raw Vegetable Salad 142

Insalata con Pomodori, Avocado, e Mozzarella ~ Salad of Tomato, Avocado, and Mozzarella 153

Insalata di Romana e Frissè ~ Salad of Romaine and Frissè 179, **180**

Insalata di Cavolo ~ Cabbage Salad 202

Insalata di Cavolo Verde ~ Salad of Shaved Green Cabbage 146

Insalata di Crescione e Foglie Verdi di Dente di Leone ~ Salad of Watercress and Dandelion Greens 130

Insalata di Gamberetti ~ Shrimp Salad 173

Insalata di Lattuga Nuova ~ Salad of Baby Lettuces 175

Insalata di Michelina con Funghi e Parmigiano ~ Romaine with Shaved Mushrooms and Parmesan 198

Insalata di Spinaci e Lattuga "Piccola Gemma" ~ Spinach and Baby Lettuce Salad 82

Insalata Mista ~ Mixed Greens 56, 63, 76, 93

Insalata Mista con Avocado, Gorgonzola, e Noci ~ Salad with Avocado, Gorgonzola, and Pecans 68

Insalata Mista con Gorgonzola, Prosciutto Fritto, e Avocado ~ Mixed Green Salad with Gorgonzola, Prosciutto, and Avocado 97

Insalata Mista con Pomodoro, Salame, e Formaggio ~ Mixed Green Salad with Tomato, Salami, and Cheese 120

Insalata Mista con Varie Cose ~ Chopped Salad with Various Things 150

Insalata Verde ~ Green Salad 53, 58, 60, 72, 79, 105, 134

Insalata Verde con Arugula in Salsa di Pesto ~ Green Salad with Dressing of Arugula Pesto 194

Insalata Verde con Gamberetti ~ Green Salad with Shrimp 166

Insalata Verde e Condimento Francese ~ Green Salad with French Dressing 205

Insalata Verde Semplice ~ Simple Green Salad 102

Insalate Miste Selvatiche ~ Salad of Wild Greens 191

Lattuga Mista con Contorni a Sorpresa ~ Mixed Green Salad with a Side of Surprises 111

Lattuga Romaine con Funghi e Parmigiano ~ Romaine Leaves with Parmesan and Mushrooms 88

Salsa per Gamberetti ~ Seafood Salad Dressing 173

IL PIATTO ROSSO

Il Piatto Rosso con Avocado e Pomodori (Gialli e Rossi) ~ The Red Plate with Avocado and Tomatoes (Yellow and Red) 60

Il Piatto Rosso con Gorgonzola e un Foglione di Basilico ~ The Red Plate with Gorgonzola, and a Large Basil Leaf 205

Il Piatto Rosso con Pomodori, Gorgonzola, e Broccoli Marinati ~ The Red Plate with Tomato, Gorgonzola and Marinated Broccoli 108

Il Piatto Rosso con Pomodoro, Basilico, Avocado, e Mozzarella di Bufala ~ The Red Plate with Tomato, Basil, Avocado, and Mozzarella di Bufala 179

Il Piatto Rosso con un Grande Pomodorone, Pomodoroni Gialli e Piccoli, Prezzemolo, Condimento di Aceto Balsamico ~ The Red Plate with a Big Heirloom Tomato, Small Yellow Tomatoes, Parsley, and Balsamic Vinegar 53

Il Piatto Rosso con un Pomodoro, Aceto Balsamico, e Gorgonzola ~ The Red Plate with Tomatoes, Gorgonzola and Balsamic Vinegar 72

Il Piatto Rosso con Zucchini, Funghi, e Cavoli di Bruxelles Marinati ~ The Red Plate with Marinated Zucchini, Mushrooms and Brussels Sprouts 93

Il Piatto Rosso di Avocado, Mozzarella, e Cetriolo ~ The Red Plate with Avocado, Mozzarella, and Cucumber 79

Il Piatto Rosso di Avocado, Pomodori, e Formaggio Pecorino ~ The Red Plate with Avocado, Tomatoes, and Sheep's Milk Feta 76

Il Piatto Rosso di Cetriolo, Pomodori, e Feta con Aceto Balsamico · The Red Plate of Cucumber, Tomato, and Feta with Balsamic Vinegar 139

Il Piatto Rosso di Mozzarella, Trota Affumicata, Zucchine Grattugiate, e Olive · The Red Plate with Mozzarella, Smoked Trout, and Olives 175

Il Piatto Rosso di Pomodori e Mozzarella nella Salsa Pesto · The Red Plate with Mozzarella and Tomatoes under Pesto 115

Il Piatto Rosso di Pomodori Gialli e Rossi, Ravanelli, e Formaggio Stilton · The Red Plate with Yellow and Red Tomatoes, Radishes and Stilton 166

Il Piatto Rosso d'Indivia con Insalata di Granchio, Pomodoro e Uova Sode · The Red Plate with Endive filled with Crab Salad, Tomatoes and Hard Boiled Eggs 194, **196**

Un Pomodorone Grande · A Big Heirloom Tomato 56

PRIMO

Carciofini Stufati · Stuffed Baby Artichokes 134

Funghi con Ripieno di Pesto e Formaggio · Mushrooms Stuffed with Pesto and Cheese 142

Funghi Stufati · Stuffed Mushrooms 184

Pasta Sfoglia con Funghi, Pomodori, e Cipolle · Puff Pastry with Mushrooms, Tomatoes, and Onion 187

Sedano con Bolognese · Celery with Meat Sauce 161

Torta di Granchio · Crab Cakes 79

Vongole in Brodo · Steamed Clams 79

MINESTRA

Cioppino di Michelina · Fisherman's Soup 97

Minestra di Piselli · Pea Soup 158

Minestra di Pollo · Chicken Soup with Pasta 161

Minestra di Verdure, Foglie Verdi di Cavolfiore, e Fagioli Bianchi · Soup with White Beans and Brussels Sprouts Greens 111

Minestrone · Minestrone 118

Zuppa di Carote · Carrot Soup 53

Zuppa di Cavolfiore · Cauliflower Soup 72

Zuppa di Pane in Brodo · Bread Soup 146

Zuppa di Pesce · Fish Soup 79, 179

Zuppa di Pomodoro · Tomato Soup 187

Zuppa di Puré di Verdure · Puréed Vegetable Soup 88

Zuppa di Verdure d'inverno · Roasted Winter Vegetable Soup 115

SECONDO

Calzone dalla Ricetta di "Chez Panisse" · Calzone 108

Cardone · Cardone or Cardoons 134

Farro · Emmer 194

Fegatini di Pollo alla Casalinga · Chicken Livers 153

Peperoncini Ripieni con Risotto e Funghi · Anaheim Chiles stuffed with Mushroom Risotto 93

Pizzette · Pizzette 161

Pancetta non Affumicata · Bacon (un-smoked) 153

PASTA, POLENTA, RISOTTO & RICE

Capellini con Verdure Verdi, Pomodorini, e Cipolle · Angel Hair Pasta with Dandelion Greens, Little Orange Tomatoes, and Onion 175

Couscous · Couscous 63

Fettuccine Alfredo · Fettuccine Alfredo 179

Gnocchi di Zucca · Roasted Squash Gnocchi 115

Lasagne · Lasagne 134

Lasagne al Forno · Baked Lasagne 58

Orecchiette con Fave · Ear Shaped Pasta with Fava Beans 146

Pasta o Polenta · Pasta or Polenta 191

Penne con Basilico, Pomodori, e Mozzarella di Bufala · Penne Pasta with Basil, Tomato, and Mozzarella di Bufala 205

Penne con Dente di Leone, Peperoncino Rosso, e Prosciutto · Penne with Dandelion Greens, Red Bell Pepper and Prosciutto 68

Penne con Verdure · Penne with Vegetables 60

Polenta · Polenta 88, 111

Ravioli al Carciofo con Burro, Limone, e Parmigiano · Artichoke Ravioli with Butter, Lemon, and Parmesan 184

Riso Bianco · White Rice 105

Riso Bianco con Aneto · White Rice with Dill 166

Riso con Verdure · Rice with Vegetables 76

Risotto ai Funghi, Finocchio, e Porri · Risotto with Mushrooms, Fennel, and Leek 72, **74**

Risotto con Funghi Selvaggi · Wild Mushroom Risotto 130

Spaghetti · Spaghetti 93

Spaghetti al Burro e all'Olio · Spaghetti with Butter and Oil 56

Spaghetti con Verdure Verdi in Padella · Spaghetti with Sautéed Greens 142, **124**

Spaghetti e Polpettine in Marinara · Spaghetti and Meatballs 53

Spaghettini · Thin Spaghetti 150

PIATTO PRINCIPALE

Agnello alla Griglia · Grilled Lamb 82

Anatra alla Griglia · Grilled Duck 130

Bistecca alla Griglia · Grilled Steak 56

Bistecca alla Griglia di Firenze · Grilled Steak in the manner of Florence 194

Bistecca "Tripunta" alla Griglia · Grilled Tri-Tip Steak 60

Braciole di Maiale alla Griglia · Grilled, Stuffed, Rolled Pork Cutlets 184

Capesante su Fettucine · Scallops on Fettuccine 139

Costole di Maiale al Forno e alla Griglia · Slow Roasted Pork Ribs Finished on the Grill 72

Costole di Maiale alla Griglia · Grilled Pork Ribs 146

Cotolette di Agnello alla Griglia · Grilled Lamb Chops 108

Cotolette di Maiale alla Griglia · Grilled Pork Chops 161

Cotolette di Manzo con Intingolo di Carne · Short Ribs and Brown Gravy 88

Fette di Carne Fredda · Sliced Cold Meat 187

Galline Farcite di Ciliege, Mandorle, Sedano, Cipolline, Finocchio, e Pangrattato · Cornish Game Hens 115

Gamberoni con Pesto e Prosciutto · Large Shrimp with Pesto and Prosciutto 76

Lombata di Maiale al Forno · Stuffed Boneless Pork Loin 198

Manzo Brasato · Pot Roast and BBQ Style Gravy 202

Medaglioni di Pescecane con Salsa di Piselli e Pomodoro · Medallions of Thresher Shark with Sauces of Pureed Peas and Roasted Tomatoes 150

Melanzane e Zucchine Stufate · Stewed Eggplant and Zucchini 194

Oca al Forno con Ripieno di Frutta Secca · Roast Goose with Fruit Stuffing 120, **124**

"Osso Buco" di Vitello · Veal Osso Buco 111

Pesce al Forno Contro Pesce alla Griglia · Whole Baked Snapper versus Grilled Yellowtail 175

Pollo al Forno · Roasted Chicken 68

Pollo al Marsala con Funghi · Chicken in a Marsala Sauce 179

Pollo alla Cacciatora · Hunter's Style Chicken 191

Pollo alla Griglia con Pesto · Grilled Chicken with Pesto 205

Pollo, Patate, e Carote al Forno · Roasted Chicken, Potatoes and Carrots 158

Rollini di Vitello Brasati · Rolled, Braised Veal 93

Salmone alla Griglia · Grilled Salmon 166

Salsicce e Agnello alla Griglia · Grilled Lamb and Sausages 134

Scaloppine di Manzo al Forno · Baked Beef Cutlets 58

Stinco di Agnello · Dry Rubbed Lamb Shanks 63, **64**

Stufato di Melanzane · Eggplant Stew 105

Tournedos di Bistecca · Individual Beef Wellington 102

Un Piatto di Carne Fredda Assortita per L'Uomo che ha fame, per favore 142

Uova Quasi Strapazzate/Quasi Omelette · Eggs Sort of Scrambled/Sort of an Omelet 153, **155**

CONTORNO

Asparagi alla Griglia 184

Asparagi con Olio di Olivo · Asparagus 130

Asparagi o Zucchine alla Griglia · Grilled Asparagus or Zucchini 161

Asparagi, Bianchi e Verdi, Arrostiti · Grilled White and Green Asparagus 150

Broccoli sotto Pangrattato · Broccoli under Breadcrumbs 53

Cavolo Rosso con Aceto e Mela · Red Cabbage with Vinegar and Apple 120

Cipolline e Carote in Brodo · Onions and Carrots Cooked in the Pan Juices 63

Contorni di Pepe, Funghi, e Cipolle · Sautéed Red and Yellow Bell Peppers with Mushrooms and Onions 150

Fagioli al Forno · Baked Beans 202

Fagiolini · Green Beans 115, 120

Fagiolini con Olio di Oliva Extra Vergine locale · Green Beans Anointed with Olive Oil 72

Foglia Verdi di Dente di Leone · Dandelion Greens 111

Melanzane alla Griglia ~ Grilled Eggplant 205

Pannocchia Cotta ~ Corn on the Cob 202

Patate e Cipolle al Forno ~ Potato Baked with Onion & Cheese 102

Patate Gratinate ~ Gratin of Potatoes with Cheeses 198

Peperoni al Forno con Formaggio ~ Baked, Stuffed Anaheim Chiles 68

Piselle ~ Peas 88

Purè di Patate con Un Bacio di Lardo ~ Mashed Potatoes with a Kiss of Goose Fat 120

Spiedini di Verdure con una sorpresa per "tutti i coraggiosi" ~ Vegetable Skewers 82

Spinaci alla Panna ~ Creamed Spinach 82, 166

Verdure al Forno (Carote, Cipolle, Finocchio, Barbabietole, e Patate) ~ Roasted Vegetables (Carrots, Onions, Fennel, Beets and Potatoes) 198

Verdure Verdi sotto Pangrattato ~ Collard Greens under Toasted Bread Crumbs 179

Zucca al Forno ~ Baked Squash 158

Zucca con Zucchero Marrone ~ Squash with Brown Sugar 120

Zucchine Gialle ~ Yellow Squash 198

Zucchine, Cotte a Vapore ~ Steamed Zucchini 58

Zucchine Gratinate ~ Baked Zucchini 60

Zucchine Grattate con un Bacio d'Olio Extra Vergine ~ Grated Zucchini with Olive Oil 60

Zucchine Grattugiate con Un Bacio d'Olio Extra Vergine ~ Grated Zucchini 68

Zucchine in Marinara con Cipolle e Peperoni Rossi e Gialli ~ Sautéed Zucchini, Onion with Red & Yellow Peppers, in Marinara 102

Zucchini Grattinati ~ Baked Zucchini 76

DOLCI, FORMAGGI E FRUTTA

Ananas alla Griglia ~ Grilled Pineapple 166

Biscotti, Biscottini ~ Biscotti, Small Hard Cookies 79, 191

Biscotti di Katerina e Gelato ~ Kate's Biscotti with Ice Cream 175

Caffèllatte con Cioccolatini ~ Brewed Moka Coffee with Chocolates 179

Ciliege, Formaggio con denti ~ Cherries and A Cheese with Some Bite 56

Cioccolatini ~ Chocolates 82, 105

Cioccolatini di T.J.s ~ Chocolates 115

Dolce di Katerina con Banana Soffritta, Gelato di Cioccolato, e Frutti di Bosco ~ Berries with Chocolate Ice Cream and Sautéed Bananas 93

Dolce Semplice ~ Simple Dessert 58

Dolce di Mary e Renae ~ Dessert by Mary and Renae 60

Fette di Arancia ~ Sliced Oranges 194

Fette di Pera con Noci ~ Sliced Pears and Pecans 161

Fette di Persimmon ~ Persimmon Slices 102

Fichi ~ Figs 198

Fragole ~ Strawberries 173

Fragole con Aceto Balsamico e Pepe ~ Strawberries with Pepper and Balsamic Vinegar 139

Fragole con Aceto Balsamico e un Biscotto ~ Strawberries with Balsamic Vinegar and a Cookie 146

Fragole Fresche e Cioccolatini con Mirtillo ~ Strawberries and Chocolate-covered Blueberries 205

Frutta ~ Fruit 153

Frutti di Bosco con Panna ~ Berries with Cream 130

Gelato ~ Savory Gelato 63

Grappoli di Uva e Biscotti ~ Bunches of Grapes and Cookies 150

Un Mandarino ~ A Tangerine 53

Mandarini, Fichi Ubriachi, e Semi di Zucca ~ Satsuma Tangerines, Drunk Figs, Pumpkin Seeds 184

Mandarino o Persimmon ~ Tangerines or Persimmons 88, 108

Mandorle di Spagna e Mandarini ~ Spanish Almonds and Tangerines 76

Melone o Frutte di Bosco ~ Melon or Berries 191

Mousse di Cioccolato di Katerina ~ Kate's Chocolate Mousse 158

Sorbetto al Limone ~ Lemon Sorbet 134

Sorbetto o Gelati con Cialde Dolci ~ Ice Cream with Sweet Wafer Cookies 68

Sorbetto o Gelato con Uva Congelate ~ Sorbet, Sherbet, or Ice Cream 202

Torta di Cioccolato con Fragole ~ Chocolate Cake with Strawberries 142

Torta di Cioccolato di Pietro ~ Chocolate Cake with Berries and Cream 130

Torta di Fichi ~ Fig Galette 162

Torta di Mela ~ Apple Tart 120

Torta di Ricotta ~ Cheesecake 97

Un Mandarino condiviso fra tutti ~ A Tangerine 53

Un Piattino d'Uva ~ A Small Plate of Grapes 63

Uva Rossa ~ Red Grapes 187

Uva, Mandorle e Taleggio ~ Grapes, Almonds, and Cheese 82

Varietà di Cioccolatini di Katerina ~ A Variety of Kate's Handmade Chocolates 118

DIGESTIVO

Acqua alla Menta ~ Water Infused with Mint 179, 191

Acqua con Frutta ~ Fruited Water 175

Acqua Frizzante ~ Sparkling Water 198

Acqua Minerale Frizzante ~ Carbonated Mineral Water 161

Acqua Minerale Naturale ~ Mineral Water 166

Caffè, Caffellatte ~ Coffee, Latte 97, 179

Digestivo a Scelta ~ After Dinner Drinks of Choice 184

Espresso ~ Espresso 93

Limoncello del Nonno, 2005 ~ Limoncello 68

Medicine per il Raffreddore ~ Cold Medicine 118

Passito di Pantelleria e Liquore ~ Sweet Sicilian Wine 93

Porto ~ Port 120

Tè ~ Tea 118

Tè di Erbe ~ Herb Tea 150

Tè di Erbe al Sole, ghiacciato ~ Sun Tea with Herbs 202

Tuaca ~ Tuaca 102

Un po' di Passito di Pantelleria ~ Sweet Sicilian Wine 82, **83**

Vin Santo ~ Saints' Wine 173, 191

Vino Dolce ~ Sweet Dessert Wine 139

RECIPE INDEX

Tri-Tip Marinade 62

"Not Enough Lettuce for a Salad" Salad 67

Jim's Favorite Couscous 67

Savory Gelato 67

Succotash 75

BIBLIOGRAPHY

Beard, James's, <u>American Cookery</u>, Little, Brown and Company, Boston, 1972

Guiliano, Mireille, <u>French Woman Don't Get Fat, The Secret Of Eating For Pleasure</u>, Alfred A. Knopf, New York, 2005

Waters, Alice, <u>Chez Panisse Menu Cookbook</u>, Random House, New York, 1982

William E. and Claire F. Marling, <u>The Marling Menu-Master for Italy</u>, Altarinda Books, La Jolla, 1971

Johns, Pamela Sheldon, <u>50 Great Pasta Sauces</u>, Andrews McMeel Publishing, Kansas City, 2006

Buford, Bill, <u>Heat: An Amateur's Adventures as Kitchen Slave, Line Cook, Pasta-Maker, and Apprentice to a Dante-Quoting Butcher in Tuscany</u>, Alfred A. Knopf, New York, 2006

National Environmental Satellite, Data and Information Service, National Climatic Data Center, http://www.ncdc.noaa.gov/oa/climate/research/2003/jul/hazards.html

<u>Climate of 2003 [:] 2003 in Historical Perspective</u>, National Climatic Data Center 15 January 2004, National Oceanic and Atmospheric Administration

La Minestra del Ringraziamento
The Thanksgiving Soup

Da noi, c'è una ricetta per la festa del Ringraziamento.	At our home, there is a recipe for the Thanksgiving dinner.
Non cambia mai.	It never changes.
C'è un tacchino, naturalmente, col ripieno, salsa di tacchino, mirtilli, cipolle in panna, patate bianche e dolci, piselli, e pane.	There is a turkey, naturally, with stuffing, gravy, cranberries, creamed onions, potatoes mashed and sweet, peas, and bread.
Per il nonno, ci vuole la torta di zucca.	The grandfather must have pumpkin pie.
Ma, la minestra, come le persone, potrebbe cambiare.	But, the soup, like the people, can change.
Un anno c'è minestra con cappelletti, un altro c'è zuppa di zucca.	One year, it was cappelletti soup, another pumpkin soup.
Quest'anno c'è una minestra vegetale.	This year, it is a vegetable soup.
Come la minestra, la tavola del Ringraziamento ha molti ingredienti.	Like the soup, the Thanksgiving table has many ingredients.
Uno fa le patate, uno apre una bottiglia di Prosecco.	Someone makes the potatoes, another opens a bottle of champagne.
Qualcuno porta aiuto, un altro una barzelletta.	One brings aid, another a funny story.
Ognuno porta conversazione, un'altra una poesia.	Everyone brings conversation, one a poem.
La piccola dice la benedizione. I vecchi portano le storie.	The youngest says the grace. The oldest ones bring stories.
Io? Mescolo, mescolo, mescolo, e qualche volta aggiungo un po' di sale.	I? I stir, I stir, I stir, and sometimes add a bit of salt.
Tutto porta sapore per la minestra;	Everything brings flavor to the soup;
tutti portano la vita alla tavola.	everyone brings life to the table.
Grazie di essere venuti a trovarci a casa nostra oggi.	Thank you for coming to visit us at our home today.